NEW ENGLAND'S GOTHIC LITERATURE

*History and Folklore of the Supernatural From the
Seventeenth Through the Twentieth Centuries*

Faye Ringel

The Edwin Mellen Press
Lewiston/Queenston/Lampeter

Library of Congress Cataloging-in-Publication Data

Ringel, Faye.
   New England's Gothic literature : history and folklore of the
supernatural from the seventeenth through the twentieth centuries /
Faye Ringel.
        p.   cm.
   Includes bibliographical references and index.

   ı. American literature--New England--History and criticism.
2. Gothic revival (Literature)--New England.   3. Supernatural in
literature.   4. New England--In literature.   5. Supernatural-
-Folklore.   6. Folklore--New England.   I. Title.
PS243.R56   1995
813'.08733093274--dc20   94-34973
                                                                     CIP

   ISBN 0-7734-0864-9

A CIP catalog record for this book is available from the British Library.

The Edwin Mellen Press   The Edwin Mellen Press
        Box 450   Box 67
   Lewiston, New York   Queenston, Ontario
   USA 14092-0450   CANADA L0S 1L0

              The Edwin Mellen Press, Ltd.
                 Lampeter, Dyfed, Wales
              UNITED KINGDOM SA48 7DY

         Printed in the United States of America

To my parents, Harold and Toube Ringel,
and to the memory of my uncle, Irving Barsky

Table of Contents

Preface

Though studies of the Gothic have proliferated in recent years, there still seems to me a contradiction inherent in doing such research. The Gothic in literature and life is about secrets, secrets of ancestral guilt, of original or individual sin. It delights in darkness. Research, on the other hand, is about seeking, finding, and exposing the results to the light of day. The emblem of the Gothic is the hidden text: the lost manuscript, the missing will, the madman's ravings. Literary scholarship, as A.S. Byatt has shown us, is about possession: the text decoded, the documents discovered, the evidence marshalled and published.

Nevertheless, undaunted by the fates of my august predecessors in Gothic research—Drs. Faustus, Heidegger, and Frankenstein, Professor Von Helsing, Charles Dexter Ward—I have opened some of New England's closets and let the skeletons dance. I discovered early on, unlike Dr. Faustus, that I did not have infinite space or time: this explains the seeming neglect of such important Gothic themes as ghosts, haunted houses, and the Faustian bargain with the Devil. For the same reason, I chose to focus on New England writers of the twentieth century Gothic: Lovecraft, King, and others less well-known. The darkness within the flowering of New England, of Hawthorne and Melville, of Mary Wilkins Freeman and Edith Wharton, of the spiritualist mediums and the psychic investigators, I have left for another volume, to be called *New England Fall.*

In this book, I use "Gothic" to encompass a wide range of phenomena in folklore, literature, and life: Chapters One and Two discuss the special sense I have tried to make of the difficult term. As a rule, I have not tampered with older texts, except to regularize long f's and "i" and "j." I have kept their inconsistency in spelling names, including those of Indian tribes. On the latter point, I have used the ii

term "Indian" throughout in preference to the more fashionable "Native American." As Melissa Fawcett Sayet, descendant of Uncas, once declared, all English terms that lump together Pequots and Mohegans, Aztecs and Maya are equally inexact and incorrect. In addition, both terms result from misrepresentations by sixteenth-century Europeans: Columbus, who believed he had discovered the Indies, and the Italian cartographers, who believed the boasts of Amerigo Vespucci. Such confusions and misreadings are entirely appropriate to a Gothic view of New England's past.

The Gothic world of secrets and hidden texts is not confined to New England's past. As I was writing this book, an art collector, Glenn Robert Smith, was researching the life of outsider artist Ellis Ruley, who lived and died (under mysterious circumstances) in my home town of Norwich, Connecticut. Smith described the town to a local paper as existing "almost in a time warp, set off from the rest of the country." He said he had been threatened and harassed by those who wished the secrets to remain buried, and described the entire experience as "like going back in Salem" (Dufresne C11). I offer to my readers the same experience, minus the physical danger. As to the spiritual danger, *caveat lector*. The Gothic, as we will see, has never been an entirely safe form of entertainment.

Acknowledgements

All books are made of books, this one, perhaps, more so than many, and acknowledgements of that kind of assistance can be found in the footnotes and Works Cited pages. This book, however, is also the culmination of my personal and scholarly history, the result of a life steeped in New England history, the Middle Ages, fantasy, and horror. While I cannot acknowledge by name all the teachers, story-tellers, students, and friends who passed along the folklore and local history of New England found herein, I will make the attempt. Once upon a time, my summer camp director, Richard Curland, told harrowing ghost stories and introduced me to the master story-tellers Chief Tantaquidgeon and Raymond "Chief" Case. The *Norwich Bulletin*, where I worked as a summer intern, was the best possible classroom in which to learn local gossip, legend, and history. In a different kind of classroom, I learned a great deal of New England lore from students in my courses in "The Supernatural in New England" at the University of Rhode Island Extension Division, the Division of Continuing Education at Connecticut College, and the Norwich Adult Education program. At Brown University, Barton St. Armand's seminar in the American Gothic was particularly inspiring. I owe him a great deal for taking H.P. Lovecraft—and me—seriously.

The last chapter of this book focuses on living writers of fantasy and horror; in a recursive process that still continues, they have made my job a delight. These writers sent copies of their works, submitted to long interviews, corrected the transcripts, and commented upon this critic's analysis of their fiction. Thank you, old friends and new: Don D'Ammassa, Greer Gilman, Delia Sherman, Paul Hazel, Les Daniels, Rick Hautala, Joe Citro.

Thank you as well to other old friends turned informants: Arastorm, Aelfwine, and the other New Hampshire Neo-Pagans; Arwen and the other Connecticut Neo-Pagans. For their expertise in Lovecraft, I thank Marc Michaud and S.T. Joshi. For her knowledge of history and the folkways of American Studies, I thank Beth Parkhurst. For founding NECON and providing a cozy corner for dark fantasy, I thank the Rhode Island Bobs, Booth and Plante. For hospitality over the years, and for *auld lang syne*, I thank Marian Walke and the Buttery.

The chapters on the New England witch belief were enriched by insights from local historians Richard Trask of Danvers, Marguerite Harris of Beverly, and Persis McMillen, descendant of witches. The staffs and collections of many museums and historical sites, including the Andover Historical Society, Andover, MA; the Beverly Historical Society, Beverly, MA; and the Sarah Orne Jewett House Museum, South Berwick, Maine were helpful. I feel privileged to have been able to work at the Northeast Archives of Folklore and Folklife, University of Maine at Orono, and to have interviewed its director, the great folklorist Sandy Ives, a national treasure.

In researching this book, I visited and received help from the following libraries: the John Hay and Rockefeller Libraries at Brown University, especially the Lovecraft Collection and its curator, Jennifer Lee; the Widener and Houghton Libraries of Harvard University; the Rare Book Collection at the University of Rhode Island's library; Connecticut College's Shain Library; and the James Duncan Phillips Library of the Peabody and Essex Museum, (the former Essex Institute of Salem, Massachusetts). In addition, I relied a great deal upon inter-library loan, thanks to the kindness of the staffs of the East Lyme Public Library, and of course, the U.S. Coast Guard Academy Library, whose I.L.L. technician, Jean Hayek, never once questioned why I was ordering all those books with "Devil" and "Witch" in their titles.

Parts of Chapters Six and Seven appeared in *Lovecraft Studies* 29 (Fall 1993); I am grateful to S.T. Joshi for printing the article and allowing me to use the material here. Chapter Six had its distant origins in a paper, "Vampires in the Fantastic Literature of New England," for the section on "Fantasy" of the 1991 NEMLA conference, Hartford, Connecticut.

The U.S. Coast Guard Academy, my employer, generously provided a one-semester sabbatical, without which the book could never have been finished. Paul Hazel gave me inspiration, encouragement, and detailed editing of the early drafts of this work. Greer Gilman, Charlotte Spivack, and David Philips reviewed and made helpful suggestions for revision of the manuscript. My parents, to whom the book is dedicated, have always provided tangible material support and less tangible but more necessary emotional support: I am grateful that long ago they decided to move to New England. I am forever inspired by the memory of Irving Barsky, my Uncle Issie, who died while the writing was in progress—if only I had not delayed this first book so long! He valued writing above any other professional activity, and he told the very best stories.

Grateful acknowledgement is made for permission to quote the following:

Brief excerpts from *Harvest Home* and from *The Other* by Thomas Tryon are reprinted by permission of Random House, Inc.

A brief excerpt from *The Witches of Eastwick* by John Updike is reprinted by permission of Random House, Inc.

Brief excerpts from *A Stranger in the Kingdom* by Howard Frank Mosher are reprinted by permission of DOUBLEDAY, a division of Bantam, Doubleday, Dell Publishing Group, Inc.

Excerpts from the letters and fiction of H.P. Lovecraft are reprinted by permission of Arkham House Publishers, Inc. Sauk City, Wisconsin.

Excerpt from "The Renegade" from THE LOTTERY by Shirley Jackson. Copyright © 1948, 1949 by Shirley Jackson, renewed © 1976, 1977 by Laurence Hyman, Barry Hyman, Mrs. Sarah Webster and Mrs. Joanne Schnurer. Reprinted by permission of Farrar, Straus & Giroux, Inc.

Excerpts from *Spirit of the New England Tribes* by William Simmons, copyright © 1986 by the University Press of New England.

Chapter One
On The Gothic in New England

> Our own backsliding hearts...plunged the whole
> country into so wonderful a degeneracy.
> --Cotton Mather

For the medieval sailor, sea monsters were one of the known hazards of navigation on the Western ocean: not as common, perhaps, as wandering rocks and ice mountains, but a threat, nevertheless. Maps used by the earliest explorers of the North American continent regularly pictured serpents, krakens, and dragons engaged in combat with hapless mariners. These drawings were not merely ornamental, though by the eighteenth century they had evolved into the decorative dragons found in the corners of maps. Instead, they marked the sites where sailors might expect to encounter such monsters.

The Pizigani map of 1367, which remained in use for the next hundred years, places one such warning not far to the northwest of the European mainland. ✓ Three Breton ships are under attack, and one "is being drawn down stern foremost by a very aggressive decapod, which drags overboard one of the crew...a dragon flies by with another seaman" (Babcock 83). A later chart, published in Venice in 1539 by the learned Swedish cleric Olaus Magnus, includes two unmistakable sea monsters in a relatively accurate map of northern lands and seas (Heuvelmans 92). Olaus's 1555 description of the nature of sea monsters, (based, he said, on eyewitness accounts), was popular in English translation throughout the seventeenth century:

> He hath commonly hair hanging from his neck a Cubit long, and
> sharp Scales, and is black, and he hath flaming shining eyes. This
> Snake disquiets the shippers, and he puts up his head on high like a
> pillar, and catcheth away men, and he devours them. (qtd. in
> Heuvelmans 92)

Supported in their beliefs by the best authorities, the earliest explorers of the New England coasts reported encounters with sea monsters. The most famous of these stories may be that of John Josselyn, who in *An Account of Two Voyages to New-England (1674)* relayed a sighting in 1639 by "two gentlemen" of his party of a "*Sea-Serpent* or *Snake*, that lay quoiled up like a Cable upon a Rock at Cape-Ann: a Boat passing by with *English* aboard, and two *Indians*, they would have shot the *Serpent*, but the *Indians* disswaded them, saying, that if he were not kill'd outright, they would be all in danger of their lives" (23). Luckily, the monster did not attack them: perhaps it lived on to spawn more of its kind. Indeed, through the eighteenth and nineteenth century, the Massachusetts coast became famous as a resort of sea serpents. Thoreau reported in his journal in 1857 that Daniel Webster had sighted one from a fishing boat off Duxbury.

While there is no evidence that any of these monsters did actual damage to ships, New Englanders continued to be haunted by the possibility of death coming to them as a mystery from the depths of the sea. Melville reminds us that all sea monsters, like Moby Dick, are kin to Leviathan; it is no light thing to go out on the deep waters, hunting him with a hook.

When did the belief in water-dwelling monsters end in New England? The answer, at least for some people, is not yet. In the twentieth century, H.P. Lovecraft, the Providence antiquarian and writer for pulp magazines, chose a sea monster as god of his fictional universe. Great Cthulhu is as indescribable as his name is unpronounceable, but, like the protean sea serpent described differently by each reporter, Lovecraft's monster combines the attributes of dragon, octopus, jellyfish, whale—and man. From the earliest explorers' sea serpents to Nessie's cousin Champ in Lake Champlain, New England's shores have been haunted by monsters and monster-hunters. From the Mathers to *Jaws*, dramas of fantasy and horror have been enacted upon those shores. The seventeenth-century explorers and settlers brought with them to the New World the nightmares, monsters, and miracles of a tradition thousands of years old and discovered that some of those nightmares, monsters, and miracles had made landfall before them and were flourishing in New England. The dark traditions, the writers who collected and re-shaped the history and traditions, and the poetry and fiction they produced make up New England Gothic.

Many critics of the literature, history, and culture of New England have emphasized that which made the new commonwealth different from the Old World. In this they follow the Hartford Wits and Washington Irving, the first writers of the new Republic, who sought to distinguish American literature from other writing in English. My intention is to do the opposite: to emphasize the continuity between the fears and wonders of the Old World and the folklore and literature of the new.

Narrowly understood, "Gothic" has come to signify the type of literature parodied in Austen's *Northanger Abbey,* those fantastic yet formulaic novels of revenge, curses, menacing villains, and menaced heroines. Yet for the creators of the Gothic novel, aristocrats such as Horace Walpole and William Beckford, the term carried a wider meaning. For them, the Gothic was a way of life. Their fictions were part of a deliberate revival of medieval taste in architecture and decoration as a way of improving upon a tedious and unsatisfactory present. The Gothic strain in New England can also be considered as part of the phenomenon of medievalism, in the survival of older traditions and in the Romantic re-creation of those traditions, since the Gothic combines nostalgia for a medieval golden age with the belief that the past, however longed for, is equally the source of horror and evil.

In this book, the term Gothic will refer to the compendium of beliefs that carried through from the European Middle Ages into New England in the Seventeenth Century. Though a few forward-looking scholars, like Cotton Mather's adversary Robert Calef, may have scoffed at the credulity of the vulgar, most New Englanders shared a fear of necromancy and the malevolent powers of the dead. In addition, belief in a Devil who delighted in tempting good Puritans led to fears of witches and others who sought to bargain with Satan for unnatural powers. At least some inhabitants of New England continued to dread Europe's legendary monsters—the merfolk, ocean serpents and lake dwellers, vampires,

4

werewolves and other shapechangers. Such fears have by no means disappeared today.[1]

Other less malevolent medieval traditions persisted in New England: the belief in fairies, elves or other nature spirits, Maypoles and rites of spring, and most of all, the search for and acceptance of signs, wonders, and "wonderful Providences."

By the nineteenth and twentieth centuries, New England Gothic also includes the conscious *re-creation* of the Middle Ages to achieve a Romantic separation from the everyday life of the world. Included are Longfellow's fascination with myths of the origin of New England, his revival of interest in Vikings and in Celtic explorers. In the twentieth century, such Romanticism continues to be manifested by Neo-Pagan medievalists, the Society for Creative Anachronism, fantasy writing groups, and by para-archaeologists who seek out Celtic Culdee settlements and find Ogham writing in glacial scratches on fieldstones.

In its medievalism, the Gothic in New England, as in Old, more often exemplifies the dark side of Romanticism, the agonies, not the quest for ecstatic transcendence. For the Romantics who followed Rousseau, children and noble savages could exist without original sin: for the Dark Romantics, there was no unfallen state. The Gothic is supremely the genre of the Fall. Who were the Goths, after all, but the tribe who brought down the glory of Rome? The word "Gothic" in its usual eighteenth-century sense conveyed disapproval, since medieval taste in life and art was considered to be as barbarous and uncivilized as the Goths and Vandals. Walpole and his followers deliberately reversed that meaning, but even in their favorable light, "Gothic" was still linked with darkness, mystery, and ignorance, was backward-looking and pessimistic rather than optimistic about the human condition.

In New England, the Gothic Fall mirrors the vision of regional decline seen by its writers and philosophers. The Fall of Man from innocence is the foundation of Puritan doctrine. Quakers, Indian wars, and contentions among the "elect" reminded writers at the end of the seventeenth century of the Puritans' failure to

---

[1]Many historians of the Gothic would dispute this statement. For the more usual opinion, see Gross 31; or Todorov.

create in Massachusetts a City on a Hill, purified and distinct from the secular society in England. In 1703, Cotton Mather lamented that *"our own backsliding hearts...plunged the whole country into so wonderful a degeneracy"* (*Magnalia* 2: 501).

In the nineteenth century, the Fall could be seen as both ethical and economic; for some, it is the loss of population from Western and Northern New England to the West. The vigorous "go-ahead" folk had left the farms, either for new lands or for industrial cities. For writers such as Hawthorne and Henry Adams, it is the perceived loss by their generation of New Englanders of the strength of purpose and dedication of the Puritan founders and the Revolutionary patriots. As Hawthorne notes in the "Custom-House" sketch that prefaces *The Scarlet Letter*, his ancestors may have been cruel and secret sinners, but they were God-fearing and productive men. He imagines that

> these stern and black-browed Puritans would have thought it quite a sufficient retribution for his sins, that ...the old trunk of the family tree...should have borne, as its topmost bough, an idler like myself.... 'A writer of story-books! What kind of business in life,– what mode of glorifying God, or being serviceable to mankind in his day and generation,–may that be?' (*The Scarlet Letter* 89).

By the end of the nineteenth century, the decline of New England is a real spiritual malaise. Boston is no longer the Hub of the universe, while the rural hinterlands are populated with throwbacks, inbred, decadent, full of atavistic superstitions, fallen from the ideal of the hardy Yankee patriot. New England comes to be seen as quaint, old-fashioned, out of the mainstream of American life. The survival of medieval beliefs or practices in backwoods places serves as a source of fascination for the Romantic medievalists, but for those who believe that New England has fallen from a happier state, from a golden age that never existed, it is further proof of degeneracy and decay.

By the twentieth century, the idea of New England as a unitary Anglo-Saxon Protestant culture has been overthrown; cast down, according to H.P. Lovecraft, before waves of Southern and Eastern European immigration, followed by blacks and Hispanics. By the 1930s, the very industries that had once attracted the immigrants began to leave the region. The textile mills that had enriched so many cities were among the earliest to leave. Then the makers of shoes, machine tools, hats, jewelry, and other products left New England, just as the nineteenth-century farmers had abandoned their fields looking for greener pastures. Cities like Fall River and Pawtucket, entire regions like Northeastern Connecticut and the Merrimack Valley of New Hampshire and Massachusetts seemed left behind by history. The abandoned factory joined the abandoned farm as a locus of horror, proof of New England's continued decline.

Such a dark view of New England's history is not the standard one, though this book is hardly the first to propose it.[2] Neither are the writers discussed here those most often studied. Its views of both history and literature, therefore, are non-canonical. Studies in American history, for the most part, have focused on the conquest of the frontier, rather than on the resulting decline of the older settlements. Local histories are usually written by amateurs or boosters; only rarely will they acknowledge declining populations or decamping industries. Studying the Gothic strain in New England can produce what Gross in *Redefining the American Gothic* describes as "an alternative history of the American experience" (3). Revisionist histories that emphasize America's victimization of native peoples and African slaves have dominated recent scholarship, but few historians with that frame of reference concern themselves with the supernatural. Leslie Fiedler, in *Love and Death in the American Novel*, may have been the first to link America's "special guilts" with "the gothic form" (134), noting that "the slaughter of the Indians, who would not yield their lands to the carriers of utopia, and the abominations of the slave trade, in which the black man, rum, and money were inextricably entwined in a knot of guilt, provided new evidence that evil did not remain with the world that had been left behind" (135). In these two "special guilts," New England merchants, soldiers, and divines had a great share.

Unlike the South, New England has no watershed event like the Civil War to mark the end of ascendancy and the old order.[3] Instead, areas decayed at differing rates. The industrial cities rose as the backwoods stagnated, the cities in their turn stagnated as new suburbs grew prosperous. The perception that "things

---

[2] Kittredge remains the authority for the continuity of Old World witch beliefs into the New; Leventhal shows how the Renaissance worldview survived in America through the eighteenth century. See Ringe for popularity of European Gothic novels; Fiedler for discussions of the Gothic legacy in New World.

[3] Although cultural historians follow Brooks in calling the Civil War the end of the "Flowering" or "Golden Age" of New England's intellectual life.

are not as grand as they once were" has a basis in fact for writers of the late nineteenth and twentieth centuries.

The darker aspects of medievalism that make up the Gothic are best exemplified in New England's obsession with death and the dead—whether expressed as burial customs or ancestor-hunting and genealogy.

Reading the *New England Primer*, Puritan children began their rise to ✓ literacy with

A   In Adam's Fall
      We Sinned All.

Thus were the children of the Saints reminded that they were doomed from birth. As they grew older, they had only to visit graveyards to be reminded, as Hamlet was, that death is natural. Gravestone carving provided one outlet for Puritan artistic expression. The earliest stones show stark images of moldering flesh and bones, in the tradition of the medieval *memento mori*. Clearly, the result of Adam's Fall was the end of human immortality; therefore, to seek to evade God's judgment on Adam by interfering with death was to re-enact Adam's sin. Those who sought out the dead or the Devil to gain knowledge or immortality were damned as necromancers. Necromancy, more so than adultery, is the secret sin of New ✓ England Gothic.

According to the *OED*, necromancy is "the pretended art of revealing future events by means of communication with the dead." The history of the word's use reveals its identity with the European conception of witchcraft. Witches, like the Biblical woman of Endor, could open the gates between life and death. But by meddling with these boundaries, the witch condemned her own soul. Necromancy was the essence of the Satanic bargain, for the witch's power over life and death could not come from God, and only Satan could stand in God's stead. Witches and wizards sought from the dead not only knowledge of the future, but the ability to cheat Death themselves.

Fear of the powers of the dead helped account for the fear of witches, who could not only cause death but perhaps even bring the dead back to life. In Salem, there was an obsession with hiding the bodies of the hanged witches. This may have been done as posthumous punishment, to keep the witches apart from the godly in death, though they had not been separate in life. It may also have been done to prevent the remaining undiscovered witches (or some of the godly) from using the bodies in unhallowed rites of necromancy. The body of one of the hanged witches, George Jacobs, hidden by his family for centuries, was re-interred only recently during the Tercentenary of the witch trials.

Raising the dead, the *OED* to the contrary, has never been confined to divination. Most necromancers sought power over the living through consulting the dead. Nineteenth-century spiritualism and the cult of mediums continued this obsession with raising the dead in a more hopeful guise, in which spirit messengers could report that the "undiscovered country" looked amazingly like New England. Not all New Englanders shared the Spiritualists' sunny view of the afterlife; some believed that tuberculosis might be caused by the depredations of the uneasy dead. The New England folkloric vampire, discussed in Chapter Six, represents death in its most horrific aspect. The native belief has little in common with fictional treatments of the subject from Byron to Coppola in which the vampire is seductive, full of the promise of eternal life. Twentieth-century horror writers have returned to and expanded the Puritan obsession with graphic images of death. H.P. Lovecraft's fiction abounds with tombs, ghouls, and the re-animated dead. The unprecedented popularity of Stephen King has brought these graveyard images into the full daylight of our culture.

New England has a long history of belief in the supernatural: what explains the persistence of such belief? From the earliest explorers through the Puritans and into the twentieth century, dwellers in New England have endowed the native peoples, the fields and the forests, and later the factories, towns, and cities, with shapes of fear. The forests were truly frightful places for the first settlers, who lost no time in cutting down the trees so that by 1800 New England was facing its first energy crisis. No less frightful were the original inhabitants of the land, the Indians who seemed like forest demons, the dark Other. The Indians' attempts to win back their lands in the Pequot Wars and King Philip's War were seen as campaigns by the Devil against the Kingdom of God. Cotton Mather's *Magnalia Christi Americana* introduces the history of the Indian wars with the observation that "nations of wretches whose whole *religion* was the most explicit sort of *devil-worship*" would naturally form the shock troops of their Satanic master "for the extinction of a plantation so contrary to his interests, as that of *New-England* was" (2: 480).

Manifestations of New England Gothic, whether expressed as nostalgia for the Puritans or, more often, horror at their excesses, have looked further back for inspiration, toward the European Middle Ages. For the most part, it has been the horrors and not the whimsies or romance of that era that were imported; though castles reassembled from European stone dot the actual landscape, the function of the castle in European Gothic is given in New England Gothic to the isolated farmhouse, the Victorian Gothic mansion, or even the deserted factory. The Fall so characteristic of traditional Gothic has its objective correlative, as we have seen, in the region's long decline from early prominence.[4]

Lovecraft followed nineteenth-century tradition in identifying the Puritans with the Gothic. Accused by critics of being "Puritanical" because he repressed sexual urges in himself and in his creations, he turned these accusations back upon one correspondent (Long; 11 Dec.1923), saying that while he did not share Puritan theology, he concurred with their "artistic" world-view:

> The Puritans unconsciously sought to do a supremely artistic thing—to mould all life into a dark poem; a macabre tapestry with quaint arabesques and patterns...in place of slovenly Nature set up a life in Gothick design... Verily, the Puritans were the only really effective diabolists and decadents the world has known;...Can you imagine anything more magnificent than the wholesale slaughter of Indians—a very epick—by our New-England ancestors in the name of the lamb? (*SL* 1: 275).

Drawing upon this view of the past, Lovecraft in his fiction establishes the age of the Puritans as our New England equivalent of the Dark Ages (St. Armand "The Roots of Horror in New England").

New England's folklore of the supernatural has been collected since the beginning of the colonies' existence. Richard Dorson's *America in Legend* provides one explanation for New England's wealth of supernatural folktales and literature. In his chapter on "The Religious Impulse" he contends that the Mathers should be studied as great folklore collectors. Because of their efforts, the lines

---

[4]See Day 96-7 for a similar discussion of the "longing and repulsion . . .toward the past" in general, not only for the Middle Ages, in the English Gothic tradition. See also Gross 23-4.

between oral and written tradition and low and high culture have always been
blurred in New England. Since stories of signs and wonders, of witches and
ghosts, have been written down from the earliest times, scholarly and popular
writers could make use of folklore materials without having to go and collect for
themselves.

Local color writing in New England, usually associated with late nineteenth-
century realism, thrives today in popular horror fiction. Magical realist Howard
Frank Mosher draws on the folklore of his native Vermont's Northeast Kingdom
whose picturesque decline is a living reminder of how New England's glories have
flown. At the University of Maine, the Northeast Archives of Folklore and Oral
History preserves in tape-recorded interviews the ancient legends of the woods and
the sea. Story-telling and folklore collecting continue in all the New England states.
Salem, whose last remaining industry is tourism, has become a center for Neo-
Pagans and the modern witch belief.

Above all, I have chosen to write about the Gothic in New England because
I have lived my life here, in the shadow of a more glorious past. I grew up in
Norwich, Connecticut, gritty city of abandoned mills that resemble ruined castles
and cathedrals, haunted by memories of Indian wars and Benedict Arnold. [5] My
nostalgia for the European Middle Ages led me as a child to an equal enthusiasm for
the earliest years of Colonial history. Then too, while very young, I discovered the
fictions of H.P. Lovecraft, who also blended antiquarian obsession with a
preoccupation with the supernatural. Like Lovecraft's, "my New England is a
dream New England—the familiar scene with certain lights and shadows
heightened ...just enough to merge it with things beyond the world" (June 1927;
SL 2: 130). Like Lovecraft's, my dream New England is most aptly described as a
nightmare.

The first part of this book focuses on the folklore and history of New
England from the sixteenth through the nineteenth centuries. After a review of

---

[5] The Falls of the Yantic River in Norwich is the actual site of Uncas's Leap, which
Cooper in *The Last of the Mohicans* moved to upstate New York. Benedict Arnold was born in
Norwich, and his ghost is said to appear on Halloween at the cemetery where his mother is buried.
By a strange coincidence, Shaun O'Connell was moved to write *Imagining Boston*, an idealized
tribute to Boston, and by extension to New England, because he grew up in a city that had failed to
realize that ideal vision. His home, Marlborough, Mass., a decayed exurb of Boston, was, like
Norwich, "a town of atrophied economic and cultural opportunities. . . . either you worked in the
declining shoe and box factories or you left town" (xii)

other definitions of the Gothic in Europe and America, the chapters are organized around motifs. Chapter Three, "Myths of Origin, Monsters in the Sea, Devils in the Forest," traces the images of fantasy and horror that emerge from the earliest European exploration of New England. Whether it is sea monsters, merfolk, or dancing demons, explorers see what they think they should see, and the European Christian mythos is superimposed on the new landscape.

The following two chapters look further at the Puritan attitude toward their new home, which at times can only be described as a kind of paranoia. The witchcraft persecutions form the most famous expression of the failure of the Puritans' attempted Utopia. Though the Salem outbreak is one of the most thoroughly-analyzed events in American history, scholars have only recently begun to treat it in the context of European witch beliefs. Chapters Five and Six ✓ emphasize the persistence of learned and popular European traditions in New England history and folklore.

Chapter Six is devoted to "The New England Vampire Belief," a tradition attested in folklore and newspaper accounts from 1790–1890. Reports of the exhumation and destruction of vampire-like revenants have been treated as fiction until recently. Startling archaeological evidence now reveals the real burial practices that support these attempts to regain power over the hungry dead.

Steeped in the history and folklore of the supernatural in New England from the earliest explorers through the nineteenth century, one writer, H.P. Lovecraft, incarnates these elements of fear and horror in his work and in so doing creates *new* New England monsters Chapter Seven, "The Local Color is Black—H.P. Lovecraft" treats Lovecraft's transformations of legends of sea monsters, haunted houses, witchcraft, and the historical vampire belief, as well as his portrayal of the decline of New England.

The final chapter traces the divergent paths New England Gothic has taken since Lovecraft: popular horror, exemplified by Stephen King and other, less well-known, writers; "mainstream Gothic," produced by such writers as Shirley Jackson and John Updike; and the continuing belief in the supernatural manifested by ghost-hunters, Neo-Pagans, worshippers of Lovecraft's invented gods, and other "true believers."

By its nature, this study blurs the lines separating fact from fiction, history ✓ from just plain story. Most authors who have chosen New England settings have made no attempt to distinguish actual events from unsubstantiated traditions. Instead, twentieth-century New England writers, like their more famous nineteenth-century progenitors Hawthorne and Melville, have drawn on historical events and folk beliefs alike to inspire horror and to make their horrors more "realistic" and convincing. In the end, the most important thing about the Gothic is that it be frightening, not that it be "real." As Fiedler says of American literature, "however shoddily or ironically treated, horror is essential" (26).

The Gothic is, essentially, dangerous entertainment. In the *Magnalia Christi*, Mather returns again and again to monsters and demons, the outward proofs of his readers' "backsliding hearts." He describes one monstrous birth to a disciple of the dissenter Anne Hutchinson in 1637. The sinful woman produced "as hideous a *monster* as pershaps[sic] the sun ever lookt upon" (2: 448).[6] It is devilish, with claws, four horns, and no forehead. Its birth is attended with signs and wonders. Its midwife was a witch, the good women present were made sick, children went into convulsions, and invisible hands shook the bed.

At this point, Mather stops, saying he is afraid to write any further. Such mouth-watering descriptions of the devices of the Enemy are too dangerous for his readers. He quotes a letter from Thomas Hooker, the founder of Connecticut, who recorded on paper the advent of this monstrosity and in so doing endangered his own soul: "...while I was thus musing, and thus writing, my study ...shook, as we thought, with an earthquake, by the space of half a quarter of an hour....My wife said, it was the devil that was displeased that we confer about this occasion" (2: 449).[7] But despite such dire warnings, New England writers continued to fill their pages with news of monsters, death, and the Devil, and readers eagerly endangered their immortal souls to seek out those pages and learn all the bad news. When did this morbid fascination with the dark side end in New England? The answer is, not yet.

---

[6]Spelling and italics are as in the original. The story is recorded in John Winthrop's *Journal* for 1638. Winthrop was probably Mather's source, since Mather follows him closely.

[7]Marion Starkey relates a similar tale in the preface to her *The Devil in Massachusetts;* a "small hurricane" invaded her house when she began her research into the witch trials. She notes that "Cotton Mather, my colleague" would appreciate her observations.

Chapter Two
History and Criticism of the Gothic

> Reason's self shall bow the knee
> To shadows and delusions here
> --Philip Freneau

Critics and historians of the Gothic have usually confined their investigations to one only of the embattled terrains of literature, whether comparative or national; history; folklore; or the history of ideas. At one point or another this study ventures onto all these terrains, freely crossing their boundaries because those boundaries are artificial. The Gothic has always been about breaking taboos. Its continued popularity in the twentieth century speaks to our untiring fascination with those who trespass forbidden ground.

The taboos challenged by Gothic fiction are those of sex and death: unnatural in the first case and both natural and unnatural in the other. The taboos on writing American Gothic history arose from an unwillingness to face the unpleasant underside of our heritage, to acknowledge the racism, intolerance, and barbarity that resulted in the persecution of Indians, religious dissenters, and witches. The idea that medieval superstition survives into the twentieth century offends all who view New England as a beacon of scholarship, enlightenment, and rational discourse. Finally, the treating of such writers as Lovecraft and Stephen King as the heirs of Nathaniel Hawthorne in a New England Gothic tradition transgresses taboos about the canon, about what literature is deserving of scholarly attention. These last taboos have been broken frequently since the 1970s;

nonetheless, most criticism of fantasy and horror remains separate from criticism of works in the literary mainstream.

1. History of the Gothic Tradition in New England

The two competing views of New England's past are embodied in works of criticism so brilliant that they have become like myths themselves. The light, vigor and optimism of Van Wyck Brooks's *The Flowering of New England* and its companion volume *New England Indian Summer* are exemplified in his titles as Harry Levin's demonic passion is exemplified in his *The Power of Blackness*. Brooks saw a Spenglerian movement in the culture of New England, in the rise to its golden age between 1840 and 1860, and in its gentle mellowing into "Indian Summer" after the Civil War. His touchstones are "vigor" and "wholesomeness," his critical judgments consistently employing metaphors of health. For example, Brooks praises Judge D.P. Thompson's *The Green Mountain Boys*, which compared Ethan Allen to a Romantic Scottish border raider, in these words: "over all one breathed the fragrant air of pine, fir and balsam, a world of sparkling lakes and flashing trout-streams...this was a Yankee tale as brisk and wholesome as any mountain-ballad"(426). For Brooks, New England in its "flowering" was as wholesome as Thoreau's Walden Pond because of "the healthy objectivity" of statesmen such as the "robust and confident" Daniel Webster and poet-philosophers such as Longfellow, Holmes, and, greatest of all, Emerson (540–1).

To this day, images of the lighter side of New England predominate in travel literature. Tourists, after all, visit back-country Vermont to wonder at its beauty while staying in quaint B&Bs, not to be horrified by cellarholes and decayed, inbred farmers. In 1990, Shaun O'Connell wrote an excellent literary history that so emphasizes the positive that it makes even the ebullient Brooks seem pessimistic and autumnal. *Imagining Boston* consistently ignores the dark side (Lovecraft's ghouls have no place in this book) in favor of the Puritans' ideal Boston, where he sees in the twentieth century the persistence of belief in "the search for personal salvation and public mission in the new world," and claims that these values "still grip the New England mind" (305). Levin's *Power of Blackness*, on the other hand, is not liable to attract new tourists to New England. He makes Hawthorne's "*no* in thunder" the center of an argument for the darker side of the American tradition, the "American Nightmare" that he opposes to the "rhetoric of the Everlasting Yea" produced by the boosters of the American Dream (7).

Critics who deny the continuity of the Gothic tradition from the Old to the New World often cite Hawthorne's preface to *The Marble Faun*, where he seems to be saying that America *has* no dark side to inspire Gothic Romance, causing him to require Italian scenes for inspiration.[1] America, he says, is not Romantic; therefore, it is impossible to write "a romance about a country where there is no shadow, no antiquity, no mystery, no picturesque and gloomy wrong, nor anything but a commonplace prosperity, in broad and simple daylight, as is happily the case with my dear native land.... Romance and poetry, ivy, lichens, and wall-flowers, need ruin to make them grow" (590). But how can we believe he does not intend all this ironically, when his writing prior to 1859 was all shadows and gloomy wrong, making Colonial New England seem an anteroom to Hell in *The Scarlet Letter* and "Young Goodman Brown." He had also, in *The House of the Seven Gables*, transformed his cousin's old wooden mansion into a Gothic ruin where moss and lichens flourished. We can only assume that in the *Marble Faun* preface he is employing the same ironic tone that he did in 1851 in the preface to *The House of the Seven Gables*, where the typical author's disclaimer of reality rings unquestionably false. He says that his "book may be read strictly as a Romance, having a great deal more to do with the clouds overhead than with any portion of the actual soil of the County of Essex" (244). Yet all who go on to read the "Romance" know that it has a stronger sense of place than any novel written in America up to that time, that its eponymous setting still stands in Salem, and that the plot is derived from Hawthorne's own family history. The Pyncheons' dream of ancestral land grants in Maine was a reality for Hawthorne's mother and for his grandparents. The wizard's curse on the Pyncheon males, "God will give him blood to drink," was hurled at Hawthorne's ancestor Judge Hathorne who, in fact, had presided at the witch trials. Knowing all this, we can assume that Hawthorne means the opposite of what he says in the novel's preface: "it has been no part of his object, however, to describe local manners, nor in any way to meddle with the characteristics of a community for whom he cherishes a proper respect and a natural

---

[1]See, among many others, Brooks 48; Levin 241; Ringe 177; Kiely 24.

regard" (244). Indeed, Hawthorne was much more successful in finding the Gothic in New England than he ever was to be in Italy.

Though this book focuses primarily on twentieth century writers of New England Gothic, the Gothic tradition can be traced in an unbroken line from the earliest settlements of the region.[2] Even before the first American novels, narratives of Indian Captivity remind us of the English Gothic romances. Though in reality the Indians of New England refused to act like proper Gothic villains and did not rape their female captives, publishers still used this image to sell the books. The "avid speculation about the sexual fate of female captives" (Kolodny 29) caused publishers to advertise exciting "barbarities" even when the redeemed captives denied that any sexual misconduct had taken place, so powerful was the image of the dark man of the forest gloating over the helpless white body of his captive.

While the first professional writers of fiction in America came from the Middle States, their work in the Gothic vein influenced the New England writers. Charles Brockden Brown's romances such as *Wieland* and *Edgar Huntly* were full of weird happenings which were rationalized according to the conventions of the "explained Gothic." Washington Irving sought out Gothic scenery in Europe and created an American Gothic landscape in the Hudson River Valley by combining and transforming folk legends that had come over with the Dutch settlers.

In New England, however, it was not the rationalized Gothic of Brown but the marvels and local color of Irving that predominated. John Greenleaf Whittier began his career by editing the earlier Connecticut poet J.G.C. Brainerd, who wrote several ballads on New England supernatural themes. In America, as in Germany, Gothic themes appeared in verse before they were transformed into prose romances. The "Graveyard School" in England was matched in the New World first by the Puritan homilies on death by Michael Wigglesworth, later by the poems of Philip Freneau. In Freneau's "The Indian Burying Ground" (1786–88), for example, Indian lore of the dead combines with the poetic convention of an elegy for a vanished race. The Indian ghosts—"the hunter and the deer, a shade!"—will

---

[2]See Attebery's *The Fantasy Tradition in American Literature*, based on his doctoral dissertation *America and the Materials of Fantasy* (Brown University, 1979) for an excellent discussion of the fantastic in New England and the rest of the United States.

force onlookers seeking Gothic melancholy to admit that "Reason's self shall bow the knee/ To shadows and delusions here."

Whittier was inspired most by Robert Burns; like his idol he wished to express local traditions in simple metrical forms and dialect. Whittier's first collection of verse, *Legends of New England* (1831), "versified stories from Mather's *Magnalia*, anticipated Longfellow's *Hiawatha* with ballads of Indian exploits, written tales of the colony times that suggested a metrical Hawthorne" (Brooks 409). Though methods of scholarship may have become more scientific, Whittier's *The Legends of New England* (1831) revised and expanded into *The Supernaturalism of New England* (1847) set a standard for the transmission and interpretation of folklore. Whittier translated to America the Gothic themes prevailing in European poetry. His retellings of ghostly legends were so popular that they re-entered the oral tradition in the form he gave them. Even his non-supernatural poetry, such as *Snow-Bound*, deals with themes of the decline. By the time *Snow-Bound* was published in 1866, many farmers had abandoned the family farms and moved West or into the industrial cities.

Hawthorne's early tales, "Twice-Told" indeed, continue the tradition of collecting and transmitting the wondrous occurrences that had fascinated the Mathers. In addition to outer manifestations of the supernatural, the darkness *within* the New England character, the secret sin within the soul haunted Melville and Hawthorne. In Melville's words, "'the power of blackness...derives its force from its appeals to that Calvinistic sense of Innate Depravity and Original Sin, from whose visitations, in some shape or other, no deeply thinking mind is always and wholly free'" (qtd. in H. Levin 26).

Melville and Poe chronicled New England's exploration of the sea, pursuing the power of blackness that is found within Whiteness, the Whale of *Moby Dick* and the Antarctic of "The Narrative of A. Gordon Pym." Poe, while simply a visitor to the region, drew on histories of New England whaling, as did Melville. The protagonist of Poe's Gothic sea story "is a native of the bleak New England island of Nantucket, which for Melville will symbolize man in self-isolation" (H. Levin 111). Besides the New England histories that underlie *Moby Dick* and *Benito Cereno*, Melville retold New England folklore in "The Lightning-Rod Man," and in "The Tartarus of Maids" compared an existing paper-mill in western Massachusetts to Hell.

While Poe, Hawthorne and Melville were bringing the Gothic into the mainstream of American literature, America in the 1840s and 1850s was freshly preoccupied with the Invisible World in the guise of new religions such as Mormonism, Seventh-Day Adventism, and Spiritualism. All three religions began in upstate New York, in an area known as the "Burned-over District," but the fire of Spiritualism spread so quickly through New England that it was as if mediums were simply waiting for a firebell in the night. New England produced the most Gothic of the physical mediums, the pale showman Daniel Dunglas Home, who was never proven to be a fraud, despite Robert Browning's claims to the contrary in "Mr. Sludge, the Medium." The wizard Home, born in Scotland but brought up in eastern Connecticut, was a protege of the Cheneys of Manchester, at whose home he met Mark Twain. Given the times, even the rationalist Twain was to turn to Spiritualism at the end of his life, hoping to contact his daughter Suzy. Spiritualism was satirized in New England's realistic literature by James and Howells, but it also occasioned a new kind of explained Gothic, where the wonders and terrors of the next world could be transformed into homely realities. Spirit hands played accordions and dropped flowers at seances, and heaven itself looked like New England in Elizabeth Stuart Phelps's spiritualist best-seller *The Gates Ajar*.

Spiritualism—like Christian Science, which originated in New England—was an arena for women's advancement. Many of the pioneering feminists were spiritualists. Raps, a male observer reported, sounded from the very table around which the women's rights advocates gathered at Seneca Falls in 1848.[3] So, too, in New England, alongside the male Gothic tradition described by Brooks and Levin, there flourished a school of local color writers who were women. Immensely popular in their time, they are only now being rediscovered by feminist scholarship.[4] Past critics of these women treated them as realists, their supernatural stories considered as aberrations. It seems to me more likely that these writers are all of a piece, belonging to their place and time, and that their use of the

---

[3]For a complete description of this unusual piece of women's history, see Ann Braude's *Radical Spirits* (58). For a contemporary view, see Epes Sargent's *Peculiar* (1863), a "feminist-Spiritualist-abolitionist" novel.

[4] See especially Josephine Donovan and Sarah Way Sherman, as well as Carpenter and Kolmar's introduction.

supernatural, rather than being uncharacteristic, reflects faithfully the New England life they knew.

The earlier generation of local colorists, notably Child, Lydia MariaLydia Maria Child and Harriet Beecher Stowe, were active in the wider world as reformers in the causes of abolition and feminism. The later generation were more exclusively professional writers. The Connecticut writer Rose Terry Cooke, Maine's Sarah Orne Jewett, Mary Wilkins Freeman, (perhaps the most commercially successful of the group), Rhode Island's Alice Brown, Massachusetts' Louise Imogen Guiney, Harriet Prescott Spofford, and Elizabeth Stuart Phelps at times even collaborated. Sometimes the "circle of friends," as they called themselves, resemble modern women's writing groups. Their writing expressed quaint customs, characters, and legends in local dialect, but their subjects included issues of feminism and racism as well. The later writers, especially, noticed the decline of New England's backwoods farms, its seaports, and its factory towns.

Edith Wharton, usually seen as a realist, set herself apart from these women: she claimed that Wilkins Freeman, in particular, had too cheerful an outlook. If so, Wharton cannot have read her ghost stories. Wilkins Freeman's "The Wind in the Rose-bush," "Luella Miller," and others are mainstream Gothic in their portrayal of child abuse and vampirism. Wharton wrote both ghost stories[5] and non-supernatural tales that mirror the decline of backwoods New England, most notably *Ethan Frome*. The tradition of Gothic feminism in the region is fittingly climaxed in Charlotte Perkins Gilman whose "The Yellow Wallpaper" has been read as ghost story, psychiatric narrative, feminist allegory, or, grandly crossing the boundaries, all three at once!

In the twentieth century, Lovecraft's fiction reflects both the masculine and the feminine traditions of the Gothic, though he acknowledged only the male line of descent, seeing himself as heir of Poe, not of Wharton. His domestic tragedies, use of dialect, and eccentric characters, however, owe much to the women's tradition, especially to the ghost stories of Mary Wilkins Freeman. Stephen King owes something to Sarah Orne Jewett, unlikely combination as this may seem. His

---

[5]See Fedorko for an analysis of several.

most recent novel, *Dolores Claiborne*, told in a woman's voice, seems a profane revisioning of Jewett's stories set in Maine coastal villages.

2. The Gothic and the Critics

Criticism of Gothic literature has flourished in the past fifteen years, with critics first seeking out traces of the Gothic in mainstream writers from Melville to Faulkner, and then expanding the canon to include less respectable works. The Gothic is only one of the "marginal literatures" that has benefited from the move toward inclusiveness in academia. Through these critics' efforts, Mary Shelley has been elevated to honorary mainstream status, (*Frankenstein* is among the most widely taught books in college literature courses), and Bram Stoker seems to be on his way to canonical status as well. Until this recent effort, however, there had been as little serious consideration of twentieth-century horror writers as there was of the earliest Gothic novelists, even though for "three decades between 1790 and 1820...the English novel and the Gothic novel were one and the same species" (Frank ix). The overwhelming popularity of the English, French, and German Gothic romances were accepted as proof of Wordsworth's charge that these books lacked "high seriousness" and "did nothing more than pander to the 'degrading thirst after outrageous stimulation'" (qtd. in Frank x). Nothing artistic could be popular, so the Gothic romances must have been literature for the non-literate. Modern fantasy for adults, as Brian Attebery shows in *Strategies of Fantasy*, has been no less condemned as escapist. Both fantasy and horror are still dismissed as "sub-literate," or, as *Time* dubbed Stephen King, "post-literate." In Chapters Seven and Eight, works that have rarely been taken seriously will be accepted on their own terms because, as William Patrick Day wrote, justifying *his* study of the Gothic, "the imaginative life of a culture is not necessarily fully embodied, or most intensely and significantly expressed, in socially acceptable forms" (10).

Some recent critics of the Gothic have discussed writers treated in this study, but from different points of departure. The literature of the Gothic has served as a mirror, reflecting critics' own preoccupations, whether economic and historical, mystical and symbolic, psychological, feminist, or post-structuralist

narrative theory.[6] One of the best treatments of the rise of the Gothic and the heirs
of that tradition remains Lovecraft's *Supernatural Horror in Literature*, written for
amateur publication in 1924 and only printed after his death.[7] The American
Gothic, as distinct from the European phenomenon, has received critical attention as
well, usually from one or another of the above perspectives.[8] An exception is
Ronald Curran, whose 1971 anthology emphasizes the continuity of Old World
beliefs in the popular culture as well as the high literature of "the American
Renaissance." Attitudes toward the supernatural differ widely among these critics,
ranging from the pioneers such as Varma and Summers, who grant it central
importance, to those like Day and Massé, who push it to the periphery, as an
embarrassing relic.

Because the Gothic looks back to the Middle Ages yet remains vigorous at
the end of the Second Millennium, it refuses to fit comfortably within the usual
divisions of literary history. Nevertheless, much criticism of the Gothic seeks to
narrow its limits. Maurice Lévy, a paradigm-setting theorist, placed the strict
temporal boundaries on the Gothic genre that can be seen in his title *Le Roman
"gothique" anglais, 1764–1824.* Aguirre, following Lévy's work, distinguishes
"modern horror" from "Gothic," and restricts the latter to a very small compass: he
assumes that "our genre starts in 1764 on Christmas Day with the publication of
Walpole's *The Castle of Otranto*," and ends in 1830, "give or take ten years for

---

[6]See, among others, Day, Punter for the first, Varma, Varnado and Aguirre for the
second, MacAndrew for the third, DeLaMotte and Massé for the fourth, and Carter for the fifth.
All have differing theories for the origin and tenacious survival of the Gothic mode. Varma
attributes the rise of Gothic to the "enthronement of Reason," which caused people to seek for
other means of "other-worldly gratification" (41). Day says, to the contrary, that Gothic "does not
offer a vision of imaginative transcendence" (192). MacAndrew claims the Gothic is not
mythopoeic but "a vehicle for ideas about psychological evil" (5). Massé focuses on the
victimized woman in Gothic, rather than the male victimizers. Baldick will not admit a tale to his
Gothic anthology unless it concerns "historical fears"(xx) in addition to the supernatural. Wolf and
Wolf influenced my focus on medievalism in the introduction to their 1974 anthology. Kiely has
excellent readings of the central Gothic texts, but treats them under the rubric of "The Romantic
Novel in England." All these recent critics acknowledge their debt to the first historians of the
Gothic, Scarborough, Birkhead, Railo, Summers, Praz.

[7]See especially pp. 23-35.

[8] Gross says his approach combines "psychoanalytical and historical analysis." Ringe
establishes the continuity with the English tradition. Fiedler is *sui generis*. See the essays in
Carpenter and Kolmar for an answer to Ringe's and Fiedler's focus on the male tradition. Malin
ignores the supernatural altogether when defining the "New American Gothic.".

vagueness' sake" (Aguirre 85). MacAndrew [9] observes the same date of genesis, noting that "it was a new literary form in the late eighteenth century," "closely allied" to the Sentimental novel which was popular at the same time because both explored the psychology of good and evil in the human mind, one through fantasy and one through realism (3–4). She does not, however, agree with the upper terminus; instead, she notes the "continuing tradition" of the Gothic in Dickens and Balzac, and the emergence of new archetypes in Stevenson and Stoker. Carpenter and Kolmar, among others, consider the ghost story a totally separate genre. I prefer to follow St. Armand, Punter, and Varnado in tracing the persistence of Gothic themes, however transmuted, from the Middle Ages into the popular fiction and culture of the twentieth century.

There have always been two strains in the cultural phenomenon of medievalism. The Gothic in New England encompasses both the light, fantastic vision and the dark, backward- and inward-looking one. Virginia Hyde compares the two strains to medieval images of the Last Judgment. In such altarpieces, the saved souls are on the right hand of God, ascending among angels and rays of light, while on the other side the Hell-mouth gapes revealing horrors (136–7). Such a distinction is not a critical anachronism. In 1804, Dr. Nathan Drake discerned these same varieties of Gothic inspiration, combining them in his now mostly forgotten novel *Henry Fitzower*. In the preface to this work, he names "the two species of Gothic superstition, the terrible and the sportive." The first species, he says, "turns chiefly on the ministration of the Spectre," while the second is characterized by "the innocent gambols of the Fairy" (qtd. in Kliger 237; 236). In the twentieth century, these same symbols of dark and light medievalism are encoded in the cover art of popular horror and fantasy: skeletons or skulls for the first, elves for the second.

Chris Baldick's introduction to his *Oxford Book of Gothic Tales* distinguishes the medievalism of a Ruskin or Morris—from whose attitudes modern fantasy derives—from the "anti-Gothicism" of those who wrote Gothic horror. Unlike the fantasy writers who admired the Middle Ages, writers of Gothic

---

[9]Also see DeLamotte who distinguishes between the "Gothic romance," found within the limits of Lévy's dates and the "Gothic tradition," later works of supernatural horror.

fiction from Clara Reeve to H.P. Lovecraft have personally repudiated medieval superstitions while relying upon them to create horrific effects. Lovecraft illustrates Baldick's theory that "when Gothic fiction has employed the ghostly apparitions and omens of archaic lore..., it has at the same time placed them under strong suspicion as part of a cruelly repressive and deluded past"(xiii). Gothic fiction has always gone far beyond Gothic revivals in architecture or landscape in emphasizing the supernatural, the barbaric, the cruel. [10]

Although it is not generally well known, the term "Gothic" had some more positive associations even during the Age of Reason. Samuel Kliger traced in *The Goths in England* the origins of this "Gothic myth" that eventually led to theories of innate Aryan supremacy. Seventeenth-century parliamentarians in England turned to their Germanic forebears, to whom they gave the collective name "Goth," in order to legitimate their desire for a strong parliament and a weak monarchy. Based on their readings of late Latin and early Christian texts, they idealized the Goths, not as the destroyers of Rome but as, in a sense, its saviors. In addition, "the early texts offered a quasi-scientific explanation of the Gothic propensity for liberty in a theory of climatic influence on character...explaining Gothic vigor, hardiness, and zeal for liberty" (Kliger 2). Their opponents the Tories, who favored a strong monarchy and a stable (i.e. non-democratic) government, tended to identify with Rome and with classical civilization. The picture Kliger paints through excerpts from seventeenth and eighteenth-century texts of brawny Gothic warriors overcoming the effete Romans who had lapsed into womanish mystery cults, also delineates the world-view of the twentieth-century *Weird Tales* writers, Lovecraft, Clark Ashton Smith, and Robert E. Howard. Because of Howard's success, the "Gothic myth" has re-entered the mass culture through films about Conan the Barbarian, played appropriately enough by the Aryan superman Arnold Schwartzenegger.

Positive associations for the Gothic emerge also from the nineteenth-century Gothic Revival whose theorists wished to revive the Middle Ages in philosophy and literature as well as architecture, the fine arts, and crafts, for social improvement, not for the *frisson* of terror. The architectural theorist A.W. Pugin,

---

[10]Praz, *The Romantic Agony*, is the classic presentation of the darkness within Romanticism.

24

who worked on the Gothic Revival Houses of Parliament, considered himself a "true Goth;" even converting to Roman Catholicism to be closer to the spirit of the Middle Ages. For him, as for these other Victorians, the Middle Ages represented perfection in art and life, an ideal social order. Through the Gothic Revival, they hoped for, in Pugin's words, "a restoration of the ancient feelings and sentiments" (qtd. in Germann 70).

The "Gothic Myth" in seventeenth- and eighteenth-century England had its counterpart in nineteenth-century America, where George Perkins Marsh of the University of Vermont delivered a discourse in 1843 on *The Goths in New England*. The scholarly Marsh, who had studied the Icelandic sagas even before Longfellow did, argued that the Puritans' racial nobility resulted from the triumph of the Gothic strain in the English make-up over the Roman (i.e. Catholic or Continental) element. He refutes at length the "prejudice which makes Gothicism and barbarism synonymous." Instead, he insists, the Goths are "the noblest branch of the Caucasian race. We are their children" (14). The racialist theories which Lovecraft was later to espouse emerge clearly from Marsh's discourse. Marsh is proud that New England had so far preserved racial purity. He favors the Vermont Yankee over the mongrelized population of "commercial towns" such as New York. Yet in the end he accepts as inevitable the decline of his homeland, whose rocky farms cannot compete with those of the Western and Southern states, predicting, accurately, that New England will yet be the schoolmaster to those regions that supplant it in political influence (39).

As Levin noted in *The Power of Blackness*, the backward-turning Gothic tradition goes against the grain of American thought, which from the Republic's founders until George Bush has preferred to see us as purveyors of a New World Order. Donald Ringe's *American Gothic* traces the profound effect of the Scottish Common Sense philosophy on the founders and writers of the Constitution. Followers of this branch of the Enlightenment distrusted all products of Fancy, let alone supernatural romance. Ringe claims that during the formative period of American literature, 1790–1830, "the rationalistic foundations of American thought are a serious hindrance not only to the writing but also to the enjoyment of fiction" (6). Nevertheless, his exhaustive research in the catalogs of booksellers of the new republic finds that "the Gothic titles increased year by year" and that "they represented a substantial part of the offerings" (14). Americans were devouring English and German tales of the supernatural, and continued to do so through the century, regardless of the pronouncements of philosophers, educators, and other representatives of the high culture. This conflict between imagination and reason remains a keynote of the American Gothic tradition.

In America, the idea of the Gothic is often linked with the grotesque or simply with the past rather than with the explicitly demonic or supernatural. We need only think of Grant Woods' painting "American Gothic," where the upraised tines of the pitchfork and the shape of the farmhouse recall upward-striving cathedral spires, and whose attenuated figures show a quaintness and austerity verging on the grotesque. There is no evidence that Grant Woods meant the farmers to be demons or the farmhouse to be haunted. Vernon Hyles's essay in *The Gothic World of Stephen King: Landscape of Nightmares* makes King part of a "new Gothicism," defined by the domination of the grotesque in the literary mainstream.[11] Grotesque figures in art may be exaggerated but recognizably human—serial killers, dried-up spinsters, Grant Woods-style farmers—or they may verge upon the supernatural—dwarfs are a popular image of the grotesque. As MacAndrew notes "the figures of the grotesque are creatures of the earth and the underworld, frequently drawn from folklore and myth" (154). Twentieth-century horror writers tend to combine grotesque characters with overtly supernatural occurrences.

The classification American Gothic has been applied more often to the twentieth-century writers of the South than to those of the North.[12] Gothic is used interchangeably with grotesque: there need be no hint of the supernatural. Instead, as in this study's view of New England, the critical emphasis in studies of Southern Gothic is on degeneracy and decay. As British critic David Punter writes, bemused at this use of the term Gothic to describe the American South, "feelings of degeneracy abound. The worlds portrayed are ones infested with psychic and social decay...the crucial tone is one of desensitised acquiescence in the horror of obsession and prevalent insanity" (3). While these words do describe the South of

---

[11]King himself analyzes the "New American Gothic" in *Danse Macabre* 280-81.

[12] See also Malin for more on the Southern writers of what he calls "New American Gothic."

Faulkner and Flannery O'Connor, it is amazing how well they also describe the New England of Lovecraft and Shirley Jackson.

3. The Gothic and the Question of Belief

In discussions of the Gothic and fantastic in literature, much depends upon whether the horrors are real. Most critics assume that the audiences of eighteenth-century Gothic did not believe in the existence of the horrors they found therein: that is, they were jaded thrill-seekers only, as critics also assume modern audiences to be. In 1804, however, Gothic novelist Nathan Drake could write that "even in the present polished period of society, there are thousands who are yet alive to all the horrors of witchcraft, to all the solemn and terrible graces of the appalling spectre" (qtd. in Kliger 235). By these terms, at least some readers of the Gothic then, as now, believed in the reality of the horrors they so eagerly sought—like Bluebeard's wife opening up one Bloody Chamber after another, both terrified and satisfied at once.

Horace Walpole's stated purpose in writing *The Castle of Otranto* was to return the sense of wonder that characterized medieval literature to the novel of his own time, that had grown too tediously realistic.[13] His Gothic castle, Strawberry Hill, had transformed the "barbarous" Middle Ages into the latest fashion for the polite aristocracy, giving the period "social standing" (K. Clark 82). The Age of Reason had produced monsters. The excesses of Gothic romance and Gothic buildings like Beckford's Fonthill Abbey (which collapsed under its own weight) mark the furthest swing of the pendulum of reaction against order and enlightenment. The Gothic, an underground stream during the first three quarters of the eighteenth century, emerged in full spate as part of the Romantic movement. By the end of the century, Imagination seemed to have won out over Reason. James Twitchell reports in his work on the vampire in Romantic literature that "In 1736 George I deemed all witchcraft foolish and imaginary" but by 1786, "Horace Walpole claimed ...that George II ...'had no doubt of the existence of vampires and

---

[13]While all the critics I have found agree on this origin of the Gothic, William Patrick Day's *In the Circles of Fear and Desire* insists that "Gothic fantasy. . . is a peculiar offshoot of the romance, because it subverts its own mythology." See Varnado on the "paradox" of Walpole's creation.

their banquets on the dead'" (32). It's hard to keep a dead man down; even harder to deny the dark night of the human soul.

Tzvetan Todorov has influenced all later theorists,[14] because he defines the genres of fantasy and horror completely in terms of belief in the wonders found within them. The genre he calls "fantastique" has boundaries so narrow that it can include only a few works of literature. The characters and readers of these selected works must remain uncertain about what they are experiencing, not knowing if it is a dream or real, or even how to define "real."

> Le fantastique occupe le temps de cette incertitude; dès qu'on choisit l'une ou l'autre réponse, on quitte le fantastique pour entrer dans un genre voisin, l'étrange ou le merveilleux. Le fantastique, c'est l'hésitation éprouvée par un être qui ne connaît que les lois naturelles, face à un événement en apparence surnaturel...(Todorov 29) [15]

He excepts from his "fantastique" works whose primary purpose is allegorical or poetic, works for which the supernatural is only a pretext. He does admit that nineteenth-century writers may have turned to Gothic themes as a way of masking forbidden subject matter such as necrophilia, homosexuality or incest. He then bars from serious consideration the modern popular literature of horror and fantasy, claiming that twentieth-century writers no longer have any need to cloak their themes in Gothic robes—free of censorship, they should be able write what they wish. Such a claim does not explain the immense popularity of Gothic horror at the end of the twentieth century, nor does it explain the persistence of belief in the supernatural even among educated people. Todorov's opinion is that "la psychanalyse a remplacé (et par là même a rendu inutile) la littérature fantastique. On n'a pas besoin aujourd'hui d'avoir recours au diable pour parler d'un désir sexuel excessif, ni aux vampires pour désigner l'attirance exercée par les cadavres"

---

[14]For a list, see Carter 7-21.

[15] [my trans.] The fantastic occupies the moment of this uncertainty; as soon as the character chooses one answer or the other, we leave the fantastic and enter a neighboring genre, the strange or the marvellous. The fantastic is the hesitation experienced by a person who is only acquainted with natural laws, facing an event which is apparently supernatural.

(169). [16] Twenty-five years after these words were written, it is clear that people still need Satan and vampires to talk about the taboos of sex and death.   More people have watched or even read *The Exorcist* or *Dracula* than have ever read the classic psychoanalytical studies of these themes by Rank, Reik and Freud cited by Todorov. Jung would never have agreed that old beliefs would lose their primacy once "explained" by psychoanalysis. His *Psychology of the Unconscious* distinguishes two types of truth, literal and psychological. He complains that "the old fogies of science have from time to time thrown away an inherited piece of ancient truth; because it was not literal but psychologic truth" (9). The Gothic is always psychologically true.

Most criticism of the Gothic in literature ignores prevailing theories about the affective fallacy because in Gothic the effect on the reader is everything. Thus critics of this mode necessarily avoid the fashionable concept of the "death of the author" or the unimportance of the author's intentions. This study relies upon information gleaned from interviews with living writers and letters of dead ones. The reciprocal effects of Gothic literature on life and of life on literature are verifiable, not fallacious. The question of belief is central to Gothic literature, as is the participation of an audience which is decidedly not a fiction.[17]

Todorov, like most critics, is uncomfortable with making literary judgments dependent upon real readers, rather than "le lecteur implicite au texte" (39). [18] The literature of horror ought to be fertile ground for the reader-response critics who have followed Todorov and Iser, but so far Terry Heller is one of the few critics to use this methodology. His *The Delights of Terror* explains why people derive aesthetic pleasure while scaring themselves with Gothic fictions, but he does not even consider the survival of superstitious beliefs. Perhaps Todorov's or Heller's definitions of what people will accept as real differ from those of the readers of Gothic fiction. This community of readers is not homogeneous: some are "true believers," but not all accept the fantastic as real. There exists, after all, a sub-genre

---

[16] [my trans.] Psychoanalysis has replaced (and by that action has rendered useless) fantastic literature. Today we don't need to turn to the devil in order to talk about excessive sexual desire, nor to vampires to designate the attraction some may feel toward corpses.

[17] See Carter, 5-7; 122-3.

[18] [my trans.] "the reader who is implicit in the text."

of "explained Gothic," just as some literary fantasy is explained, like *Alice in Wonderland*, as being "all just a dream."

There is ambiguity within these texts and in the readers' minds as well. The narrator is often unreliable, yet the authors take great pains to build up a structure that supports belief through witnesses' testimony, letters, and documents. "The novelist's decision to tell a story through multiple voices or to filter the main narrator's voice through one or more frames impels consideration of the validity of testimony" (Carter 119). When readers accept such products of the imagination as though they were real and historical, the Gothic is liable to be censored. One of the earliest "historical Gothics," Daniel Defoe's *A Political History of the Devil*, which mixes Satanism and sedition with satire, has been banned since the early eighteenth century. Nor has the censorship ended: horror comic books in the 1950s and slasher movies today have been blamed for violent behavior in teenagers, and books by Lovecraft and King have been removed from libraries for promoting Satanism.

The Gothic will never really be safe entertainment with dangerous subjects, though theorists of horror including Stephen King have explained its appeal in those terms. People are attracted to the Gothic, according to Heller, because "safe terror is distanced terror" and readers can find reassurance that the monsters are only on the screen, or in a book. We *are* fascinated by horrible things happening to other people. King often states that he will continue to attract readers as long as people slow down to look at traffic accidents. This is certainly one appeal of the Gothic, yet it does not account for the power of Gothic fictions to create *fresh* uneasiness in the reader who might not have expressed such fears before or to maintain beliefs that might have died out without the transmission mechanisms of fiction and film. "The Power of Blackness" in Hawthorne, Melville, Lovecraft, Wilkins Freeman, and King de-familiarizes the New England landscape. The sensitive reader of their fiction cannot walk the streets of Salem, New Bedford, Providence, Boston, or Bangor without seeing what these authors saw as if superimposed upon the everyday scenes. Vampires, hybrid monsters, cannibals, and necromancers can all be found in their Gothic vision of a declining New England, and all the urban renewal in the world will not reassure their reader otherwise.

30

This book analyzes literary works of many degrees of skill and artistic merit, but such fiction, like the earlier Gothic novels, should not be seen as merely escapist. Fantasy and horror mirror themes that are universal as well as particular to the history and culture of New England. As Sir Devendra Varma notes, "The 'fantastic' in literature is the surrealistic expression of those historical and social factors which the ordinary chronicle of events in history does not consider significant" (46). In our case, we can find the decline of New England chronicled by writers of Gothic tales before we can find it in most histories of life or art. Frank's description of the English Gothic novel serves as well to describe, in their separate times, the fictions of Hawthorne, Lovecraft, and King:

> Homes and other places of former security are forbidding and dehumanizing; ... figures of authority such as parents or clergymen ...are sinister and despotic; ...even children are fiendish and malicious.... Although the Gothic traditionally requires some degree of a willing suspension of disbelief, it is not... escapist literature; rather it relates in some intimate symbolic ways to the politics, culture, art, and psychology of its time and ours.   (Frank xii)

Just as the Gothic in art has survived the attentions of critics and censors, so belief in the supernatural has proved remarkably tenacious in life. Since Plato, "vulgar superstition" and "mythological thinking" have regularly been declared dead, only to be rediscovered a few years later to the surprise of the literate community, though perhaps in a slightly changed form. As Daniel Lawrence O'Keefe notes in *Stolen Lightning: The Social Theory of Magic*, "magic persists" (458-9). Today's anthropologists have ceased expressing shock at the primitive beliefs of their informants; instead, they collect rural and urban folklore of the supernatural. [19] New legends of the supernatural keep arising—even in the age of television. Many of these "urban belief stories"—the Death Car, the Ghostly Hitchhiker, sightings of Elvis revenants—seem like Gothic tales in modern dress.[20]

It is difficult to measure the exact level of belief in the supernatural in past civilizations, but a few examples must serve to demonstrate the persistence of

---

[19] Duncan Emrich estimates in *Folklore on the American Land* (1972) that based on the number of superstitious beliefs collected in the archives at UCLA, "there must be in the United States today . . .fifty million *different* folk beliefs and superstitions" (600).

[20] Attebery does not think these "belief tales" represent the true fantastic imagination (*Fantasy Tradition* 26).

Fancy and Imagination in the face of Reason and Science. When Cotton Mather's account of the Salem witch trials, *Wonders of the Invisible World*, was published in England in 1693 it was an immediate best-seller. The canny bookseller-publisher, John Dunton, emphasized the sensational "Account of the Tryals of Several Witches, Lately Executed in New-England" and omitted the sermons and theological discussions included in Mather's first edition. Dunton's advertisement for the book "seems formulated to address a skeptical attitude about the whole subject of witches in general and about the credulity of the colonists in particular" (Cook 305). The mass audience who responded to the book, however, were attracted by the author's sensational subject, not the publisher's "skeptical attitude"; they were the same type of audience who 70 years later would welcome the Gothic novels. In 1788, an anonymous treatise on Romantic architecture was published in Germany which praised the style of the medieval period because it was sure to "produce a universal effect" on all who enter such a building, "since a belief in magic, stories of mediaeval knights, etc. is firmly established amongst the people" (qtd. in Germann 84). The author is speaking of the people of his own time who would visit new buildings designed in the Gothic style. He must be assuming that the old beliefs have not vanished, if such magical associations can be styled "universal."

Throughout the nineteenth century, intellectuals reported, to their disgust, that outmoded beliefs lingered in New England. In the novel *Locke Amsden, or The Schoolmaster* (1847), the hero, teaching in a Vermont town called *Horn-of-the-Moon,* an apt name for the superstitious locale, is accused of sorcery as evidenced by his unnatural proficiency in advanced arithmetic. [21] Such brilliance could only have come "from one who should be nameless, but who always exacted his pay for his assistance" (130). The author D.P. Thompson, a judge and local historian, [22] explains to the reader that most Vermonters were not this credulous, but that "isolated neighborhoods, even in the heart of intelligent communities" were "uncultured" (130). In these backwaters, Thompson says, "we found all the exploded notions of witchcraft, sorcery, divination, and the like, still

---

[21]The identification of mathematics with occult knowledge is ancient. In the seventeenth century, "mathematical books" meant books on prognostication and astrology (Parker 89).

[22]Brooks does not discuss this novel; it is probably not healthy enough, though its hero eventually triumphs over the superstition.

entertained...that led us almost to doubt whether we had not, by some miracle or other, been carried back a century and a half, and set down among a clan of the immediate disciples of old Cotton Mather" (130–31). In 1892, the *Providence Journal* used almost the same language to describe an outbreak of vampirism in South County, in which the similarly benighted inhabitants were exhuming corpses and burning their hearts. Hawthorne's contemporaries believed in the reality of the tales they told him of ghosts, curses, of meetings with the Devil, and quests for the Great Carbuncle. Hawthorne himself reported being haunted literally as much as figuratively, by apparitions as well as by existential guilt.

While some English intellectuals might have mocked the credulity of the colonists, our history has usually been pictured as the triumph of rationalism, the climb upward from naive believers to those admirably rational and agnostic gentlemen,the Founding Fathers, and thence upward again to the triumph of science and industry. The Gothic quest, however, is Hell-bent, spiraling down and out. New England's history, far from supporting Day's contention that "the Gothic world...has no real existence outside fantasy" (4) has been marked by intrusions from the Invisible World. Day's claim *is* justified only to the degree that all art creates a secondary world having questionable existence outside its own boundaries. For New England, Gothic fiction can be at least as faithful a mirror of reality as so-called realistic or mimetic fiction. Despite the best advances of reason and science, belief in the reality of the unknowable or supernatural persists. While no one can prove beyond a shadow of a doubt that the machinery of the Gothic— the vampires, witches, sea serpents, devils—exists, throughout the history of New England, in one way or another, that machinery has been and still is believed to be true. More important, these beliefs have continued to inspire interest even among those who, like Todorov's reader of the "fantastique," have not yet settled the question of the reality of wonders and horrors.

For the earliest explorers of America, however, the question of belief that would later define the Gothic arose only rarely. Magic existed, as did sea serpents, demons, and witches. The New World was dangerous terrain, the locus of all the night terrors of an Old World childhood. The forests were dark and deep, darker still their inhabitants, human and otherwise. Long before the Puritans, Europeans pursued an errand into the wilderness that would become New England. The tales they brought with them and those they published upon their return helped create the darker image that is New England Gothic.

Chapter Three
Myths of Origin, Monsters in the Sea, Devils in the Forest

...it seems a matter of surprise, that any person who has examined
the testimony, can doubt the existence of the Sea-serpent.
--Benjamin Silliman

At low tide at the mouth of the Taunton River, on the southern coast of
Massachusetts near Fall River, a boulder reveals carvings near its base. While
these petroglyphs have been denounced as Romantic forgeries, they are usually
accepted as ancient, having been attributed at different times to Indians, English
settlers, the Viking Leif Erikson, the Portuguese Miguel Corte Real, the Italian
Verrazano, and nameless Phoenician explorers. Scratches on the boulder have been
identified as Ogham and assigned to the Irish St. Brendan or the Culdees. In 1712,
Cotton Mather described the inscriptions to the Royal Society in England as one of
his American *Curiosa*. In 1974, the State of Massachusetts set aside the area as a
park, having earlier moved the boulder to protect its carvings from erosion. To
celebrate the opening of Dighton Rock State Park, officials invited representatives
of each ethnic group who had ever claimed title to the carvings to staff booths at a
festival. Fearing that these lodges and religious groups (a Lebanese Christian
church stood in for the Phoenicians) might not sufficiently resemble their medieval
ancestors, the organizers also invited the Society for Creative Anachronism, which
recreates the life and culture of the Middle Ages, to hold a tournament and other
knightly entertainments. The day was a great success, with pizza sellers competing
(not always amicably) with shish kebab vendors, and races between the Sons of
Norway's rubber Dragonship and the Wampanoag tribe's canoe. It was a triumph

for the fantasy of medievalism in New England, the Gothic vision of the region's history.

New England's English explorers came, as did the Conquistadores, with minds well furnished in fantasy. Just as the Spanish and Portuguese explorers found Amazons and enchanted islands while searching for the Seven Cities of Cibola and the Fountain of Youth, phenomena they first encountered in the novels of chivalry that drove Don Quixote mad, so English explorers came expecting to find Fortunate Isles as well as the horrors of Hell. Expecting to find devil-worshippers, they found heathen Indians. Expecting monsters, they found sea-serpents, mermaids, lions, and werewolves.[1]

Those who came searching for commercial gain tended to paint the brightest picture of the worlds they encountered. The earliest propagandists for colonization sent back favorable reports of the North American natives. Indians were abducted and exhibited in Shakespeare's London, where they were a ninety-days' wonder. As Trinculo observes in *The Tempest*, so popular were these exhibitions that folk who would not "give a doit to relieve a lame beggar" would gladly "lay out ten to see a dead Indian" (2.2.32). When De Champlain portrayed the Algonkians as "good Indians" and supported their cause against the Iroquois "bad Indians," he shaped the course of French and English colonization in North America. As a result of his 1615 voyage, Jesuits immediately ministered to and converted the "good" Hurons, while the "bloodthirsty" Iroquois became allies of the English. But the pamphleteers protested too much. The more often they insist, as did William Wood in 1634, that emigrants to the New World should judge the Indians to be "wise, lofty-spirited...true in their promise" (Wood 61), the more it seems that his readers must have believed the opposite. As Wood admits, most Englishmen shared a "needlesse feare ...deeply rooted in the conceits of many" (69), that the Indian was probably a devil or a bloodthirsty savage, the gargoyle on the Gothic cathedral come to life.

Besides medieval superstitions, explorers and settlers brought medieval material culture and foodways with them into the New World. Once there, the in-comers were amazingly adaptable, whether it was in keeping English squash pie

---

[1]See Flint, *The Imaginative Landscape of Christopher Columbus* for an analysis of that explorer's medieval mindset.

recipes, while substituting American pumpkins, or devising new forms of governance, while retaining English common law. Nevertheless, as we have seen, most studies of American cultural history have emphasized disjunction rather than continuity. Thomas Wentworth Higginson, editor and mentor of Emily Dickinson, in 1898 published *Tales of the Enchanted Islands of the Atlantic*, which traced the origins of New England to the myths of medieval European civilization. In his introduction, he notes that "these hazy legends were altogether disdained by the earlier historians; indeed, George Bancroft made it a matter of actual pride that the beginning of the American annals was bare and literal. But in truth no national history has been less prosaic as to its earlier traditions, because every visitor had to cross the sea to reach it, and the sea has always been...the foreordained land of romance" (vii). These "hazy legends" of medievalism light and dark were the common heritage of all who visited New England.

1. Sailing West: Isles of Fortune and Misfortune

Underlying the practical business of exploration were centuries of myths about sailing into the sunset which could simultaneously (and without apparent contradiction) be a metaphor for death as well as the quest for immortality and eternal youth. As Lovecraft wrote to Frederic Jay Pabody (19 June 1936; *SL* 5: 266–69) explaining Classical references to Atlantis and the tradition of enchanted islands in the Western Ocean, "the notion of a glorious western land of happiness (after death or otherwise) arising from the glories of the sunset [was]...coloured by prehistoric rumours of both America and such islands as Iceland, the Canaries, the Madeiras, and the Cape Verdes" (268). An earlier Rhode Island local colorist, Thomas Robinson Hazard, known as "Shepherd Tom," identified his native state's South County with the "Ancient Atlantis," claiming that the Narragansett country matched in every particular the Greek descriptions of the paradisiacal place.

The Paradise of the Celts was achieved by sailing westward. The legendary St. Brendan voyaging in a skin boat, found both Heaven and Hell on islands in the Western Ocean. These twelfth-century narratives were part of the Irish tradition of *imrama*, or sea sagas, such as the pagan "Voyage of Bran." The Saint's sea stories found their way into oral and written tradition throughout Europe. Well into the seventeenth century, maps identified various islands where the Saint made landfall as the "Fortunate Isles." Initially these islands were indicated as the Madeira group, but as the Age of Exploration continued, the site of the "Fortunate Isles" was pushed farther out into the Northern and Western Atlantic, until, with mystery gone, the islands vanished from cartography.[2]

Still, mystery is persistent. When it was realized that the Americas were in fact vast continents rather than a string of archipelagoes, Renaissance scholars remembered Plato's description of the drowned land of Atlantis. As DeCamp notes in his *Lost Continents,* Spanish as well as English experts maintained that North America was either part of Atlantis or that the Indians were refugees from the island's destruction. The Elizabethan wizard John Dee gave the name Atlantis to the North American continent, while Sir Francis Bacon's utopia, *The New Atlantis*, was set in America (DeCamp 28–9). Islets and reefs were marked on maps as remnants of the Lost Continent. The Atlantis myth has remained popular in fiction. Lovecraft was fond of the idea of mysterious sunken lands, as he tells correspondent Elizabeth Toldridge (20 Nov. 1928), but he shrugs off the question of the reality of Atlantis, saying he doubts if any mid-Atlantic continent could have existed within human memory (*SL* 2: 253).

Though perhaps only a few classical scholars expected voyagers to run aground upon Atlantis, every seventeenth-century seaman would have feared the Sargasso Sea. Babcock's theory in *Legendary Islands of the Atlantic: A Study in Medieval Geography* is that the "Sargasso Sea" *was* Atlantis. As he describes it, "Somewhere in that ocean of obscurity and mystery there was a vast dead and stagnant sea...Gigantic entrapping weeds and wallowing sea monsters ...were recognized,too, as among the standing terrors of the Atlantic" (29). Well into the twentieth century, fantasy writers speculated about this "graveyard of lost ships." Nor has the delusion ended. Babcock's 1922 map shows the "Sargasso Sea" as coterminous with what is now dubbed the "Bermuda Triangle." Some myths just never die.

In addition to the "Fortunate Isles," other mythical islands lured travelers westward. Throughout the Middle Ages and Renaissance, "Brazil" or "Breasil" appears on maps of the Western Ocean. Babcock finds it on the map of Dalorto in

---

[2]The legends of the Fortunate Isles exercised "a most profound effect" upon Columbus's explorations, according to Flint, *The Imaginative Landscape of Christopher Columbus* (91; 97).

1325, noting that at this time ordinary sailors would have assumed it to be "Hy Breasil" or Country of the Forever Young, the Paradise of pagan Irish myth (65). Professional explorers and adventurers, however, were looking for real places. Surely it is not strange that the Portuguese, certain they had found the mythical paradise at last in the South Atlantic, gave the name Brazil to a new continent. Ortelius's authoritative map of 1570, showing our world in nearly recognizable shape, still indicates both the continental and the insular Brazils, as well as the "Isle of the Seven Cities," and St. Brendan's Isle.

Explorers of the northern and the southern New World were familiar with the legend of the Seven Cities of Cibola. This legend had a truly Gothic origin, deriving from the ballad hero Rodrigo "el ultimo godo," Spain's last Visigothic king, who was conquered by the Moors in 714. According to this legend, seven bishops with their congregations fled the Moorish ascendancy, sailing westward with the fallen kingdom's golden treasures, founding cities on "Antilla" (or Ante-Isla, the "counter-island"). When Cuba and the smaller islands surrounding it were discovered, they were dubbed the Antilles, so closely did they correspond to the shape of the mythical islands. But when no great stores of gold or Visigothic Christians were found there, the site of the bishops' golden cities once again migrated westward, drawing Coronado into the Southwestern wastes searching for them.

Rumors of a similar city of gold drew explorers to New England: Norumbega. Situated in various places on early maps, it was first visited by the French adventurer Jean Alfonse in 1542, who placed it on the Penobscot River in Maine, at a site commemorated by present-day Bangor's Norumbega Mall. Later explorers, however, could find no trace of a thriving Indian metropolis, with its gold- and fur-bedecked king.[3] De Champlain says in 1604 that he has thoroughly surveyed the Penobscot region and found only a wilderness, with "none of the marvels there which some persons have described" (*The Voyages of 1604–1607* 52–53). This did not discourage dreamers from searching: as late as the 1890s, the baking-powder millionaire Eben Horsford, a Harvard professor, erected a Gothic

---

[3]See De Champlain 44n.

tower at the head of the Charles River in Waltham, Massachusetts, to mark what he thought to be the real location of golden Norumbega.[4]

Sailing westward might find you gold or an Earthly Paradise, but as with St. Brendan, it was just as likely to take you to Hell. Before English explorers had encountered Native Americans, they had heard legends of cursed islands inhabited by demons, the darker counterpart of the Fortunate Islands in the Western Ocean. The explorers brought this notion with them and reported confirmation of the legends.

There are numerous cartographic warnings about cursed islands of "imported diabolism" (Babcock 178), one of the earliest being a map from 1436 with an island called "The Hand of Satan." This chart, attributed to one Bianco, drew, according to Higginson, on an Irish legend about three evil brothers encountering the Hand of Satan at sea (134–142). That such an island existed was confirmed by sixteenth-century explorers who reported an "Island of Demons" where they found "eager and capering imps at the bleak and savage northern end of Newfoundland" (Babcock 178). Such names appear on maps into the seventeenth century, confirming a "belief in diabolical evil in the northeastern coast of America" (Babcock 180). On Jacques Cartier's first voyage in 1534, he declared that the new lands were all "stones and wild cragges" with nothing worth exporting, and nothing to attract a civilized man. He calls Labrador, with no perceivable ironic intent, "the Land that God allotted to Caine" (*Early English and French Voyages* 10), a nickname still in use. Based on these reports of diabolical inhabitants, it is not strange that the first explorers of New England should have seen uncanny rites on those shores. Seeing Indians dancing around campfires, they describe it in terms of Devil-worshippers or tempting apparitions.

Josselyn in his 1639 voyage recounts one case of demonic revelry, based on the report of Mr. Foxwell, whose vessel lay off Cape Ann:

> about midnight they were wakened with a loud voice from the shore, calling upon *Foxwell, Foxwell*, come a shore, two or three times: upon the Sands they saw a great fire, and Men and Women

---

[4]The tower, described by Skinner (2: 33), later became the centerpiece of an amusement park. The park is long gone but the derelict tower still stands. See Tree for more about Norumbega, which she calls an "American Shangri-La" (5). Stephen Williams describes Horsford's contributions to the field of "Fantastic Archaeology" (206-209).

hand in hand dancing round about it in a ring, after an hour or two they vanished, and as soon as the day appeared, *Foxwell* puts into a small *Cove*, it being about three quarters floud, and traces along the shore, where he found the footing of Men, Women and Children shod with shoos, ...but neither *Indian* nor *English* could he meet with on the shore, nor in the woods.   (21)

Later in the voyage, Josselyn sailed by "an inchanted Island," though he gives us no more details. Two weeks later, he saw an iceberg, "an Island of Ice...mountain high." This, too, must have been an enchanted place, since he notes that "We saw likewise two or three Foxes or Devils skipping upon it" (10).

Such revelry on the shores seemed to call forth pagan abandon in the English crews. Some explorers seem to have brought the European pagan tradition with them, and the results were Maypoles and spring revels. There is evidence in history and folklore for a persistence of the European Old Religion in Thomas Morton's colony at Merrymount with its famous Maypole.

The explorer Pratt in his *Narrative* reported finding white fishermen behaving like pagans off the coast of Maine in the spring of 1622: "The men y† belong to ye ship, ther fishing, had newly set up a May pole & weare very mery" (7). A wonderful anecdote in Martin Pring's *Voyage* of 1603 pictures a musically-talented young sailor charming the wild savages into dancing with him, "twenty in a Ring, and the Gitterne in the middest of them, using many Savage gestures, singing lo,la,la,la,lo" (*Early English and French Voyages* 347).

The most famous episode of the Old Religion in the New World was immortalized by Hawthorne as "The Maypole of Merrymount." Thomas Morton founded a colony at Mount Wollaston, which he renamed "Mare-Mount," or "sea-mountain," but which his enemies more appropriately nicknamed Merrymount. Morton's own account of that colony's rise and fall, *The New English Canaan*, disagrees in many instances with Bradford's official history. Morton was no Puritan and may not have been speaking allegorically when he claimed that the water of the "fountaine at Ma-re Mountæ" cures melancholy. "Mine host of Ma-re Mount," as he calls himself, apparently welcomed to his new seigniory Indians and renegade Puritans alike, and sold guns to both. This policy rather than the orgies and worship of the Old Gods may have been the reason that the Puritan government vowed that "his Plantation should be burned downe to the ground, ...and his

person banished from those territories, and this put in execution with all speede"
(Morton 163).

It is not only nineteenth-century anthropologists who saw May games and
the Faerie belief as remnants of a pre-Christian religion. Bradford chose similar
words to describe the practices he so abhorred at Merrymount: "They set up a May-
Pole, drinking and dancing ...dancing and frisking togeather like so many *fairies* or
furies rather" (qtd. in A. Earle 228; emphasis mine). Their May-pole was no small
affair, but "a stately pine-tree 80 feet high, and with 'sundry rimes and verses
affixed.'" (qtd. in A. Earle 228). Hawthorne wove the history of the place into "a
kind of allegory" of the attempt to transplant the spirit of Merrie Old England into
the New Israel of the Puritans. He says of the masked and costumed Maypole
revellers that "These were New England Gothic, definition of monsters." He
imagines dancers costumed as wolves and bears paired with a real dancing bear,
and "the salvage man," the Green Man of English tradition, matched with a colonist
costumed as an Indian hunter, the real man of the woods. (*Twice-Told Tales* 34–
35). Thus Hawthorne represents allegorically the process of New England Gothic,
linking the demons and bogeys of the old world with those of the new.

When the Puritans had driven out Morton's colony, they decreed that the
place be called Mount Dagon, after the worshippers of false gods who were
punished by Samson. This Philistine god, believed to be half-man, half-fish, was
found carved on Puritan tombstones in Massachusetts during the seventeenth
century, a coincidence that may have inspired H.P. Lovecraft, who wrote of a
revived worship of Dagon in "The Shadow Over Innsmouth."[5] Despite the
obliteration of Morton's colony, New Englanders persisted in celebrating the rites
of spring. As Samuel Sewall wrote, on May 26, 1687, "It seems the May-pole at
Charlestown was cut down last week and now a bigger is set up, and a garland
upon it" (qtd. in McMillen 162).

2. Strange Creatures of the Land and Sea

---

[5]See Will Murray's article in *Lovecraft Studies* which traces down the complex trail of
"Dagon in Puritan Massachusetts."

Having reached North America, travelers remembered what they had been taught by oral tradition and schoolbook authorities. Many of their medieval beliefs found echoes in Indian traditions. For the Europeans, the medieval doctrine that all creatures on land had counterparts in the ocean led to finding catfish, dogfish—and sea-serpents and merfolk.[6] From Josselyn to Barnum and on to the present, mermaids and sea monsters have been at home in New England.

The standard work on the subject of sea monsters is Heuvelmans's *In the Wake of the Sea-Serpents*. This Belgian biologist devoted a lifetime to tracking down sea-serpent sightings. Though he acknowledges hoaxes and admits to misidentifications with basking sharks or other marine life, he concludes that many of these beasts will eventually be proven as real as the giant squid, once thought to be mythical. Based on the salient points of their reported descriptions, he calls his sea-beasts, "long-necked;" "merhorse;" "many-humped;" (this is the animal most often reported off New England) "many finned;" "super-otter;" "super-eel;" "marine saurian;" "father-of-all-turtles;" and "yellow-belly." Heuvelmans's log of sightings misses one that "got away" from Christopher Levett, who declines, in his account of *A Voyage into New England* (1628) to relate at greater length his experiences at sea, where he saw flying fish and, apparently, Heuvelmans's "mer-horse," strange fish "with manes, ears, and heads, and chasing one another with open mouths like stone horses in a park" (35).

Some New England scholars were convinced of the sea-monster's reality. Benjamin Silliman, one of nineteenth-century Yale's greatest scientists, was one such believer, saying in 1827 that "'To us it seems a matter of surprise, that any person who has examined the testimony, can doubt the existence of the Sea-serpent'" (qtd. in Heuvelmans 25). The Linnean Society of New England investigated the sightings off Cape Ann in 1817; after taking witnesses' depositions, they agreed that the creature was real (repr. in Botkin 194–99). Many still concur in this belief. Edward Rowe Snow, who published over 70 volumes of folklore of the sea, says that he accepts the reality of sea serpents. In 1967, he mentioned that their skeletons could be seen at Berkeley and Harvard, but whether

---

[6]This doctrine was current in the eighteenth century in the form of the great chain of being, discussed by Leventhal in connection with mermaids (237-239).

by this he means extinct plesiosaurs or their more fabulous descendants he does not say (*Incredible Mysteries* 101).

Medieval voyagers had encountered all sorts and kinds of sea monsters. On each voyage, St. Brendan would spend Easter on the back of the monster Jascoyne, biggest of all fishes. This mother of all fish stories, based on Talmudic legends of the Biblical Leviathan, can be found in the *Physiologus*, whose Greek text dates from the mid-fourth century. The eighth-century Latin translation calls the monster "Aspidoceleon," saying that it is "large like an island, heavier than sand.... Ignorant sailors tie their ships to the beast as to an island and plant their anchors and stakes in it" (*Physiologus* 45). In the Bestiary tale, the monster is irritated by the sailors' cooking fires and dives, taking them down with it. St. Brendan, being holy, escapes this fate. This is not his only encounter with a sea-monster: at another point in his story, fire-breathing sea-serpents pursue the Brendan voyagers.

Scandinavian scholars such as Olaus Magnus were the acknowledged authorities in the Renaissance on the habits of sea-beasts. Perhaps Christian Norsemen retained some ancestral memories of the pagan myth of the Midgard serpent, *Jörmundgandr*, who "strove to bite his own tail as he encircled the world at the sea's bottom, heaving scaly coils to create storms" (Baker 128).

After Josselyn's famous encounter story, narrated above in Chapter One, sea-serpents continued to be a common sight off the Massachusetts coast. Thoreau's journal gives his account of the sightings investigated by the Linnean Society at Cape Ann. It seems that the Massachusetts sea-serpent was then as great a tourist attraction as the Loch Ness monster is today in Scotland.

> Mr. Buffum says that in 1817 or 1819 he saw the sea-serpent at Swampscott, and so did several hundred others. He was to be seen off and on for some time. There were many people on the beach the first time, in carriages partly in the water, and the serpent came so near that they, thinking that he might come ashore, involuntarily turned their horses to the shore as with a general consent, and this movement caused him to shear off also. The road from Boston was lined with people directly, coming to see the monster. Prince came with his spy-glass, saw, and printed his account of him. Buffum says he has seen him twenty times, once alone, from the rocks at Little Nahant, when he passed along close to the shore just beneath the surface, and within fifty or sixty feet of him, so that he could have touched him with a very long pole, if he had dared to. (Jan. 14, 1858; 10: 243–4)

Thoreau, unlike the Linneans, seems unconvinced by the account, undercutting his narrative by adding that "Buffum is about sixty, and it should be said, as affecting the value of his evidence, that he is a firm believer in Spiritualism" (Jan. 14, 1858; 10: 243–4).

Sightings seemed to come in waves, with crests in 1817–20 and again in the late 1840s. Somewhere in the latter years, although Thoreau did not recount the story until 1857, Daniel Webster went out off the coast at Duxbury to see the sea-serpent. Thoreau gives the story in his journal, in classic folktale style, at several removes from the original source:

> B.M. Watson tells me that he learns from pretty good authority that Webster once saw the sea-serpent. It seems it was first seen, in the bay between Manomet and Plymouth Beach, by a perfectly reliable witness (many years ago), who was accustomed to look out on the sea with his glass every morning the first thing as regularly as he ate his breakfast. One morning he saw this monster, with a head somewhat like a horse's raised some six feet above the water, and his body the size of a cask trailing behind. He was careering over the bay, chasing the mackerel, which ran ashore in their fright and were washed up and died in great numbers.

After establishing the veracity of his witness, Thoreau continues:

> The story is that Webster had appointed to meet some Plymouth gentlemen at Manomet and spend the day fishing with them. After the fishing was [over], he set out to return to Duxbury in his sailboat with Peterson, as he had come, and on the way they saw the sea-serpent, which answered to the common account of this creature. It passed directly across their bows only six or seven rods off and then disappeared. On the sail homeward, Webster having had time to reflect on what had occurred, at length said to Peterson, "For God's sake, never say a word about this to any one, for if it should be known that I have seen the sea-serpent, I should never hear the last of it, but wherever I went should have to tell the story to every one I met." So it has not leaked out till now. (June 14, 1857; 9: 415–6)

Shades of the Ancient Mariner, who also encountered "sea-snakes," and was thereafter condemned to tell the story to every passing ear!

Thoreau made note of Webster's close encounter only after the great statesman's death, and his journal was not published until 1906. Perhaps this brush with the mysterious or supernatural later led Stephen Vincent Benet to match Daniel Webster with the Devil. In *The Flowering of New England*, published the same year as Benet's short story, Van Wyck Brooks seems to see something of the pretematural about Webster. Brooks retells the legend of Webster commanding that his horses be buried standing up, a legend transformed into a haunting ballad by Maine regionalist Elizabeth Coatsworth, together with an explanation.

> Daniel Webster's horses—
> he said as he grew old:
> 'Flesh, I loved riding,
> shall I not love it, cold?
>
> 'Shall I not love to ride
> bone astride bone,
> when the cold wind blows
> and snow covers stone?
>
> 'Bury them on their feet
> with bridle and bit.
> They were fine horses—
> see their shoes fit.'   (56)[7]

Perhaps Webster was himself responsible for the legends that grew about him after his death, since "I still live" were his last words (Brooks 416). Webster was a larger than life figure. According to Brooks, strangers felt bereft by his death. "Countless boys...felt that life had grown suddenly small and lonely and wondered how the sun could rise without Daniel Webster" (415).

Webster was hardly the last New Englander to see the sea-serpent. One sighting off Provincetown in 1890, reported by Reynard in her collection of Cape Cod folklore *The Narrow Land*, comes from the Town Crier, who claims that "I was not unduly excited by liquor or otherwise." The Crier compares the great serpent's head to a "two hundred gallon cask" as it rose from the deeps. This monster, however, did not remain in the deep water; instead, she left the sea, "undulated over the dunes, keeping her head thirty feet in the air" and dove into Pasture Pond, where soundings failed to produce the monster—or a bottom for the pond (249).

---

[7]The legend also reminds us of the Norse pagan custom of burying the horses of great chiefs and warriors along with their masters. See Gwyn Jones, Plate 16, which shows one such grave in Iceland.

Algonkian Indians had their own accounts of sea-serpents, which apparently antedated European contact. The Maine Indians were plagued by a lake-dwelling monster, the *Wi-will-mekq'*, described variously as resembling an outsize snail or a huge, slimy worm. The folktale "Uliske" in Alger's *In Indian Tents* is a sort of "Beauty and the Beast" in reverse. Uliske, whose name means "Beauty," is seduced by one of these lake monsters who has bewitched her into thinking he is a handsome young man. She marries one human husband after another, delivering them to the lakeside to feed the serpent's appetite.

The Penobscots have a hero-legend of a great shaman who defeats the *wiwilimecq'* by transforming himself into another water creature and waging underwater battle. The ancient legend became attached to a historical figure, the chief and shaman Old John Neptune (1767–1865), whose *poohigan* or familiar spirit was the eel; the tale was circulating in oral tradition in the 1930s (Eckstorm 39–48).

Skinner, in *Myths and Legends of Our Own Land* (1896) reports a water-snake in the Twin Lakes in the Berkshire Hills, last seen in 1890, as well as "a snake with a head like a dog's" which haunted Sysladobosis Lake in Maine in his time (2: 298–9). This monster was still being sighted in the nearby Chain Lakes into the twentieth century, according to folklore collector Alice Bryant, whose father told her about the lake serpent, which was huge—"30 feet from hump to hump." Its passing during the winter left an unmistakable imprint in the ice of the lake (NA 23.009).

Though the salt-water variety is little seen these days off the Massachusetts coast, the Indians' fresh-water monster is thriving.[8] "Champ," resident in Lake Champlain, was photographed in 1977. Sightings of a long-necked, many-humped beast have been common since the early nineteenth century. Tourist literature claims that the Sieur De Champlain was the first European to document the existence of "Champ." This pleasing fiction is not supported by De Champlain's own *Voyages*, which never mention a lake-dwelling serpent. He does, however, report hearing about a great fish swimming in the lake he named after himself, "the largest being. . .eight or ten feet long"; in form it resembles a huge pike, "but it is

---

[8]One of the few surveys of lake-dwelling serpents is Peter Costello's "American Lake Monsters."

armed with scales so strong that a poniard could not pierce them." This creature is wily, sounding more like a crocodile than a fish in this Indian legend reported by the explorer: "When it wants to capture birds, it swims in among the rushes . . .where it puts its snout out of water and keeps perfectly still...when the birds come and light on its snout...it adroitly closes it, which it had kept ajar, and pulls the birds by the feet down under water" (*The Voyages of 1608–1610* 161). Even this hint of the preternatural is unusual for DeChamplain, whose journals generally reveal him to be a notable skeptic, constantly undercutting earlier, more credulous, travelers' tales such as that of golden Norumbega.

Europeans and Indians shared a belief in other water monsters, this time in human or partly-human form. The mermaid belief in Europe can be traced to Lilith and Dagon, or to the Sirens and sea-nymphs of the Mediterranean. Merfolk, like sea-serpents, were hazards of navigation, for seeing a mermaid sitting on a rock portended storm. In addition, the creatures themselves, though fascinating, were no friends to human sailors. "As custodians of drowned souls, they were ever eager to increase their stock of prisoners. *Speculum Regali* spoke of a twelfth-century mermaid haunting a deep near Greenland, fish in hand. If she cast it towards a ship, it was certain to sink by tempest; if away, the ship would reach port" (Baker 140).

Eric Pontopildon, one of Heuvelmans's main authorities for the reality of sea serpents, claims to have dissected a merman found in the North Sea. His Viking ancestors were equally pragmatic. In the *Landnamabok*, the twelfth-century Icelandic *Book of the Settlements*, merfolk were an expected part of the seascape. One fisherman, Grim, "pulled up a merman, and when he came up asked him: 'What do you prophesy of our fortune?'" (Jones 135). This was a dangerous question, for the merman foresaw Grim's death and the death of all his men. Though belief in these merfolk was widespread, there were not as many attempts to exhibit specimens during the medieval period as there were in the eighteenth and the nineteenth century, when Barnum capitalized on New Englanders' credulity by exhibiting the "Fiji Mermaid" (which proved to be the upper torso of a monkey sewn to the tail of a fish). Barnum also offered a bounty for the Lake Champlain monster, whole or flayed.

For sailors, the merfolk of the early narratives, rather than being curiosities, were dangerous temptations.[9] No wonder explorers were ready to clout merfolk on the head or hack off their arms! Josselyn did not only report sea serpents. He also knew of a Merman in Casco Bay, off the Maine coast. This "Triton" attacked the canoe of a fowler, Mr. Mittin. The Englishman's response was to chop off one of its hands with a hatchet. As a result, "the Triton presently sunk, dying the water with his purple blood, and was no more seen" (Josselyn 21). Such reports should not surprise the reader, Josselyn says, for *"there are many stranger things in the world, than are to be seen between* London *and* Stanes" (25).

Captain Richard Whitbourne, on a 1610 voyage to Newfoundland, encountered a mermaid, confirming what the ancient authorities had taught him. He describes her as "looking cheerfully, as it had beene a woman, by the Face, Eyes, Nose, Mouth, Chin, Eares, Necke, and Forehead." He took a long look at her, noting her lovely "haire, downe to the Necke." The mermaid was just as curious about the Englishmen, for she swam around their ship, but when she tried to climb into the ship's boat, the sailors were frightened, "and one of them strooke it a full blow on the head." Despite this harsh treatment, the mermaid persisted, visiting two other boats in the St. John's harbor, whose sailors also "for feare fled to land" (Purchas 19.439–440).

The great adventurer and self-propagandist Captain John Smith saw a mermaid in 1614, during the same voyage on which he discovered Maine and Monhegan Island.... She was "'swimming about with all possible grace...long green hair imparted to her an original character by no means unattractive.'" (qtd. in Snow, *Incredible Mysteries* 102). Snow says that "he had already begun 'to experience the first effect of love' toward the creature until the moment when she revealed that from the waist down she was in reality a fish" (*Incredible Mysteries* 102; *Legends* 108-9). The Dutch explorer Nicholas Denys reported that in 1656 Capt. Rouleau and three French vessels tried to catch a merman with ropes off the coast of Nova Scotia but failed in the attempt (Eckstorm 85)[10] All these explorers

---

[9]See Briggs, *The Vanishing People* for gruesome tales of blood-drinking, ship-cursing merfolk "so dangerous that the mere sight of them is enough to cause a shipwreck"(70). Also see Beck, *Folklore and the Sea* 230-243, for other fearful tales of the mermaid belief. Walter Map, *De Nugis Curialium* xiii: 232-3 reports the "marvel" of "Nicholas Pipe, a merman" who could dwell on land and sea, and who put his abilities to forecast storms at the service of the English.

[10]Also described in Snow, *Incredible Mysteries* 103.

were following in the tradition of Columbus, who reported seeing "sirens" off the Rio del Oro on his first voyage to the New World. These "sirens," unlike their northern cousins, made no aggressive moves, but Columbus reports in his journal that "they were not as beautiful as they are depicted, for somehow their faces had the appearance of a man" (qtd. in Flint, *The Imaginative Landscape* 85).

No account of the prevalence of the merfolk tradition in New England could be complete without a story by one of the Mathers, yet none are found in their published collections of wonders. In a manuscript letter to the Royal Society, however, Cotton Mather reported his conversion to belief in "the common tradition of tritons, or fishes in a shape near human," based on the account of "three honest and credible men." (*Selected Letters* 210; 211). On Feb. 22, 1716, these fishermen came upon a merman on the rocks "near the shore of Brainford-harbor" [Branford, Connecticut]. The merman offered them no violence; still, they determined to capture the creature, who they described as all human from the waist up, though his arms were shorter than natural, but whose "lower parts were those of a fish, and colored like a mackerel." This "triton" having escaped, the witnesses hastened to report the occurrence to Mather, who bolstered their first-person narrative with learned references to authorities Classical and modern (*Selected Letters*, July 5, 1716; 210). Everyone must have sent Mather accounts of fascinating monsters. In a letter dated two days earlier, he promises to forward on to the Royal Society a sketch and "a short narrative" of "a calf, which had so much of a human visage as to make the attentive spectators apprehensive that the poor animal had been impregnated by a beastly Negro" (*Selected Letters*, July 3, 1716; 210).

The belief in merfolk is not confined to Europe: Native Americans had their own versions of the legend. Eckstorm cites the *Jesuit Relations* for 1669 and 1672–3 to prove the ancient origin of Upper Algonquian Indian beliefs in half-fish men who are the ancestors of some of their clans. Their water-god, whom the Jesuits compared to Neptune, gave his name to the Mississippi. In New England, the greatest chiefs of the Maine Indians also claimed descent from the water-god and his merfolk. Their name was transcribed into English as "Neptune" perhaps because, as Eckstorm theorizes, the Algonkin root "n'be," meaning water, reminded early explorers of the Roman sea-god. She reports, from Lescarbot's *New France*, another convergence of New and Old World myths. In 1606, near what is now Orono, Maine, Lescarbot staged a grand mythological masque, "Neptune's Theatre," featuring the sea-god, Tritons—and Indian actors. It does seem likely that the Indian participants would have found in this entertainment confirmation of their own legends, and might have therefore adopted the name Neptune for their leading family (Eckstorm 88–9). Beck reports the same ancestry for the Neptune family in his *Folklore of Maine*, saying that "They were descended from a half-man, half-fish who lived in a hole under Indian island and who could foretell danger to the tribe. This creature drowned those who fell into the water and plugged up their eyes, ears and mouth with mud" (247). Eckstorm gives the merman's name as "Nodumkanwéts," while the Passamaquoddy word is "Hapodamquen." Alger reports a legend of Hapodamquen, "The Merman," whose enemy is another merman, "Lampeguen." Hapodamquen wins an epic underwater battle, commanding an army of fish, lobsters, and marine mammals. The story-teller notes that he "still lives to destroy little children who disobey their mother by going near the water" (Alger 71).

Cape Cod's Wampanoag Indians believed in a sea-goddess, who evolved into the shore-dwelling Granny Squannit and the sea-witch, Squant. Tales of the latter were known to whites as well, in her guise of a "mer-woman with a sea-green tail" who could slow ships down by hanging on like a barnacle. "Cape sailors knew that Squant would abide unless...the mate sang the Doxology, or the moon's path cut across her tail, or star-spikes, sharp in the water, pricked her and drove her below" (Reynard 59).

In Harriet Beecher Stowe's local color novel of life on the coast of Maine, *The Pearl of Orr's Island*, a sea captain recounts a fanciful story of the merfolk. This tall tale, in which a merman accuses him of dropping anchor on top of his house on the sea floor, is given credence only by the children in his audience. The captain's daughter assures her young friends that "father saw mermen and mermaids a plenty of them in the West Indies" (127), thus making it clear that in 1862 merfolk were no longer commonly found swimming in Casco Bay.

Not only for information on inhabitants of the sea did early explorers depend on ancient authorities and medieval bestiaries. The first accounts of New World fauna are a fascinating mixture of accurate reporting of real creatures unknown to European eyes—moose, porcupines, raccoons—with fabulous creatures unseen by the reporter but expected to be lurking somewhere in the wilderness. William Wood in his *New Englands Prospect* (1634) listed "the kingly Lyon" as an American beast, along with the "tripping Deare" and "Quill-darting Porcupines," but was forced to add "Concerning Lyons, I will not say that I ever saw any my selfe." Still, reliable men have told him about roaring in the woods; therefore according to all authorities, there "must eyther be Devills or Lyons; there being no other creatures which use to roare" (19). This roaring "Lyon" was still believed to haunt the marshes of coastal Massachusetts in the nineteenth century, according to a note in the *Journal of American Folklore*, when someone in Marblehead "who looked unkempt or fierce was compared to 'a rumbling marsh lion'" (Farmer 252).

Wood did not report any unicorns in the forests of Massachusetts, unlike the earlier explorer John Hawkins, who used medieval Bestiary lore to prove them native to Florida. In his *Voyage of 1565*, he reported seeing beasts of one horn, "Which comming to the river to drinke, putteth the same into the water" (*Early English and French Voyages* 127) to clear the spring of poison, as shown in the scene woven into the Unicorn Tapestries at the Cloisters. By the same logic, where there are unicorns, Hawkins claims, there must be lions, the natural enemies of unicorns, though he has not seen any himself.

More horrifying beasts haunted the shadows of New England's forests. French settlers brought legends of the *loup-garou*, the man-wolf, stories of whom had been told as well in the English Middle Ages. Kittredge, in *Witchcraft in Old and New England*, traces the werewolf belief in England back to the Anglo-Saxon Laws of Cnut (175; 492–494n). Lycanthropy, the disease in which a man imagines himself to be a wolf, was a concern of Renaissance science. This European belief found its echo in the native American traditions of totems and animal souls, though Indian shape-changers were held more in awe than in horror. Indian shamans were known for the ability to transform themselves into animals. As late as 1981, Nosapocket of the Mashpee Indians related an account of an Indian who changed himself into a weasel in church, "and then he collapsed back into the weasel form and darted out the door never to be seen again" (qtd. in Simmons, *Spirit* 285).

The fear of flesh and blood wolves lay at the heart of the settlers' werewolf belief, though the optimistic Wood swears he never heard of an American wolf attacking a grown man. Still, those who wished to extirpate the Indians and knew of shamans' boasts found it easy to believe that these fierce warriors might at times take on the shapes of four-legged beasts. Mather in the *Magnalia Christi* describes in slasher-movie detail the massacre of a captive child by the Indian Hope-Hood. This Indian, alive at the time he was writing, Mather calls "that hideous *loup-garou*." (*Magnalia* 2:519). Since those who would go up against supernatural lycanthropy were themselves larger than life, General Israel Putnam's eighteenth-century defeat of an almost unkillable wolf, the last one in Connecticut, cast an otherworldly aura over the stalwart hero. With the extinction of wolves in Southern New England, however, tales of the *loup-garou* became confined to areas of French Canadian settlement, where they have been collected by folklorists to the present day.[11]

The Northern Algonkians had legends of two-footed night-walkers, corresponding to Old World beliefs in hairy wild men of the woods (who were identified by many Europeans with the Indians themselves). The Windigo or Wendigo was feared by white and Indian lumberjacks well into the twentieth century, and tales of this monster were widespread through upper New England into Canada. It made its presence known through huge tracks, each with a drop of blood. In some versions of the legend, the Wendigo is an Indian transformed by starvation into a cannibalistic monster. The search for such "Big-foot" creatures continues today, primarily in the Pacific Northwest, but Connecticut has its own version of the monster, reported for over a hundred years as the "Winsted Wild Man." Frightened witnesses of the creature, (some accounts date from as recently as the 1970s), describe it as very tall, naked, and covered with hair (Philips 166–168).

3. Indian Gods, the Devil, and the Little People

---

[11]Richard Dorson collected French-Indian *loup-garou* tales in the Upper Peninsula of Michigan from "Aunt Jane Goudreau, *Roup-Garou* Storyteller"; The Federal Writers' Project found similar tales among the French-Canadian community of Woonsocket, R.I. (repr. in Botkin, *A Treasury of New England Folklore* 222-3). The nineteenth-century Vermont local-colorist Rowland Robinson tells a French-Canadian dialect story of the *loup-garou* in his *Danvis Folks* (repr. in Botkin, *A Treasury of New England Folklore* 221). The University of Maine's Northeast Archive contains many accounts of *loup-garous* in the lumber camps. By the 1960s, the belief had become confused with stories of the *lutin*, the mischievous goblin of medieval France, who was often blamed for mishaps. One former lumberjack, Maynard Jalbert of Limestone, Maine, told of "the loup-garou that came to the lumber camp where he worked and rode the horses all night" (J. Anderson 3.011).

The encounter between Puritan and Indian has been the subject of many books, though of necessity the written testimony from the Early Contact Period comes from those who could write—the European explorers and settlers. No one can settle in a few words the controversy over whether the Puritans were Gothic villains and the Indians innocent victims, (the currently fashionable view), or the other way around, (the Puritans' own vision). The Puritans produced reams of self-exculpating material, and they have not lacked for defenders even in this century. Vaughan's *New England Frontier: Puritans and Indians 1620-1675*, for example, takes the position that "the Puritan record is impressive" in their treatment of the Indians as in all other aspects, thus reducing displacement and near-genocide to "some misunderstandings and injustices" (viii).

One such "misunderstanding" shocks us today: neither the Pilgrims under Bradford nor the founders of Massachusetts Bay wondered why so many Indians had died of a plague just before they arrived. Instead, chroniclers recorded their joy at the fortuitous death of so many Indians that had cleared the land for their occupation. They could only see the hand of God at work in that action. Edward Johnson, writing in 1652, considered the smallpox raging among the Indians as one of his proofs of God's intervention in New England, an example of God's *Wonder-Working Providence*. It is true that Puritan settlers could not have known that the plagues that so decimated the native population had been brought by earlier European visitors, a process that was thoroughly chronicled only recently in William Cronon's *Changes in the Land*.

This section can not begin to summarize the wars and displacements, the treaties honored or dishonored by Indians and descendants of Puritans. Instead, it will focus on the Puritans' initial misreadings of Indian religion, as they viewed their New Canaan through a dark Gothic lens. Though it is more difficult to narrate the Indians' side of the story, their mythology and folklore does include beliefs in a "Little People" and a wealth of Trickster legends which soon became identified with the Christian Devil. It may be that the stories preserved by non-Indian folklorists were those best fitting the European Gothic tradition.

Based on explorers' reports from North America and New Spain, the Puritans had expected to encounter more organized, armed resistance from the Indians. Psychologically, the less learned settler was prepared to find devils in the forest; all the written reassurances to the contrary could hardly prevail against such primal fears. It does not matter that in reality "the forests of New England were not teeming with wild savages" that, instead, "the population density was probably less than .22 per square mile" (Vaughan 29). Demons are not so easily exorcised. It does not help to know that there is only one vampire in town, not 200. Creatures like that can always make more unless dealt with properly, with fire and the stake.

It is no wonder that Puritans believed the Indians were Devil-worshippers. Those few who observed Indian rituals must have found substantiation for their worst nightmares. Belief in the powers of Indian sorcerers declined as the settlements grew, but in the early years of the Contact Period the belief was well-attested on both sides. That most sympathetic of the Puritan divines, Roger Williams, wrote in *A Key into the Language of America* that Indian powwows "most certainly (by the help of the Divell) worke great Cures" (1: 212). Because of the infernal origin of these cures, Williams was afraid to attend Indian religious ceremonies. He notes that "after once being in their Houses and beholding what their Worship was, I durst never bee an eye witnesse, Spectatour, or looker on, least I should have been partaker of Sathans Inventions and Worships" (1: 152). Wood thought the powwows were necromancers, "betaking themselves to their exorcismes and necromanticke charmes, by which they bring to passe strange things" (82). Wood gives what sounds like a genuine first-person account of a successful shamanistic healing ritual, explaining that "sometimes the Devill for requitall of their worship, recovers the partie, to nuzzle them up in their divellish Religion" (83).[12] John Winthrop in his *Journal* for 1639 notes that there was a huge storm of violent wind. "The Indians near Aquiday [Aquidneck Island, now Newport, Rhode Island] being pawwawing in this tempest, the devil came and fetched away five of them" (1: 297).

Indian shamans encouraged such beliefs among Europeans as well as their own peoples. They boasted that their magic could make them and their followers invulnerable, according to battle reports from the Pequot Wars and King Philip's War. Roger Williams wrote to John Winthrop during the earlier war that one Pequot powwow was planning to sink the white man's ships by swimming underneath them, but, he adds, "I hope their dreams ...shall vanish, and the devil

---

[12]For other, similar accounts of Indian rituals, see De Champlain, *The Voyages of 1608-1610* 159-60; and *The Voyage of 1615* 321-322; Rosier's *True Relation* (*Early English and French Voyages*, 374); Levett 52-53; and Josselyn 96-97.

and his lying sorcerers shall be confounded" (qtd. in Simmons, *Spirit* 62). Tales collected after the defeat of King Philip, however, made it clear that while some Indians may have continued to believe in the effectiveness of their own magic, they believed that the English could somehow ward it off, through a greater counter-magic.[13] According to Eckstorm, the shamanistic tradition endured among Maine Indian chiefs, who were feared for their wonder-working powers well into the nineteenth century (101–6).

Based on Old Testament accounts of pagan practices, the Puritans expected the Indians to perform human sacrifice. It is to the credit of the first generation of Puritan writers that most do not give credence to this rumor, although they report at length the torments that warriors would inflict on captives from other tribes.[14] Still, the rumor that Indians, like the Biblical worshippers of Moloch, sacrificed babies to the Devil had a long life—as late as 1851, when DeForest's *History of the Indians of Connecticut* describes such ceremonies: "At these times they brought their furs, their wampum, and, it was told, even their children, and throwing them upon the fire, sacrificed them to Hobbamocko, the author of evil" (29).

Everyone did not concur in the characterization of Indians as active diabolists. Morton of Merrymount, unlike Roger Williams, did not believe the Indians worshipped *any* supernatural beings, gods or devils—he seemed to grasp the idea that pantheism or nature-worship was inexplicable in Christian terms. In a report "of their pretty coniuring tricks" he thinks of the Indian's *Powahs* as mere tricksters and conjurers; they were "but weake witches" (34–5), not wizards or worshippers of Satan. De Champlain made the same observation when he visited the Massachusetts coast in 1606. He says that these savages "pray no more than the beasts" (*The Voyages of 1604–1607* 96). Even more sympathetic observers such as Morton and De Champlain were incorrect in their readings of Indian religions, but at least their misunderstandings led to tolerance. The Puritans' misreadings of Indian religious practices could be used to justify their extirpation.

Misunderstandings of alien religions were not confined to the Europeans. In a shamanistic society, those who experience visions of new gods are honored.

---

[13]Whittier, in *The Supernaturalism of New England*, reports a sorcerer's dual between the Indian preacher Hiacoomes and a Martha's Vineyard shaman (34-36).

[14]Edward Winslow, an early explorer, in *Good Newes from New England* does say that the Indians sacrifice their children (Purchas 19: 385).

Bearing the names of two gods of the vision quest, the "friendly Indians" of the Plymouth Colony, Squanto and Hobomock, must have been such god-seekers. If so, they probably intended to add the new God of the white man to their collection (Simmons, *Spirit* 40; Eckstorm 102). Nor were the Europeans the only ones to demonize the unknown Other. The early explorer William Wood records a different kind of "first encounter" tale, reporting that two or three Indians in Massachusetts in the 1630s were frightened by their first sight of a Black man. "Seeing a Blackmore in the top of a tree, looking out for his way which he had lost, surmised that he was *Abamacho* or the Devill, deeming all Devils that are blacker than themselves" (Wood 77). In another instance of cross-cultural confusion, Josselyn tells of "two *Indians* and an *Indess*" who witnessed an apparition of the god *Cheepie*. He was flying through the air above them, and when Josselyn asked what this fearsome Devil looked like, they answered "all wone *Englishman*, clothed with hat and coat, shooes and stockins" (95).

Because the first European visitors to North America were not twentieth-century cultural anthropologists, we do not possess any "unbiased" versions of Algonquian religion and mythology.[15] By the time American Romantics became interested in Indian legends and began to write them down, these tales of creation, gods, and devils had been "contaminated" by European influences. For example, Abby Alger, collecting stories "Told by Penobscot, Passamaquoddy and Micmac Indians" in the 1890s, reports this creation myth as authentically Indian: "In the beginning God made Adam out of the earth, but he did not make Glus-kabé (the Indian God). Gluskabé made himself out of the dirt that was kicked up in the creation of Adam" (11). Many other Indian legends are equally syncretistic, seamlessly combining motifs from European and African traditions. We must also keep in mind the changes introduced by the editors.

Since the late eighteenth century, collectors of Indian lore have tended to be Romantic, echoing Pope's "Lo! the poor Indian," or hostile, or both at once. Even the supposedly objective anthropological surveys done in the 1890s and 1930s now seem culturally biased. When the Maine Writers Research Club in 1952 compiled a celebratory volume dedicated to *Maine Indians in History and Legend*, the editor

---

[15]See Simmons, who *is* a cultural anthropologist, for a lengthy analysis of the European bias, 37-64. He, in turn, has been accused by Mohegan tribal historians of distortions and inaccuracy in his reporting.

could write of the Passamaquoddys of her acquaintance that "Though they may be characterized as mystics and dreamers, with rather vague uncritical minds, ready to believe anything as long as it contains an element of supernatural and miraculous force, yet there is an abundance of simple charm and romance in their traditions which amply rewards the patient researcher" (E. Earle 122).[16]

Believing that Indians were different in some essential way from those of European descent could lead to horrifying results. The explorer John Josselyn, who reported on sea-serpents and merfolk, declared that the Indians were instinctual swimmers from birth, so much so that "if they suspect the child to be gotten by other Nation" they would throw the infant into the water, where, if he were Indian, he would swim like any animal (92). Levett makes almost the same observation in 1628, saying that the Indians take their babies "and cast them into the sea, like a little dog or cat, to learn them to swim" (54). A Maine legend says that some white sailors tried the truth of this experiment with the wife and baby of a local sachem, deliberately overturning their canoe into the Saco River. The mother survived, but the papoose, tightly swaddled, drowned. This led the sachem to ally himself with King Philip and raid the Saco River settlements. The tale is told to explain the curse on the Saco River, which "must each year drown three of his hated [white] race" (Sturtevant 150).[17] True or not, this tale illustrates the nasty underside of the Romantic view of the Noble Savage. If They are more instinctual and natural than We, They are also closer to animals, and can be treated with the same casual cruelty.

The first generation of settlers who recorded Indian theology usually forced it into a Manichean Christian scheme, with an equally powerful God of Good, or Great Manitou, and a Spirit of Evil, who, as Edward Winslow says in *Good Newes from New England*, "as farre as wee can conceive is the Devill" (Purchas 19: 383). The idea that this Spirit, Hobomok (Wood's *Abamacho*) or Cheepie, might instead be a trickster, and thus malevolent and benevolent by turns, that he was the god who answered the vision quests, would not occur to seventeenth-

---

[16]Eckstorm expresses the same sentiments (96-7), though her knowledge of her Indian informants is superior to Earle's.

[17]The Saco River Curse remains one of the most widespread belief tales in Maine folklore; brought into print again with every new drowning, it appears over twenty times in the collections of the Northeast Archive.

century, or indeed to many twentieth-century observers. On this point, Roger Williams came closer to comprehension than most, recording multiple gods of the winds, fire and "Squauanit, The Womans God" (who may be Squanit, the Goddess of Cape Cod legend) in his *Key into the Language of America*. Continuing his research, he wrote to Gov. Winthrop that "I brought home lately from the Nanhiggonsicks the names of 38 of their Gods, all they could remember" (208n). Shocked, he revised his conversion estimates, for he realized that these Indians had merely *added* to their pantheon the Christian God, who could be appropriately worshipped one day in seven.

Such a discrepancy in numbers can be accounted for if the Algonquians had an earlier animistic religion underlying a later theistic one. When Williams asked for names of gods, the informant might just have reeled off the 38 nearest numens. Perhaps the elves or forest spirits of Indian legends were the numinous remnants of the earlier faith, when every little stream and rock had its guardian. Or perhaps the Algonquians had experienced something similar to what had happened in Ireland, the process by which the old gods were gradually reduced in size, influence, and power until they became "the little people"—the elves or fairies.[18] The great Celtic god Lugh became the Leprecaun (sometimes translated "little stooping Lugh"). The sun-god, who in the *Mabinogion* has to turn his hand to shoe-making, became the full-time fairy cobbler.

Elusive as the elves themselves, the belief in small nature spirits, not humans, not gods, was shared by the Algonquian Indians and the Europeans who conquered them. I first learned the legends in the proper manner, through oral transmission. I heard tales of the little people—"elves, you would call them, or leprecauns," from Chief Harold Tantaquidgeon of the Mohegan Tribe in Uncasville, Connecticut.[19] Since then, students in my local history classes have reported hearing of a little people haunting the Thames River banks in the Mohegan sacred lands that were taken to become Fort Shantok State Park. These beliefs remained unpublished until the 1980s, when anthropologist William Simmons

---

[18]See Briggs, *The Vanishing People* 36-37 for discussion of this theory of the origin of the fairy belief.

[19]How I regret not writing the stories down at the time, but at age 9 or 10 I could not know what priceless folklore I was hearing. Luckily, Simmons more than made up for my lack of foresight.

studied the folklore of the Indians of southern New England in *Spirit of the New England Tribes*. One of his main informants, Gladys Tantaquidgeon, (sister of Harold), had herself trained as an anthropologist with Dr. Frank Speck, who studied the Mohegans in the early part of the century. She had collected folklore in the 1920s and 1930s among the Indians of Martha's Vineyard. The Mohegans, along with the Narragansetts and the Wampanoags, retained memories of ghosts, witches, and heroes even when they had assimilated in all other ways to the culture of their white neighbors (5). Simmons reports that the belief in the "muhkeahweesug" or little men is unique to the Tantaquidgeons in Southern New England, but their memories of it stretch unbroken from the nineteenth century to the present. The last native speaker of Mohegan, Fidelia Fielding, Gladys Tantaquidgeon's great-aunt, may also have been the last New Englander to see the Little People. Melissa Fawcett Sayet, tribal historian of the Mohegans, writes of *her* great-aunt Gladys Tantaquidgeon's memory of "one family dinner at which Great Aunt Fidelia abruptly excused herself to talk to these magical mischievous beings" (qtd. in Simmons, *Spirit* 298n).

Like English and Irish fairies, the Mohegans' Little People were given offerings of food and drink and dwelt in underground mounds. In another parallel to the British Isles tradition, the Mohegans associated the "muhkeahweesug" with mounds containing the artifacts and petroglyphs of an older civilization. A similar word means "whippoorwill" in the Pequot language, perhaps demonstrating a link between this particular bird and the fairy people (Simmons, *Spirit* 298n; Hazard, *Recollections* 138). Perhaps the legend of the whippoorwill as a psychopomp, a guide for dead souls, has a Native American origin.[20] Living members of the Mashantucket Pequot Nation, whose reservation is located in Eastern Connecticut, retain memories of a belief in the Little People. In 1987, one informant told anthropologist William Simmons that in her childhood she had seen "Wooden People," lay figures carved from wood and displayed, representing the hidden people of the woods. These Little People haunted hot springs and wells, and older people would leave food out for them ("Pequot Folklore" 170–1).

Alger's Maine Indians call their Puck-like figure "Mikumwess," which might be a variant rendering of the Mohegan word. In one tale, he is the *poohegan*

---

[20]See Chapter Seven for Lovecraft's use of this motif.

or familiar spirit of the sorcerer Wild Goose, and the elf takes the shape of a beautiful girl to lure the Giant Witch from his enchanted cave, so that the hero Gluskabé [or Glooscap] can kill him (26–7). In Maine, reports of "elves of the woods" appear in stories transmitted in the 1940s by Charles Watkins. The "outdoor Gods" had to meet on Mount Katahdin because their council fires were being disturbed by the "elves of the woods" ("Why Katahdin" 167). These elves are afraid of the evil spirit Pamola, and so they "wept for many moons. Their tears are still seen flowing down the big valley" on Mt. Katahdin. (Watkins, "The Coming of Pamola" 169; Whittier, *Supernaturalism* 63).

The term in Ojibwa folklore for these little people is something like "Pukwudgee" or "Pukwudji."[21] The Mashpee Pukwudgees are not nice fairies, pygmies really, tricksters, like Puck. Like Robin Goodfellow, they are identified by Wampanoag storytellers with the will-o'-the-wisps, Tei-Pai-Wankas. "Travelling Indians followed these lights and were lured into the marshes where Mahtahdou, the Devil, trapped their feet in quicksands and sucked them into the earth" (Reynard 30). Also like Puck, they could appear as bears or wild cats and so frighten humans. They even attack the family of the gentle giant Maushop and blind his sons with bad medicine,"so potent was their magic (even a common Pukwudgee had charms greater than those of the tribal medicine-men)" (Reynard 29).

It is strange that there were not more mergings of Old and New World fairy beliefs, but one such story does turn up on Cape Cod, where stable goblins from Whitby, Yorkshire arrive in a horse's mane, "the first dobbies to reach New England." Shipwrecked along with their horse on the dunes of Cape Cod, they trudge the beach with mooncussers[22], and end up feeling right at home: living in haunted mounds on the dunes, and riding at night on an immortal wild colt. Reynard claims that in her time oldsters on Cape Cod remembered these tales that

---

[21]It was used by Reynard's informant among the Mashpee in the 1930s, but Simmons claims he had learned it from published accounts of Ojibwa myths; Whittier spells it "Puckweedjinees"(*Supernaturalism* 62).

[22]Familiar figures on Cape Cod's haunted beaches, mooncussers were wreckers. They were accused of leading horses with lanterns tied to their tails up and down the beach in storms in order to lure ships onto the rocks so they could be looted.

so blended pukwudgee and English pixie lore (325).[23]   PukwudgeeA similar tale
was collected in 1966 in Maine, where Gram Smart remembered that in her
childhood, when the horses were heard whinnying in the stables at night, she was
told that "the horses were being ridden by fairies and their manes were braided for
stirrups for them to put their tiny feet in."   When she attempted to check the
accuracy of this tale, "sure as anything the manes of the horses would be braided in
very small pleats" (G. Stevens 390.19).   A nineteenth-century folklorist
remembered fairy beliefs from her own childhood in Marblehead, an isolated
fishing village known for retaining traditions lost to urban Massachusetts.   She
relates tales of fairies living underground and emerging to dance in fairy rings as
well as malicious pixies who loved to lead travelers astray, thus explaining the New
England dialectal adjective "pixilated" for a confused elderly person (Farmer 252).
A final narrative comes from "Shepherd Tom" Hazard, who praised the beauty of
"Worden's Pond, more generally called 'the Great Pond,'" in Rhode Island's South
County, "where the fairies used to congregate and dance by moonlight" (*The
Jonny-Cake Papers* 245).   "Shepherd Tom" was perfectly capable of inventing
"ancient folk-tales," but in this case the perpetual mist that enshrouds swampy
Worden's Pond might well have given rise to legends of fairies.

The legends of Hobomok, the trickster god, of benevolent giants such as
Maushop, and of evil nature spirits were all easily assimilated to tales of the
Christian Devil.   The Maine Indians feared Mount Katahdin as the haunt of a
particularly monstrous spirit, Pamola, who had carved the mountain's "knife edge"
with his wings.   The Indian storyteller may have been influenced by Christian
demonology in this description: "huge wings that dragged on the ground,...horrible
beak, and claws like big arrows" (Watkins,"The Coming of Pamola" 169).   Belief
in this "evil avenging spirit" who haunted the mountain continued into the twentieth
century, according to Watkins ("The Story of John Neptune" 170–1).

The giant Maushop is the hero of stories from Cape Cod and the Islands, so
often wreathed in the fog that was the smoke from his pipe.[24]   He is a culture hero,

---

[23]See Kittredge 219, for the English ancestry of these dobbies; Attebery, *Fantasy Tradition* in Chapter Two discusses the paucity of fairy sightings in the New World, as does Leventhal 137.
[24]Reynard published these re-tellings in 1935, based on recollections of stories told her by "Chief Red Shell, Historian of the Nauset Wampanoag Tribe, and by Chief Wild Horse, Wampanoag Champion of Mashpee" who "retain and treasure the legendary beliefs"(23).

benevolent toward humans. Roger Williams reported that tales of the Indian giant were common in his time among the Wampanoags. A correspondingly malevolent being is Squant the Sea-hag, dweller in an Underseas Cave near the cliffs at Gay Head on Martha's Vineyard, whose descendant Granny Squannit, though shrunken in power, remained a bogey for naughty Indian children at the time Reynard compiled her book. The Praying Indians, according to Reynard, accepted the Christian identification of Maushop with Lucifer, "who was obviously of great stature, since he managed to perform mischief now in one part of the land, now in another" (35). Maushop is credited with transforming the landscape and creating the rocky islets of Cuttyhunk and the Elizabeth Islands. In a story collected by Gladys Tantaquidgeon in 1928, "Maushop attempted to build a bridge from Gay Head to Cuttyhunk by placing huge boulders in the sea, but before he had accomplished his task, a crab caught him by the heel and he was obliged to stop work. This made the giant so angry that he threw the crab toward the Nantucket shoals; threw several of the boulders far out to sea and broke off a portion of Gay Head which he cast into the sea, thus forming No Man's Land" (qtd. in Simmons, *Spirit* 212). Simmons collected an abbreviated version of the same legend in 1983 from a waiter of Wampanoag descent working in Roger Williams' city of Providence (233).

The Devil must have been a frequent visitor to New England, judging from the proliferation of Devil's Dens, Footprints, Bridges, Ash Heaps and other such places on the map. Most of these were either Indian holy ground, sites where powwows held the rituals identified with devil worship by the Puritans, or else they had already been associated by the Indians with the deeds of Hobomok or Maushop, as in the Cape Cod legends. Some have been linked both with Indian powwows and witches' meetings. Among the most famous of these haunted places is Devil's Hopyard, in East Haddam, Connecticut. Now a state park, it has been a nexus of legends from the time of the earliest settlements.[25] There at Chapman's Falls, according to folktales, witches would gather to brew their hellish potions in

---

[25]These legends have had a long life in print and oral tradition; I learned them while at summer camp on nearby Gardner's Lake. Print sources include DeForest 57; Skinner 43-45.; Barber, *Connecticut Historical Collection* 525-8; Botkin 180-2; Drake 427-8; Bell 127; White 1: 23-25. David Philips collects still more legends of Devil's Hopyard and explicates the origins of more than 30 other Devil-sites in Connecticut alone (117-123).

64

the circular pot-holes found in the rock below the Falls. The Devil would sit at his ease at the top of Chapman's Falls, playing his fiddle while the witches stirred their brew. A similar folk explanation is given for North Kingstown, Rhode Island's Kettle Hole and Hell Hollow, where witches and spooks would gather to frighten the godly (Gardiner 70).

To this day, the East Haddam area remains a center for Indian worship; powwows are held in the Haddam Meadows next to the Connecticut River. The Moodus section of East Haddam takes its name from the Indian word "Machimoodus," meaning "place of noises." It is an area of unstable geology, where the phenomenon known as the "Moodus noises" has been observed by Europeans for over three hundred years. The noises went through an active period in the early 1980s, with "swarms" of small quakes recorded. The "noises," which have varied over the years from rumbles to earthquake proportions, seem to center on Mount Tom, a hill near the confluence of the Moodus, Salmon, and Connecticut Rivers. Indian tales adapted by the settlers claim that the Haddam witches, famed for Black Magic, and the East Haddam witches, who practiced a benign White Magic, would meet in mortal combat under the rivers and in caves under Mt. Tom. Finally the Great Spirit tired of their commotion and banished them with a sapphire wand.

Another explanation, given by an Indian to a minister in 1729, was that the Great Spirit was angry because the new God and his followers had trespassed upon a sacred place. The noises, by all reports, were more violent in the eighteenth century than they are today, climaxing in an earthquake in 1791 strong enough to be perceived in Boston and New York. Geologist Michael Bell believes that "the potential remains for another moderate quake, or even a repeat of 1791" in this seismically active area (129). One "scientific" explanation for the Moodus Noises appealed to Nathaniel Hawthorne, who immortalized the alchemist Dr. Steel as Doctor Cacaphodel in his "The Great Carbuncle." The rest of this *Twice-Told Tale* derives from analogous legends of the White Mountains. [26] Connecticut history records Dr. Steel's visit to Moodus from England in the late eighteenth century. He attributed the tremors to carbuncles, mammoth gems with alchemical properties. Exploring the caves under Mt. Tom, he supposedly emerged with two huge organic

[26]See Haskell for an attempt at a natural explanation for the phenomenon.

pearls, the mysterious carbuncles, which he pocketed. He left the area, warning
that the noises would return when the remaining miniature carbuncles had grown to
full size. No further carbuncles have been excavated from under Mt. Tom.

The deeds of Hobomok—identified by the Puritans with Satan—inspired
New England place-name legends. According to Narragansett legends, he stole a
squaw and leaped from Devil's Foot Rock at Quonset Point, Rhode Island (where
his cloven footprint can be seen) to Aquidneck Island.[27] There he flung the squaw
into a living death in Purgatory Chasm, where Middletown and Newport meet.
Many ghost stories cling to this cursed beach: in one version, Hobomok was
condemned for his crime to swim there, killing Indians and whites. Another,
current in oral tradition, concerns a wicked sea captain who "cursed the briny deep"
as he went down with his ship off Purgatory Chasm. The captain was transformed
into an ogre who feeds on swimmers.[28]

Satan's Kingdom in New Hartford, Connecticut, received its name in the
eighteenth century because these rugged hills and gorges in the northwestern part of
the state had become home to renegade whites, blacks, and Indians who were
suspected of combining devil-worship, robbery, and miscegenation.[29] Still other
Devil places were known to be haunts of rattlesnakes, manifestations of The Old
Serpent: the "Devil's Dens" in Weston and Franklin, Connecticut share this origin,
while Weston's has a "Devil's Footprint" rock as well. The Ayer family, who are
still the owners of Franklin's Devil's Den, were braver or less credulous than other
Puritans. A family legend says that when they took up the land in the seventeenth
century, they exorcised the Old Serpent by importing a herd of vicious snake-eating
pigs from Massachusetts, and were never troubled thereafter.

Snakes were identified with the preternatural in the Old World; in the New,
the rattler seemed peculiarly apt for the role of Satanic avatar. *Winthrop's Journal*
recounts how one such snake disrupted the Synod at Cambridge in 1648, until an
elder stood upon its head and speared it with a trident. In accordance with Puritan
belief, "nothing falling out but by divine providence," Winthrop was quick to

---

[27] Another Devil's Footprint rock at Portland, CT next to the Connecticut River has a
similar folktale attached (White 1: 7).

[28] These stories have circulated in print in Rhode Island as well. See Farrington;
Bourgaize 29-32; 86.

[29] See Mills for legends of *Satan's Kingdom in New Hartford* composed in the meter of
Hiawatha.

66

allegorize the incident as follows: "the serpent is the devil; the synod, the representative of the churches of Christ in New England." For the moment, the devil had been routed—but not forever (2: 347). The first ballad recorded in New England, "Springfield Mountain, or The Pesky Sarpent," on the death of a laborer by rattlesnake bite, explained it as a judgment upon him.[30] A Rhode Island legend combines snakelore with another "Great Carbuncle." In this tale explaining the origin of Coventry's Carbuncle Pond, Indians captured a great serpent whose head contained a radiant gem. This carbuncle was a talisman, warning of danger to the tribe. When the white men came, they coveted the gem. In the ensuing battle, all the Indians were killed except for their chief who threw the carbuncle into a small lake, rather than see it fall into enemy hands (Bourgaize 91–2).

Few modern New Englanders may be able to explain precisely why their land is so be-Devilled, but many have visited Devil's Hopyard or know of its sinister reputation. Connecticut's famous demonologist Ed Warren calls that park one of the most haunted spots in America. He claims to have investigated an inordinate number of cases of malevolent ghosts and demonic possession within its boundaries. The folklore of places and the place names themselves have inscribed the Puritans' vision of devil-worshipping Indians deep into our consciousness.

4. Myths of Origin: or, the Quest for Whiteman's Land

Were the Indians of New England really, as the currently fashionable term has it, "The First Peoples" to dwell there? Were the English the first Europeans in New England? Or did New England have a medieval, and indeed a prehistoric, European presence? The question of "who got here first?" interested Cotton Mather, but it became an obsession only in the nineteenth century, an obsession by no means abated as 1992 saw rival commemorations of the quincentenary of Columbus's voyage and the millennium of Leif Erikson's. The nineteenth century "Romantic Revival" in Europe and America seized on the necessity for myths of origins, as national literatures and political nationalism grew up together.

---

[30]See Leventhal for a discussion on the folklore of the rattlesnake in America; see also Botkin 337; White 2: 49–50.

In New England, discovering proofs of early European visits developed into a quest to remake the region into what *Eirik the Red's Saga* fortuitously called *Hvitramannaland*, or Whiteman's Land, a place in the New World where whites ruled over kingdoms of aborigines.[31] Since the eleventh century, descendants of European immigrants have indulged in this kind of wish-fulfillment, based on evidence that is slender or non-existent. Speculations about ancient Irish, Scottish, Phoenician, and Norse visitors have formed a kind of alternate reality, a secret history of New England more romantic than the textbook version. Stephen Williams calls theories and evidence of this sort "Fantastic Archaeology." Those who practice it favor the conspiracy theory of historiography, an attitude which makes their published writing, despite impressive documentation, seem closer to myth than to science. Their claims of suppressed evidence and secrets divulged only to certain families remind us of the lost, forbidden manuscripts of Gothic fiction.

In North Salem, New Hampshire lies Mystery Hill, now open to the public as "America's Stonehenge." There the curious can find numerous small buildings made of unmortared stones and an "altar of sacrifice" (a flat rock with deep grooves in the top). The construction of these wonders has been ascribed to everyone from Irish monks or Culdees, to pagan Celtiberians and Phoenicians, to Vikings, to a hitherto unknown pre-Indian race. While these explanations seem equally fantastic, attempts to explain away the small rocky chambers as Colonial-period sheep-folds are not very convincing either.[32]

The Irish voyager St. Brendan was thought to have visited New England, though not to found a colony. Mystery Hill, however, is promoted by its owners as the product of even earlier Irish visitors. In 1936, William B. Goodwin bought the site. In his opinion, it was built by the Culdees, a secular monkish order of the time of St. Patrick (and he has been accused of changing the rock formations around to match his theory). In the 1970s, Barry Fell conducted studies of the

---

[31]See Gwyn Jones 186 and 186n for other references to this mysterious country. Ingstad dismisses it as purely legendary (80, 29), a strange stance for someone who accepts the rest of the sagas as factual.

[32]For more about the history of Mystery Hill, see Stephen Williams, *Fantastic Archaeology* 258-64.

inscriptions and layouts of the chambers, and concluded that Culdees of 600–900 A.D. would have been latecomers, that the place was much older.

To support his theory, Goodwin had studied the Norse sagas, which do refer, as described above, to a "Great Ireland" or "Whiteman's Land;" Goodwin interpreted the cryptic words to mean an inland kingdom extending from Connecticut into Vermont and New Hampshire with outposts in (where else?) the Wampanoag country near Dighton Rock. He does note that "Curiously enough, there is no record in Irish history of the aforesaid Great Ireland" (176). This would not be surprising, he says, if the New England Irish had been Culdees, the mysterious sect that supposedly tolerated pagan, Druidical practices, whereas the official historians of Ireland were Romanized Christians, eager to suppress knowledge of the earlier independent Celtic Church. Goodwin believed that Mystery Hill was the religious center for the Culdees, from which they established posts all over New England to convert the Indians.

More recently, Barry Fell, in *America B.C.* and in television appearances on the "In Search of . . ." series, has popularized a vision of New England as a veritable crossroads of Old World visitors. He views Mystery Hill as a *pagan* cult center, founded by Bronze Age Celts about 1000 B.C. They were joined in their worship by Phoenician traders, and later Egyptian miners. His evidence for all this traffic is literally carved in stone. Fell claims that his training in epigraphy, the study of alphabets and codes, has enabled him to identify six different scripts incised into New England sites. The Celtic inscriptions, he says, are in Ogham— including the writing Cotton Mather observed on Dighton Rock. At Mystery Hill, Fell found Iberian characters in the Punic language on a triangular rock, reading, he says, "To Baal of the Canaanites, this in dedication" thereby proving to his satisfaction that "ancient Celts had built the New England megalithic chambers and that Phoenician mariners were welcome visitors" (91).[33] Since Fell began his work, similar stone chambers have been located all over New England, with members of organizations such as the New England Antiquities Research Association, the Early Sites Research Society, and the Gungywamp Society dedicated to reading the record of the rocks. While Fell admits that the up-and-down strokes of Ogham "can be produced occasionally by fortuitous means" (91)

---

[33]For serious debunking of Fell and his *ouevre*, see Stephen Williams 264-73; 320.

(i.e. glaciers), he has found other alphabets carved into New England rocks. At the Gungywamp site in North Groton, Connecticut, Fell has identified Christograms [IC and XC] and Chi Rho symbols [the Greek equivalents] on rock outcroppings, which would imply European visitors from the first millennium (Barron and Mason 42). Research at these sites continues, as fantastic archaeologists enthusiastically promote the true history of New England which they claim is being suppressed by the archaeological orthodoxy, just as the Romanized Irish suppressed memories of the Culdees.

More so than the Irish, the Vikings have long been popular choices as the "true discoverers" of the New World. They were pure Nordics, after all, and their explorations were not sponsored by the Catholic Church or Spain. Also, the "Gothic Myth" (discussed in Chapter Two) favored these pure-blooded conquerors. In this case, the romantic secret history has proven to be based on fact. Until early in the nineteenth century, Norse sagas relating voyages beyond Iceland and Greenland to "Markland" and "Vinland" were judged by English-speaking scholars to be as mythical as legends of Thor and Odin. At this time, Leif Erikson's Vinland was identified as New England. Since then, proponents of the Gothic Myth have been locating boatyards, campsites, inscriptions, and cellar holes all around the coasts of New England which they have attributed to the Vikings. One enthusiastic proponent of the Viking theory was Longfellow, who translated the Norse sagas. His poem "The Skeleton in Armor," linking the Stone Mill in Newport with the Vikings, convinced many of the theory's accuracy. Another Harvard Professor, Eben Horsford, construed the name of the Indians' lost golden city of Norumbega as "Norvega" or Norway. The "Vinland Map of 1440" that so embarrassed Yale University when it was proven to be a fake in the early 1970s, nevertheless demonstrates the continuing wish to populate early New England with white men. Speculations about Norse settlement remained in the realm of fantastic archaeology until the work of Helge Ingstad, who in the late 1960s discovered the Viking encampment at L'Anse aux Meadows in Newfoundland by diligently searching the sea-coast from Rhode Island northward. Carbon-14 dating placed the construction of these stone houses at the time of Leif the Lucky, ca.1000 A.D. The homely artifacts Ingstad found there—a cloak brooch, a smithy, a spindle whorl—have

70

made Newfoundland the only well-documented incursion of the Vikings into North America.[34]

Nor were the Vikings the only medieval freebooters to be credited with colonizing New England. The idea that a Scottish prince founded a colony in the New World in the 1390s and explored south as far as Massachusetts was put forward in the nineteenth century, but seems to have made few converts at that time. The strength of the quest for Whiteman's Land continues undiminished, however, as 1992 saw the publication of Andrew Sinclair's *The Sword and the Grail*. This study of the Scottish Prince Henry St. Clair of Rosslyn blends the fate of the Templars, the Grail, the Masons, the Illuminati, and the Scots colonization of the New World into yet another convincing secret history of conspiracy.[35] The Sinclair theory rests on the *Zeno Narrative*, an account printed in 1558 purporting to reproduce family documents of the fourteenth-century navigators Niccolo and Antonio Zeno. Sinclair offers as his other evidence "the tombstone of William de St. Clair in Rosslyn Chapel,...the Vopell and Vavassatore map of the New World, with its figure of a crowned knight in Nova Scotia and its inscription" and the carving of a knight with a broken sword etched into a hillside in Westford, Massachusetts (109). According to the *Zeno Narrative*, the sixteenth-century writer's ancestors sailed with a Scottish Prince first to Greenland, and then to the other side of the Atlantic, to "Estotiland" where they founded a colony. They had been convinced to sail north and west by a fisherman, who claimed to have been blown off course, landing in "a very great country and, as it were, *a new world*" (qtd. in Sinclair 203).

Origin myths that attempt to push back the pedigree of the white man in New England have proved relatively harmless in the grander scheme of history. Theories that attempt to explain the origin of the native inhabitants of the Americas, however, have had more serious consequences. European treatment of the Indians

---

[34]In addition to the writers named here, see Skelton, Marston and Painter whose Yale University Press book was supposed to have authenticated the Vinland Map in 1965. Another enthusiastic popularizer of the Gothic Myth is Frederick Julius Pohl, especially in *The Lost Discovery* and *The Viking Settlements of North America*. In the latter work, Pohl uses evidence from the sagas to extend the range of Norse contact to Florida.

[35]Sinclair's work follows that of Frederick Julius Pohl (who favored the Scots as well as the Vikings) in *Prince Henry Sinclair: His Expedition to the New World in 1398*.

in the seventeenth century and thereafter may have been influenced by whether the new arrivals inclined towards light or dark medievalism. Did they consider the Indians to be descendants of the lost tribes of Israel? Of Prince Madoc? Survivors of Drowned Atlantis? Or were they something other than human, perhaps devil-worshippers settled by Satan in the outlying marches of his realm?

All these theories originated in the necessity to explain how there could be a race of human beings not previously mentioned by authorities Biblical or Classical. Nor has this attitude totally disappeared: as Charlotte Hill wrote in 1952, many still suffer from a "hemisphere complex," that is, they cannot imagine a people or a high culture arising first in the Western Hemisphere (160). Only the Old World can be the cradle of civilization. The Puritan idea, found in the writing of the Mathers, that Satan must have expressly placed the Indians here, so far West of Eden, or the more humane attempts to give the Indians Jewish or Welsh ancestry find their equivalents today among those who would believe that alien astronauts built the Mayan pyramids rather than credit a brown-skinned, native race with such a feat.

Many Puritan divines and lay leaders subscribed to the Ten Lost Tribe theory; Vaughan cites Roger Williams, John Eliot and the English Puritan Thomas Thorowgood (20). Williams noticed certain customs the Indians held in common with the Jews, including the taboos on menstruating women and the practice of anointing the head with oil (1: 24). The Jewish descent theory had been put forward earlier by Diego de Landa, the monk who in the 1560s destroyed nearly all the Mayan codices because they were the work of the Devil. While collecting local myths, he heard Mayan elders say "that this land was occupied by a race of people, who came from the East and whom God had delivered by opening twelve paths through the sea. If this were true...all the inhabitants of the Indes are descendants of the Jews" (qtd. in DeCamp 32).

In support of this theory of Jewish origin, Roger Williams and William Penn published lists of corresponding words demonstrating that American Indian languages had affinities with Hebrew. Skeptical of these correspondences, Wood says in *New Englands Prospect.* (1634) that "by the same rule they [the Indians] may ...be some of the gleanings of all Nations, because they have words which sound after the Greeke, Latine, French, and other tongues" (91). Other Britons were less skeptical: Hakluyt and Raleigh heard the Indians speaking what sounded to them like Welsh. From this evidence, they swiftly concluded that the Indians must be descendants of Prince Madoc, who in Welsh legend had sailed westward in the twelfth century. This theory of origin was especially attractive to the British, as it served to strengthen Britain's historical claims to North America. Stranger origins than these have been put forward for America's aborigines. Rock inscriptions like those at Dighton Rock have been cited as evidence that the Indians were descendants of the survivors of "Atlantean" civilization.[36] Even today, popular literature and television programs link the Mayan and Aztec temples with the Egyptian pyramids as evidence for the survival of Atlantean science in America.

Not all European contacts with the original inhabitants of North America led to disaster. Throughout the sixteenth century, until the founding of the Massachusetts Bay Colony, explorers alternately traded peacefully with Indians and carried them off into slavery. Writing in 1628, one English visitor, Christopher Levett, praised the hospitality of the Maine sagamores whom he considered true kings and queens. He had settled at "Quack," which he renamed York, and had begun to fish with the permission of the local sagamores, "glad of this opportunity, that I had gained the consent of them, who as I conceive hath a natural right of inheritance, as they are the sons of Noah, and therefore do think it fit to carry things very fairly without compulsion" (45). His respect for the Indians, growing out of the belief that they were not merely errant Israelites but sons of a patriarch, made Levett's behavior considerate and may have made his mission a success.[37] Unfortunately, the devil in the forest theory seemed to settle itself more firmly into the Puritan consciousness, with the result being what can only be called paranoia, as the next chapters will explore.

---

[36]The Indians had their own folktales about Dighton Rock, which they retained in oral tradition into the nineteenth century (Simmons, *Spirit* 70). Skinner says that in his time (1896), "the Indians said there were other rocks near it which bore similar markings until effaced by tides and drifting ice" (2: 26). The Portuguese explorer theory has been championed by the large Portuguese-American community of Rhode Island and Southeastern Massachusetts: see da Silva, *Portuguese Pilgrims and Dighton Rock*. For even more about the inscriptions on the rock, which he calls "litmus paper for testing the tides of current archaeological interpretations," see Stephen Williams 213-217.

[37]Of course, descent from Noah's sons was not an unmixed blessing; Winthrop notes in his *Journal* that some magistrates of Roger Williams's colony, the "politically correct" of their day, went on record condemning those Puritans who "would have the Indians rooted out, as being of the cursed race of Ham" (2: 18). The curse on the descendants of Ham was also used to justify enslaving African blacks. In some medieval texts, Ham was described as a magus, a practitioner of forbidden arts (Flint, *The Rise of Magic* 333-38). This, too, might have linked Ham to the Indians in the learned imagination.

The book has not yet been written on how beliefs, practices, and material culture from the Old World were naturalized in the New. The examples given in this chapter only scratch the surface. In England, as in the Americas, survival of medieval techniques and Gothic traditions continued unrecognized side by side with Romantic revivals of the same. American Romantics like Longfellow who immersed themselves in the Viking sagas probably did not realize that the typical New England barn of his time was constructed with medieval methods of framing, following the general design of Anglo-Saxon mead halls. According to Kenneth Clark's essay *The Gothic Revival*, Horace Walpole in 1764, thoroughgoing antiquarian that he was, did not realize that Cotswold village architecture had survived unchanged from the fifteenth century, and that "the average barn was more truly Gothic than his bepinnacled Strawberry [Hill]" (29). The Romantic attempt to superimpose upon New England a *proper* Gothic past, filled with Viking longships, mysterious stone monasteries, and Knights Templar, has had much less influence on American civilization than has the Gothic manner of envisioning the real inhabitants of the new land.

If the Indians were worshippers of Satan, and their country part of his dominion, then it was only logical that Satan would single out Christian interlopers as particular targets of his wrath. In such an environment, beliefs in malevolent witchcraft and diabolism that were weakening on their native soil in Europe would continue to flourish where they had been transplanted.

Chapter Four
The New England Witch Belief

The Divill would sett up his Kingdom their & we should have happy days...
--Mary Lacey, Jr.

The belief in the efficacy of witchcraft is alive and well in New England in the 1990s. Some people assuage a fascination with the supernatural by watching horror films and reading Stephen King. Others go further, guiding their lives according to the advice of the astrologers, mediums, and fortunetellers who have subsumed the functions of witches in earlier times. These modern-day witches claim powers of healing, predicting the future, and controlling the dead. Their customers seek blessings, curses, and charms for wealth and for love, the same reasons New Englanders were accused of seeking out witches in the seventeenth century. Today's customers hazard only their wealth, but in Puritan Massachusetts and Connecticut, client and witch alike were risking their lives and their immortal souls in the bargain.

The most notorious manifestation of the Gothic spirit in New England remains the Salem witchcraft trials. The events of three hundred years ago cast a shadow over American history, an intrusion of the supernatural no one can explain away as mere illusion. Unlike the other supernatural visitations discussed in this book—sea serpents, vampires, werewolves—the witchcraft outbreak in Salem Village and Town has been exhaustively chronicled and analyzed by authorities, from the Mathers to Governor Hutchinson in the eighteenth century to modern historians, feminists, and sociologists. While for many years scholars treated the

Salem trials as an anomaly, more recent research has demonstrated that the witch belief was prevalent throughout seventeenth-century New England, and that studying it is necessary for a complete understanding of Colonial history. Only recently have a few researchers admitted that the complex of paranormal beliefs making up the witchcraft phenomenon remains part of the continuum of human experience: such beliefs cannot be relegated to primitive societies or the distant past. Instead, witches and the fear of witchcraft, however transformed and displaced, remain part of the culture of New England and the rest of the United States.

These two chapters do not pretend to be a comprehensive history of witchcraft in New England.[1] In addition to various analyses mentioned above, the primary source documents recording indictments, testimony, and executions are available in modern editions.[2] Instead, this chapter focuses on the striking survivals in the New World of older beliefs from both the scholarly and the folk traditions of the Middle Ages and Renaissance, as shown in accusations of witchcraft in Connecticut and Massachusetts. The Puritan attitude toward Indian religion, discussed above in Chapter Three, may have influenced the New England witch belief. Certain strange visions as well as the wonders produced by demonic possession also confirmed Puritan fears that they had been singled out for special attention by Satan. Chapter Five narrows the focus to the events at Salem and their aftermath in folklore, literature and life.

The witchcraft belief is the best-documented manifestation of New England Gothic because it is the single instance where fear of the supernatural intersected with the resort to common law. With other supernatural threats, there was no

[1] Such a history already exists: Demos's *Entertaining Satan: Witchcraft and the Culture of Early New England*. I have also relied upon the excellent work of Karlsen, *The Devil in the Shape of a Woman: Witchcraft in Colonial New England*, and Weisman, *Witchcraft, Magic, and Religion in 17th-Century Massachusetts*.

[2] Among the compilations of seventeenth-century documents that I draw on in this chapter are Hall, whose *Witch-hunting in Seventeenth-Century New England* reprints cases from Connecticut as well as Massachusetts; Tomlinson, *Witchcraft Trials of Connecticut*; Harris, et al. *John Hale: A Man Beset by Witches*, for Hale's own *A Modest Enquiry into the Nature of Witchcraft*; Trask, *"The Devil hath been Raised"* for the Salem Village outbreak of March, 1692. Among the older sources are Fowler, who reprints Mather and Calef; Drake, *Annals of Witchcraft in New England*; and Burr, *Narratives of the Witchcraft Cases*. I have relied heavily on the verbatim transcripts of the trials in Essex and Suffolk County, published by Boyer and Nissenbaum as *The Salem Witchcraft Papers (SWP)*.

available legal remedy: victims of the Wendigo, mermaids, or vampires, as far as we know, did not dream of retribution through lawsuits. Even Indian shamans were apparently outside the rule of English law: very rarely is an Indian accused by a white of malefic witchcraft. English witches, however, could be found out through legal means. We therefore have records of the cases that were brought to trial. By the same token, when the trials stopped, when common law ceased to give credence to supernatural (spectral) evidence, it can seem to us today as if the witch belief stopped, too. Despite historians' focus on the events in 1692, the New England witch belief did not begin in Salem, nor did it end there.[3] The Puritans brought with them popular and scholarly traditions of magic high and low. The trials may have been confined to a few parts of Massachusetts and Connecticut, but all of New England has been troubled by fear of witches. That fear is by no means ended.

Though the exact number of those accused, tried, and condemned may never be known, more accurate records exist for Colonial New England than for the more extensive witch-hunts of Britain and the Continent. Diligent researchers have tracked down over 30 cases of witchcraft in Massachusetts and over 20 in Connecticut before 1692; over 150 were charged during the outbreaks that year in Massachusetts and Connecticut. Of the many accused of witchcraft, 20 were executed in 1692, and at least 15 were hanged prior to that time in Connecticut and Massachusetts.[4] There may be others who, once accused, fled to Rhode Island or New York before they could be indicted thus leaving no court records. We know that some of the wealthier folk who were indicted in Salem and Connecticut were able to escape to other states and continue their lives.

Though the witch belief remained strong in frontier New England through the nineteenth century, it is an interesting historical note that no trials for witchcraft

---

[3]See Hansen, "Andover" 48, for more on this subject. Richard Godbeer's *The Devil's Dominion* (1992), the most comprehensive work I have seen so far on the status of magic in New England, arrived after I had composed this argument. He treats many of the same cases, and he also collates the history and folklore of magic and witchcraft.

[4] A slightly different reckoning is given by Demos 11. He discovers, by careful correlation of his research with Alan MacFarlane's for England, that the New England record of executions as compared to overall population is higher than England's, but is closest to the record in Essex, England, from which many of Massachusetts' inhabitants (particularly in Essex County) originated. Karlsen, by including every person whose life was touched by witchcraft accusations, whether they were indicted or not, brings the tally up to 344 (47).

are recorded in New Hampshire, Vermont, what is now Maine, (then part of Massachusetts), Northeastern or Northwestern Connecticut. Instead, the seventeenth-century trials emerge from the oldest cities and their immediate hinterlands—Hartford, New Haven, Old Saybrook, Boston, Springfield, Salem. This may be because citizens of the frontier had more material things to worry about without blaming invisible forces, or, more likely, that they distrusted courts and magistrates even more than they feared witches, and so they resorted to folk remedies against witchcraft that left no traces upon the written record.[5]

The witch belief links American history with unbreakable chains to medieval and Renaissance Europe. Followers of the doctrine of American exceptionalism, which prevailed virtually unquestioned from the beginnings of the Republic until quite recently, preferred to ignore such links: instead, historians treated the events at Salem as an aberration and sought causes that had nothing to do with the traditions of European witchcraft. [6] Recent scholarship on the witch-hunts in Europe and America has demonstrated that the opposite is true. Belief in the existence and power of witches was part of the legacy of popular religion brought from the Old World to the New. As John Demos notes in *Entertaining Satan*, "Witchcraft was no meandering side-show, isolated from the larger history of early New England. On the contrary: it belonged to—and in—that history virtually from beginning to end" (386) When did New Englanders cease to believe in witches? The answer is, not yet.

1. "The Whole Plot of the Devil against New England": Puritan Paranoia

The transcripts of the trials for witchcraft in seventeenth-century New England are a record of collective paranoia, a seeming confirmation of the Puritan belief that Satan had enlisted Indians, schismatics, and witches in a conspiracy to destroy the godly. In his account of the Salem hysteria, *Wonders of the Invisible*

---

[5] A similar theory is posited by the social historian Muchembled to explain the uneven pattern of witch-hunting in early modern France. He notes that some rural areas were "closed" to the extension of power by the central government, whereas cities and some villages were "open" and thus allowed government investigators free access ("Satanic Myths and Cultural Reality").

[6] For an excellent survey of the doctrine and its critics, see "The Problem of American Exceptionalism: A Reconsideration," by cultural historian Michael Kammen.

World, Cotton Mather paints a vivid picture of Massachusetts Bay as an outpost fortress of God in the lands of the Devil.

> The *New Englanders* are a People of God settled in those which were once the *Devils* territories, and it may easily be supposed that the *Devil* was exceedingly disturbed, when he perceived such a People here...
>
> An Army of *Devils* is horribly broke in upon the place [Massachusetts] which is the *Center*, and, after a sort, the *First Born* of our *English* settlements; and the Houses of the Good People there are filled with the doleful Shrieks of their Children and Servants, Tormented by Invisible Hands, with Tortures altogether preternatural .... (387–90)

As we have seen, from the time of the earliest settlements, New Englanders felt themselves to be the especial targets of Satan's attentions. Their preachers taught them to regard Indians not simply as non-Christians but as active Devil-worshippers, making all pagan idols and gods aspects of Satan. Since Satan lurked so close, it was only natural that he would try to recruit the people of Massachusetts Bay as agents for subverting their own godly brethren. John Greenleaf Whittier, whose own Quaker family had suffered from the witch persecutions, wrote in 1831 of this attitude, remnants of which lingered in his own time. The Puritans, he said, "stood there on their little patch of sanctified territory...within were prayer and fasting, unmelodious psalmody, and solemn hewing of heretics ...without were 'dogs and sorcerers,' red children of perdition, Powah wizards, and 'the foul fiend'" (*Supernaturalism* 75).

Cotton Mather, though today the most famous, was hardly the first Puritan to fear a Satanic conspiracy. John Winthrop, whose *Journal* of New England's history is not overly concerned, as a rule, with the supernatural, conveys the same paranoid feeling about Satan's intentions against the colonists. He makes note of "Another plot the old serpent had against us" (1: 287). Because the schismatic Roger Williams had taken refuge in Rhode Island, making it a haven for Quakers, Jews, and accused witches from the other colonies, Winthrop says, laconically, that "At Providence,... the devil was not idle" (1: 286).

The possession of so many innocent girls at Salem, like the capture of other maidens by Indians, and the massacres of King Philip's War, seemed designed to substantiate Puritan conspiracy theories. For the witchcraft in 1692 was not confined to Salem Village and Town: all Essex County was alive with witches. When the afflicted girls were taken to nearby Andover, confessions and accusations grew apace. One "Susannah Post testified that she had attended a witch meeting of two hundred, where she heard that there were five hundred witches in the country" (Silverman 106). Such huge numbers could only confirm Mather's fears that a great conspiracy, organized and led by the Prince of Angelic Plotters, had targeted the new Israel in the wilderness. But why had these evil days come to Essex County? According to the testimony of one of the accused Andover witches, Mary Lacey, Jr., it was because "The Divill would sett up his Kingdom their & we should have happy days & it would be bett'r times for me if I would obay him" (*SWP* 2: 522).

Fears of conspiracies, natural and preternatural, were manifested by Puritan settlers in ways other than the persecution of witches. Puritan paranoia led to episodes that they called "providences" or "wonders,"[7] and which modern psychologists might refer to as "collective hallucinations." In the same year that witches were hanged in Salem, soldiers in the garrison at Cape Ann reported that they were under attack by French Canadians or perhaps by devils in human shape. Reinforcements were called in, but no physical evidence of these "phantom leaguers" was ever found.[8] During a similarly tense period, the 1750s, when the New Englanders were once again under threat of French and Indian attack, the militia of Windham, Connecticut registered a similar false alarm. They stood to arms on the town green, ready to repel any invaders material or otherwise. In this instance, the attacking phantoms with their harrowing cries were identified the next morning as bullfrogs in a dried-up pond, and the incident passed into local history as the "Windham Frog-Fight."[9] As a sign of the town's good-natured acceptance

---

[7]See Hall, *Witch-hunting* 8 for a discussion of the role of "wonders," as well as his detailed study of Puritan popular religion *Worlds of Wonder; Days of Judgment*. For an entirely different explanation of some results of Puritan paranoia (a word he never would have used!), see Perry Miller's *The New England Mind*, which traces America's faith in a federal covenant of governance back to Puritan attempts to protect mankind from inimical forces through the "integument of the Covenant" with the divine (490).

[8]The story is told by Mather in the *Magnalia Christi*; it is the subject of a poem by Whittier, "The Garrison of Cape Ann." See also Drake, *New England Legends* 253-260.

[9]For this oft-told tale, see, among many others, Hazard, *Jonny-Cake* 361-2; Skinner 2: 40; Drake, *New England Legends* 436; White 1: 41. Philips, *Legendary Connecticut* 207-210 has the "last word" on the frog fight.

of the story, "in the center of the official Seal of the Town of Windham squats a baleful bullfrog" (Philips 210), just as a witch on a broom constitutes Salem's official heraldry. In each case, what is remembered is the ludicrous aftermath of the incident, not the genuine fears that occasioned it.

The best-attested Puritan "collective hallucination," however, comes from the earliest days of the New Haven Colony, which in the 1630s outfitted a ship to attempt to open trade and secure the faltering colony's future. So many hopes were pinned on the success of that mission that all were anxious for any news of the ship's whereabouts. One day, a large part of New Haven's population saw a verific vision of the ship sail through the clouds above the harbor, and, overwhelmed in a fiery sunset, disappear from view. This was assumed to be a representation of the ship's fate, for it was never seen again in life. The story is told by Winthrop and Edward Johnson. Cotton Mather recounts it as the clearest indication of God's Providence vouchsafed to the New Haven Colony.[10] New Haven's Phantom Ship never became part of jocular folklore as did Windham's Frog Fight, perhaps because those who saw the vision as well as those who wrote of it never doubted the reality of their experience. God's hand was clearly visible, but perhaps Satan's intervention in human affairs was visible as well, in the ship's fiery end, as it was in the accusations of witchcraft. These legends remind us how strong was the hold of signs and wonders on the popular imagination in early New England.

2. The Gothic Heritage of Witchcraft: Learned and Popular Beliefs

The Puritan attitude toward the invisible world did not develop in isolation in America. The witchcraft belief is one of the clearest examples of the Gothic heritage the colonists brought from medieval and Renaissance Europe. Puritan settlers brought with them the laws, customs, and the superstitions of Old England, where laws against witchcraft remained in force well into the eighteenth century. Apologists for England and the Protestants have attempted to blame the persecution of witches on the Spanish Inquisition, but more witches were charged and executed in Protestant countries than ever were in Spain.

---

[10]*Magnalia Christi* 1: Chap. 6.

The Puritans were not the first to emphasize the active role of Satan in human affairs. The Catholic Church in the Middle Ages incorporated the concept of Satan as enemy of God and Man into its dogma. Satan was manifest in the activities of heretics and witches (often the same people), and the Inquisition was empowered to deal with both. Though statutes against witchcraft are as old as Christianity, only in the late fifteenth and sixteenth centuries did the prevalence of the witch belief result in mass persecutions, justifying the name "epidemics." What scholars refer to as the "mature" or "composite" theory of witchcraft took shape in Europe beginning around 1435, with the demonology of John Nider, and culminated in the *Malleus Maleficarum* (ca. 1485), the "Hammer against Witches," by the Dominican Inquisitors Heinrich Institoris and Jakob Sprenger (Kieckhefer 23; Eisenach). Of the latter work, Jeffrey Russell in *Witchcraft in the Middle Ages* notes that its "ideas were eagerly borrowed even by Protestants who wholeheartedly rejected other aspects of Catholicism" (231). Most historians believe that the availability of scholarly manuals such as the *Malleus* spurred the persecutions; very few agree with Montague Summers, who claimed that those accused of witchcraft really were worshipping the Devil. Though for many years the witches' confessions have been viewed as nothing but hallucinations, the inevitable result of tortures, or even as fabrications by the Inquisitors themselves, the brilliant work of Carlo Ginzburg and those who have followed him has shown that there may have been truth underlying the confessions. As Ginzburg has proven, there *were* "agrarian cults" in the Italian Alps whose adherents called themselves *benandanti*, benevolent night-walkers. When first denounced to the Inquisition, *benandanti* narrated shamanistic visions of night battles against malevolent witches in defense of the crops. Only after many years of torture did their testimony change, conflating good and evil witches in accordance with the learned "mature theory" that required all magic to be Satanic in origin.

Neither the European Inquisitors, the Puritan inhabitants of New England, nor modern scholars agree on the exact definition of witch. In some cases, the term wizard is used for a male, in others witch is used for both sexes. Other terms such as sorcerer, necromancer, and cunning folk turn up in the trial transcripts. Current practitioners of the Old Religion employ the term "wicca," from the Anglo-Saxon word for witch. Known as "Wiccans" or "Neo-Pagans," they claim to be adepts of healing traditions and worshippers of the Goddess. The Puritans would not have listened to such claims. For those who conducted the New England trials:

> *A witch is a Magician, who either by open or secret league, wittingly, and willingly, consenteth to use the aide and assistance of the Devill, in the working of Wonders.*
> ...in this generall tearme, I comprehend both sexes or kinds of persons, men and women, excluding neither from beeing Witches. (Perkins 636; italics original)

This was the definition of William Perkins whose *A Discourse of the Damned Art of Witchcraft* (1618) originated as a sermon in Cambridge, England in 1608. A copy of this volume was part of the library of the Rev. Samuel Parris, whose household became the focus of the Salem hysteria. [11]

By common law in America and England of the seventeenth century, if a person denied the existence of witchcraft in the past he was an atheist; if he denied its power in the present he was a lawbreaker. To doubt the existence of witches was to doubt the existence of Satan, and so of God. Atheism was already seen as a danger in seventeenth-century England and America: some at least had begun to question the physical powers of Satan and his instruments. The very existence of books written in or popular in America such as those of the Mathers and Joseph Glanvill's *Saducismus Triumphatus* (1681), can be seen as proof that the reality of witchcraft powers had to be defended (Carter 24). The Salem persecutions gave more ammunition to those who doubted the existence of witches, the most famous being Robert Calef, whose attack on Cotton Mather, *More Wonders of the Invisible World* (1700) was burnt in Harvard Yard. Even so, six years after Salem, when an account of a poltergeist episode in New Hampshire, *Lithobolia: or The Stone-Throwing Devil*, was published in London, the author warns that any reader who doubts the veracity of this tale of demons, spirits and witches "must temerariously unhinge, or undermine the Fundamentals of the best Religion in the World; and he must ...abandon that of the Three Theologick Virtues or Graces" (Burr 76–7). While belief in the existence of witches was required, good Puritans, like good

---

[11] Keeney's annotated bibliography notes the presence of Perkins's sermons in Parris's library; Nevius concurs and also locates copies of Perkins in the libraries of John Cotton, Thomas Hooker, John Harvard, and both Mathers. In quoting Perkins, I change all the long *f*'s to *s*, and regularize *u* and *v*; otherwise transcription is exact.

Catholics before them, were warned not to give full credence to the superhuman powers witches claimed for themselves, but rather to believe that Satan deluded them into thinking they could fly, raise storms, or read minds. Scholarly commentators on witchcraft were inclined to set limits on the witches' powers, so as not to grant the Enemy unlimited sway over God-fearing Christians. Following in a long tradition of Catholic and Lutheran scholarship, Perkins, Hale, and Mather make an effort to explain rationally some of the seemingly inexplicable events and powers claimed by confessing witches and their accusers. Perkins, for example, answers objections made by some skeptics that accused witches are only crazy persons, "of a melancholy humor," and not really in covenant with the Devil because the witches' confessions are too full of "things false and impossible"

> ...as that they can raise tempests, that they are carried through the aire in a moment...that they passe through key-holes, and clifts of doores, that they be sometimes turned into cats, hares, and other creatures; lastly, that they are brought into farre countries, to meete with Herodias, Diana, and the Devill, and such like; all which are meere fables, and things impossible. (641)

Perkins explains the discrepancies between intellectual and folk beliefs by asserting that witches are "sober, and their understanding sound" (641) when they first enter their covenant with the Devil, but once they have been in league for a while, they begin to lose their minds, and the Devil deludes them in this way through a kind of intoxication. Recent analysis of the hallucinogenic ingredients in the witches' "flying ointment" and the ritual consumption of intoxicating substances in the witchcraft traditions of some cultures may mean that Perkins was not so far from wrong on this question.[12]

Perkins' reference to "Diana and Herodias" in the passage quoted above links him directly with nearly a thousand years of banning sorcery and persecuting witches as heretics in Europe. The passage derives ultimately from the *Canon Episcopi* which scholars now date from about 960, but which was believed during the Middle Ages to be the product of a synod of the fourth or fifth century.[13]

---

[12]See Weisman 1; Larner 127-150.

[13]John of Salisbury, a twelfth-century scholastic, may be the originator of Perkins's theory that the Devil deludes the minds of witches into believing in the night-rides and other powers (Russell 115). See also Kieckhefer 38-40.

According to Russell, successive Catholic and Protestant theologians re-translated the *Canon Episcopi* which set forth the witches' claims to night-rides under the leadership of the Roman Goddess Diana and Herod's sister, Herodias. These claims were to provide the basis for Margaret Murray's theory that a fertility cult, descended from classical rites, survived in Western Europe until the witch persecutions of the Renaissance. Her theory, in turn, represents the historical justification for modern Neo-Pagans' re-creation of witchcraft. Why Diana and Herodias were associated with the fear of secret witch-meetings is uncertain, but it seems that by the seventeenth century, only learned clerics could have been familiar with these names. Certainly they were never invoked by any witches questioned in New England.

As we have seen, the Manichean strain in Puritanism endowed the Devil with great powers. Like the Inquisitors, Puritans believed that *all* magical powers derived from Satan. There could, therefore, be no such thing as white magic, apart from Satan's influence. All magic users were assumed to have signed a contract with the Devil, and to be allied with their fellow witches in a great conspiracy. This conspiracy theory, while peculiarly appropriate to the circumstances of New England, characterizes the entire history of the suppression of witchcraft by Christianity. As Ginzburg notes, from the early fourteenth century on, witches were blamed for disasters ranging from cattle disease to the Black Plague. "The schema of a hostile group conspiring against society was progressively renewed at all levels ...The supposed nocturnal meetings of witches and wizards ...embodied the image of an organized, omnipresent enemy with superhuman powers" ("Deciphering" 124). The learned beliefs recorded by Perkins, Hale, and the Mathers were the end result of centuries of scholarly inquiry into witchcraft and demonology. The Catholic Church, and later the Protestants, saw witches as worshippers of the Devil and enemies of God and man. Not only did they harm the bodies of their victims, but they endangered their immortal souls. Perkins epitomizes the religious and intellectual view that justified killing every witch, even those who have not been proven to be murderers, those we might term "healers" or "white witches." He is suspicious of all the "occult sciences;" in another sermon, he opposes the use of almanacs, because they rely on astrology, a forbidden pagan science. In sum, he does not believe that there is a distinction between healing and killing witchcraft:

> But some Witches there be that cannot bee convicted of killing any:
> what shall become of them? Ans.: As the killing Witch must die by
> another Law, though he were no Witch; so the healing and
> harmlesse Witch must die by this Law, though he kill not, onely for
> covenant made with Sathan. For this must alwaies be remembred as
> a conclusion, that by Witches we understand not those onely which
> kill and torment; but all Diviners, Charmers, Iuglers, all Wizzards
> commonly called wise men and wise women; yea, whosoever doe
> any thing (knowing what they do) which cannot be effected by
> nature or art; and in the same number we reckon all good Witches,
> which do no hurt but good, which do not spoile and destroy, but
> save and deliver. All these come under this sentence of Moses,
> because they deny God, and are confederates with Sathan. ...it
> were a thousand times better for the land, if all witches, but
> especially the blessing *Witch* might suffer death.... Death therefore
> is the iust and deserved portion of the good Witch. (Perkins 652)

Through such interdictions, we can catch a glimpse of the folk economy of magic
and counter-magic, existing as an alternative to the remedies offered by learned
divines and physicians. The Rev. John Hale, writing after the Salem outbreak,
continues to rely on Perkins' authority. Hale, too, condemns those who profess to
be diviners and the sinners who frequent such "cunning men," since "all of them, if
they have their knowledge, or skill, or working by the Devil, are in Satan's black
list of Witches" (Hale 111). Increase Mather in *Remarkable Providences* expands
upon Perkins' ban against "healing witches" to include the traveling conjurers,
sometimes called "cunning folk," whose descendants were found in England by
Thomas Hardy as late as the nineteenth century. Their business consisted of
"unbewitching" people; they would practice counter-magic, discover the cursing
witch, and remove the curse. Increase Mather damns them all together: how such
practitioners "can wholly clear themselves from being white witches I am not able
to understand" (190–1).

Professional unbewitchers were found under different names throughout
medieval and Renaissance Europe. The Inquisition, like the Puritan divines,
considered them witches, and thus liable for prosecution. As a woman testified
before the Modenese Inquisition in 1499, "'who knows how to heal knows how to
destroy'" (qtd. in Ginzburg, *Night Battles* 78). Since Ginzburg's book was
published, European scholars have found other traditional unbewitchers who were

also swept up by the great witch-hunts.[14] Thus were folk beliefs demonized to fit more securely into the official scenarios of pact and diabolism.

While some historians have denied the transmission of traditional witch beliefs to the New World, Puritan scholars such as Perkins, Hale, Deodat Lawson, and Cotton Mather record and condemn the use of counter-magic, folk remedies against witchcraft diabolical in themselves and leading to the further corruption of the souls of those who employed them. Lawson, writing during the Salem outbreak, repeats Increase Mather's warnings, saying that "these indirect means...Burning the Afflicted Persons Hair; parings of Nails, stopping up and Boyling the Urine. Their Scratching the Accused, or otherwise fetching Blood of them ...[is] a Giving place to the Devil." (qtd. in Trask 99) The Puritan divines' insistence that no magic could be done without Satanic assistance meant that the learned witch belief was concerned with details of the pact with Satan almost to the exclusion of all else.

Regardless of whether they were in truth innocent healers and midwives, Jews, heretics, or surviving pagan fertility cultists, witches in the European trials were accused of worshipping Satan and attacking the Church. In the scholarly Puritan view, witches in New England were also attempting to render back to Satan the forest lands so recently part of his earthly kingdom. Just as witches in Catholic France and Spain were accused of desecrating the Mass, communion, and the elaborate ceremonial of the Catholic Church, so New England witches were said to parody the congregationalism and *lack* of ritual that characterized Puritanism. The learned witch belief insisted upon a conspiracy and a congregational organization for witches' meetings. The Puritans were not the first to propose a conspiracy theory of witchcraft: Russell theorizes that the medieval Catholic Church identified witches with heretics such as the Cathars, the Waldensians, the Protestant reformers, or supposed converts who remained secret Muslims or Jews, all of whom represented conspiratorial threats to Church hegemony. Moreover, Russell suggests that most of the accused witches of Europe *were* heretics or crypto-Jews,

---

[14]See Klaniczay for the Hungarian *taltos*, and Henningsen for Sicilian and Romanian "cunning folk." The *Malleus Maleficarum* records these customs of counter-magic in detail, in order to declare them heretical and diabolical (Part II, Question 2; 155-164).

since the term "sabbat" for a witch-meeting, and the earlier term, "synagogue," (common before the fifteenth century) seem to derive from anti-Semitism.[15]

Unlike the confessions obtained during the European witch-hunts, there is nothing in the Salem transcripts about child sacrifice or cannibalism, and little about abnormal sexuality. The mass orgies synonymous with Satanism in European trials from the Middle Ages through the nineteenth century are missing from the record in Massachusetts. In Connecticut, however, there are a few references to orgies in the trial of Rebecca and Nathaniel Greensmith, who were hanged in Hartford in 1663. Increase Mather wrote in *Remarkable Providences* that Rebecca Greensmith had confessed that "the Devil told her that at Christmass they would have a merry Meeting," thus justifying Puritan attempts to ban that pagan holy day. She also admitted "that the Devil had frequently the carnal knowledge of her Body" (Burr 20). Some of those accused in Salem in 1692 did describe a blood baptism by Satan, and there is some mention of red bread and red drink. The Rev. Hale takes note of "their Witch meetings, and that they had their mock Sacraments of Baptism and the Supper...their signing of the Devils book" (45). Belief by educated clergy in such practices provided justification to kill them all: even if the accused witches had murdered no one, even if they appeared in the harmless guise of children or senile women.

Like the ancient Hebrews, the Puritans were a people of the book; it is therefore appropriate that the Devil's book stood at the center of the Salem trials. In this, the Puritans departed from English practice: as Kittredge notes, "with the general run of English witches, who belonged to the illiterate class, the agreement with Satan was implicit only, or at most oral" (242). In Puritan terms, the witch's covenant with the Devil was like a distorted mirror image of the holy covenant between God and the elect, or between a righteous government and its people.

It is the learned view of witchcraft—of pacts, sabbats, and perverse sexuality—that has become familiar to us from the eighteenth-century Gothic novel and its descendants in popular fiction and film. The witch's curse and the tortures of the Inquisition swiftly became Gothic clichés along with evil monks and crumbling castles. At the same time, French aristocrats were enacting Gothic

---

[15]This may be an example of an old theory come around again, as Montague Summers cites scholars before him, including the authors of the *Malleus*, who affirm the identity of heresy and witchcraft. (*History of Witchcraft* 24).

cruelties in life. The Satanism of the Marquis de Sade and Madame de Montespan was game and earnest, their dark medievalism commingling the "terrible" and the "sportive." Anacharsis Clootz, guillotined in 1794, called himself "the personal enemy of Jesus Christ" (Summers, *Malleus* xviii). Congregations who worshipped Satan with the Black Mass, using a virgin as the altar; orgies; and attempted poisonings by witchcraft did exist in the late eighteenth century, the time of the Gothic novel's birth, rather than in the medieval times that were the Gothic novel's setting. Such practices have no connection with the New England witch belief, and not until twentieth century rebels and decadents sought a model were they naturalized upon American soil. Yet Gothic fiction; films such as *Rosemary's Baby, The Witches of Eastwick*, and *Hocus Pocus*; and Fundamentalist Christian preachers have ensured that in the popular imagination the archetype of witchcraft remains the Satanic conspiracy.

The scholarly vision of witchcraft, as we have seen in Perkins' definitions, encompassed what we would now call "occult science," those sciences of the Renaissance which persisted, as Leventhal shows, into the eighteenth-century "Enlightenment." Such a view of witchcraft was more syncretistic than the popular one, drawing not only on traditions of England and of the Indians, but on close readings of the Bible in the original languages, on Classical mythology, and on the findings of Catholic witch-hunters. According to Leventhal, well into the eighteenth century, a Harvard education would have included some study of astrology and alchemy, and medical practice was still based on the medieval theory of humors. Though esoteric subjects could be studied in college, there were few professional mages in Colonial America, Hawthorne's Chillingworth to the contrary; books on divination and astrology, however, were widely popular among the educated and the less-educated. Katherine Harrison of Wethersfield, CT, accused of witchcraft in 1668, was alleged by her neighbors to be acquainted with Lilly's *Astrology*. William Lilly was the most successful of the seventeenth-century English astrologers, at a time when astrologers were not automatically expected to be witches. Indeed, according to the *Malleus Maleficarum*, witches could not override the influence of the stars on human affairs, since the stars were ruled by good angels, not evil spirits (Parker 73; *Malleus* Part I, Question 3, p. 27). *Christian Astrology*, Lilly's *magnum opus*, was approved by Puritans and Royalists alike. It is a long and difficult book, which inspired numerous imitations and abridgements. Perhaps Katherine Harrison owned one of the latter, or else one of Lilly's many almanacs, which contained hints for fortune-telling along with calendrical and astronomical data.

The "cunning folk" or professional unbewitchers discussed above often claimed knowledge of the forbidden sciences. Caleb Powell, a sailor, attempted in 1679 to quell the Morse family poltergeist by using his expertise in astrology and knowledge of the spirits. For his pains, he was indicted for witchcraft; the bosun of his ship testified "that if there were any wizards he was sure that Caleb Powell was a wizard" (Hall, *Witch-hunting* 239). Another sailor, Job Tuckey of Beverly, may have boasted of his familiarity with Satan, leading to his indictment for witchcraft in 1692. Edwin Stone in his *History of Beverly* (1843) guesses that Tuckey was not a professional wizard, but that he "probably was fond of exciting wonders by marvellous speeches" (215). During the trials, James Darling testified that "Job Tookey Said he was not the Devills servant but the Devill was his" (*SWP* 3: 760). Tuckey showed some knowledge of scholarly demonology when he claimed in his defense that he was no witch, but it was "the divell in his shape that hurts the people" (*SWP* 3: 759). This hair-splitting did not avail against the afflicted girls, who called him a murderer as well as a wizard, because he had claimed in their hearing "that he had Learneing and could Raise the Divell W'n he pleased" (*SWP* 3: 759). Sailors may have been under unusual suspicion, especially when they had pretensions to learning not appropriate to their class. Maybe in ordinary times they encouraged suspicions that they knew strange arts—maybe it got them free drinks or the attention of women—but during witch-hunts, Caleb Powell and Job Tuckey nearly paid for their learning with their lives.

In the scholarly view, witchcraft was worthy of close attention primarily because of the pact with the Devil. In the Catholic Church, the pact raised witchcraft from the status of noxious superstition to that of heresy; in Puritan theology, the pact confirmed the existence of a conspiracy against the saints.

The testimony given by accusers and accused in the New England witch-hunts does not only reflect what the examiners had read in the *Malleus Maleficarum* or in Perkins. When neighbors of the accused testified, they complained about the everyday harms committed by witches, spooking cattle or preventing cream from turning to butter, and they related the remedies they had employed against these harms, the ancient methods of detecting and countering witchcraft. This sort of testimony in itself rarely convinced educated judges of a witch's guilt, but it provides for modern scholars an unusual concentration of oral traditions that rarely make their way into print. As Kieckhefer notes, referring to the continental witch trials, "it is notoriously difficult to glean the beliefs of the illiterate masses when the only sources are texts drawn up by the literate elite" (2). The gulf between learned and folk traditions was narrower in seventeenth-century New England, with its greater literacy, than in, for example, sixteenth-century Italy, but by and large, the two views of witchcraft remained distinct. In the popular view, witchcraft was not about great conspiracies marshalling in the Invisible World: it was about human malice in the Visible World.[16]

Some of those brought to trial for witchcraft in New England had long been suspected by their neighbors of possessing uncanny powers. Unlike the randomly-accused victims of the Salem hysteria, Margaret Jones of Charlestown who was hanged in 1648 [17] *was* a professed witch, one of the "healing witches" condemned by Perkins' *Discourse of the Damned Art of Witchcraft*. Like many of those burned by the Inquisition, she was a folk healer: simple medicines in her hands may have had extraordinary effects. Eventually, however, she must have lost a few of her patients, and she was indicted for malefic witchcraft. Winthrop records in his journal that she was accused of having a "malignant touch," with neighbors testifying that "many persons ....whom she stroked or touched...were taken with deafness, or vomiting, or other violent pains or sickness" (2: 344). The Rev. John Hale, who as a boy witnessed her execution, implies that her accusers had experimented with traditional methods of counter-magic before going to the courts: he says that "She was suspected ...partly because some things supposed to be bewitched, or have a Charm upon them, being burned, she came to the fire and seemed concerned" (39). According to testimony at her trial, she would threaten those who feared to consult her with endless pains as punishment. She was clairvoyant, foretelling events, and knowing others' secret speeches. She was

---

[16]See also Hall, *Witch-hunting* 9; Kieckhefer; Demos, 172-4.

[17]Governor John Winthrop presided over the case. Jones was not the first witch executed in New England; here, apparently, Connecticut bears the palm. All we know of the earlier case is Winthrop's laconic notation in 1647 "One [*blank*] of Windsor arraigned and executed at Hartford for a witch" (2: 323). No court records exist for this trial, but in 1904, the diary of a Windsor town clerk was found, identifying the witch as "Alse Young" (Tomlinson 4).

accused of possessing a familiar, in the shape of a little child, that suckled her even in prison and vanished when an officer appeared. She died, like many later witches, cursing judge, jury, and witnesses.

Another woman fitting the traditional model of the witch, Ann Hibbins was executed at Boston in 1656 merely for possessing highly-developed clairaudient abilities, and, according to a Boston minister, "more wit than her neighbors" (Hall, *Witch-hunting* 91). She was arrested for witchcraft, and though none of the customary proofs were found—no witchmarks, familiars, dolls—yet she was convicted for knowing too many of her neighbors' secrets. She also had the uncanny knack (although apparently useless for her) of knowing when other people were talking about her.[18]

Anything at all out of the ordinary could provide potent evidence for witchcraft in the popular mind. Hugh Parsons of Springfield, who was tried along with his wife Mary in 1651, was accused by his neighbors of bewitching their puddings as they steamed in the bag.

> George Lancton and Hannah his wife do jointly testify upon oath:...they had a pudding in the same bag and that as soon as it was slipped out of the bag it was cut lengthwise like the former pudding, and like another...as smooth as any knife could cut it namely one slice all along wanting but very little from end to end. (Hall, *Witch-hunting* 32)

In contradiction to the orders of the Puritan divines, before going to the law, the Lanctons tried some counter-magic. They threw a piece of the bewitched pudding in the fire, and after about an hour, Hugh Parsons appeared, in accordance with folk beliefs about discovering witchcraft, or, as Lancton deposed, "that the spirit that bewitched the pudding brought him thither" (Hall, *Witch-hunting* 33). Another accusation of pudding-tampering comes from the transcripts of the Salem witch trials, where Sarah Cole of Lynn was accused by a neighbor of turning his fine white Indian pudding as red as a blood pudding (*SWP* 1: 231).

The accused witch Katherine Harrison, discussed above, was described as a "common and professed fortune teller;" her neighbors were not afraid to confess that they had resorted to her frequently because of this skill (Hall 173, 178;

---

[18]Karlsen gives a totally different interpretation of the case against Ann Hibbins, *passim*.

Tomlinson 44–45). Samuel Wardwell of Andover, one of those executed in 1692, was also known as a fortune-teller. According to the testimony of Thomas Chandler: "I have often hard Samuel Wardle of Andovr till yung person thire fortine and he was much adicted to that and mayd sport of it" (*SWP* 3: 787). Katherine Harrison was also a folk healer, but as with Margaret Jones, when one of her patients died, her neighbors charged her with *maleficia*. In their testimonies, they remembered that she could spin more than any other woman, and that she had bewitched their cattle.

The latter accusation may be one of the most enduring harms attributed to witches, condemned in the earliest penitentials of the Christian era and current today in cattle-raising areas of Europe, the Americas, and Africa. In the trial of Susanna Martin, one of the few executed at Salem who had a prior reputation for witchcraft, reports put her powers over cattle at a truly supernatural level. When John Allen of Salisbury refused to carry some wheat for her in his ox-cart, she cursed him, saying "his oxen should never do him much more service." Not content with merely striking his oxen with a disease, Allen deposed, Martin had caused his oxen and others to run from Salisbury beach to Plum Island, where they stampeded "with a violence that seemed wholly diabolical," straight into the water and swam out to sea, never to be seen again (Mather in Calef, Fowler 305).[19]

On the whole, folk witch beliefs in New England, as in Renaissance Europe, are concerned with divination, inflicting small personal harms, blessing, and cursing, not with sin, devil-worship, or possession. Weisman distinguishes the malefic revenge of the cursing witch, "ordinary witchcrafts," from "bewitchments," the torments of the afflicted girls at Salem, done for no apparent reason and resembling Biblical accounts of demonic possession[20]. He believes that the resort to law answered the misfit between the popular and the official beliefs by a search for guilt through confessions and spectral evidence. After 1700, however,

---

[19]The *Malleus Maleficarum* devotes an entire chapter to folk beliefs concerning the witch's power over cattle (Part II, Question 1, Chapter 14; 144-147). Demos (171-2) gives numerous examples of cattle-bewitchment claims from the Connecticut and Massachusetts trials. In Maine in 1964, the following tale was collected as true: "There was a woman living in Limington some years ago. Cattle driven along the road by her house would refuse to go by the house. . . . One man went into her house, and threatened to whip her with a bull whip unless she took the spell off the cattle. . . Fearing the whipping, she took off the spell and the cattle went by her house without any trouble from that time on" (Sawyer 377.35).

[20]See also Leventhal 124.

the reversal of convictions and reparations paid to the victims caused courts and the learned to wonder whether any rules of evidence could determine guilt in witchcraft cases, or indeed "whether witchcraft was discoverable at all" (Weisman 176), and witchcraft cases moved back into the domain of folklore.

Just because much of the mischief credited to witches—spoiled butter and puddings, contrary cattle—may now seem trivial, we must remember that the folk witch belief also encompassed the witch's ability to cause illness and even the death of her victim. While accused witches often had long-standing quarrels or land disputes with their neighbors, the accusers nevertheless seem sincere in their convictions that they are being grievously harmed through supernatural means. The idea that they are somehow taking advantage of an outmoded belief to win court cases is anachronistic. Instead, in Cotton Mather's words, most people believed that "our dear neighbors are most really tormented, really murdered, and really acquainted with hidden things, which are afterwards proved plainly to have been realities" (*Selected Letters* 37). Whatever their actual causes may have been, the injuries to self and property reported in the transcripts of the witch trials were real, as real as the harms inflicted upon themselves by followers of today's cult leaders, as measurable as the millions of dollars spent calling in to psychic hot-lines.

As a result of a millennium of trials and two hundred years of intensive persecution, the laws of evidence regarding witchcraft were on the books in Old and New England, but applying them was another matter. What constituted evidence of familiarity with the Devil? Any form of supernatural ability as attested by witnesses or confessions, and physical evidence such as witchmarks, extra nipples to suckle familiars sent by the Devil. Continental witch-hunters had long identified witchmarks as acceptable evidence for the pact with Satan. Witches' teats did not have to resemble genuine nipples (though woe betide the woman born with supernumerary nipples!). Any mole or spot that appeared to be insensitive to pain or was cold to the touch could be a witchmark. If pricked by a pin, blood would not flow from it. The infamous Mathew Hopkins, Witchfinder General in seventeenth-century England, would use a special pin when convictions were slowing down. The pin looked huge and fierce, but, like a stage dagger, it would fold in on itself when pressed to the body. The judges would "see" three inches of steel disappearing into a mole, but the accused witch would feel nothing.

To doubt the efficacy of witchmarks as evidence could be dangerous. In Connecticut, it led to one doubter, Mary Staples, being accused of witchcraft herself. In 1653, she had protested the hanging of Goody Knapp of Fairfield, who had been convicted primarily on the evidence of witch's teats. A year later, at Staples' trial for witchcraft, one witness after another testified to their shock at watching Staples search Goody Knapp's hanged body, and hearing her declare, as Susan Lockwood deposed, "here are no more teats than I myself have, or any other women, or you either if you would search your body" (Hall, *Witch-hunting* 80; Tomlinson 8). This early feminist was attacked by the experts of the time, including a midwife, who insisted that Knapp *and* Staples possessed more excrescences than women normally had.

In Fairfield in 1692, women were again charged with witchcraft because of witch marks. In these cases the committee of pious women appointed to examine them were explicit in their reports, leading us to marvel at their ignorance of female anatomy. On one of the accused, Mercy or Marcy Desborough, the examiners insisted that they had found a classic witch's teat, even though rather than being cold and insensitive to pain, it caused the accused to convulse when it was touched. The searchers had found "on her secret parts growing within ye lip of same a lose piece of skin and when pulled it is near an inch long. Somewhat in the form of ye finger of a glove flatted. That lose skin we judge more than common to women" (Tomlinson 60). Desborough was condemned to death, but earned a reprieve because the minister Gershom Bulkeley petitioned the court in late 1692, saying that the Fairfield court had acted under an illegal charter. Upon appeal, Desborough's lawyers argued that, by 1693, Massachusetts had repudiated folk traditions of "'teats, water trials and the like,'" since "'those that will make witchcraft of such things will make hanging work apace and we are informed of no other but such as these brought against this woman'" (Tomlinson 63).

But regardless of learned doubts as to the efficacy of this type of evidence, in Salem in 1692, accused women were still being strip-searched for witch marks. A jury of women set *their* marks to a report that a "chyrugen," J. Barton, signed, saying that they had found "preternathurall Excresence of flesh between the pudendum and the anus" on the bodies of Bridget Bishop, Rebecca Nurse, and Elizabeth Proctor (*SWP* 1: 107). Strangely enough, the same jury of women conducted a second search and could not find any witches' teats, but the magistrates must have disregarded the second report and relied on the first one. The three accused were convicted of witchcraft and sentenced to death, though Proctor was reprieved for her pregnancy; by the time the child was delivered her husband had been executed, but the hysteria was over.

Other legal methods of determining a witch's guilt were the "swimming" test (the "water trial" mentioned above) and the fire test; neither were used in Massachusetts. In both cases the theory seems to have been that if the pure element—water or fire—rejected the witch—that is, if she floated or did not burn, she was guilty. If she sank or burned she was innocent—though probably dead! Connecticut apparently did use the swimming test, first in the trials in Hartford in 1662, again in the case of Elizabeth Clawson of Stamford, (who had also been searched for witch marks), and probably in the later case of Winfred Benham, described in Chapter Five. Clawson floated when she was thrown into the water on June 2, 1692, and floating was presumed to prove the witch's guilt. Despite the evidence of the water test, she was acquitted "primarily because of an affidavit signed by 76 individuals, including many elected officials" who swore that she was not "contentious" nor did she wish harm toward her neighbors (Stanko; Tomlinson 56).

Although the traditional methods of counter-magic were not found in the law-books, everyone, not just the professional "cunning folk," seemed to know infallible methods for discovering a witch. These might include burning or boiling the victims' hair or urine, pinning down the suspected witch with cold iron in her tracks, or baking a witch cake. These beliefs, condemned by Perkins at the start of the seventeenth century, were flourishing in Puritan New England as evidenced by the space that both Increase and Cotton Mather devoted to blasting them. In *Remarkable Providences*, Chapter Eight, Increase Mather reiterates Perkins' condemnation of the supposed "healing" or "white" witch, even if their cures seem to end an afflicted person's suffering. Anyone who consults the "cunning folk," or who attempts such counter-magic for themselves, he says "do honour and worship the devil, by hoping in his salvation" (I. Mather, *Remarkable* 189). Despite these condemnations, during the Salem outbreak in 1692, a witch-cake was baked from rye meal and the urine of some of the suspected victims of bewitchment.

Hardest of all to define, yet the focus of the Salem outbreak, was "spectral evidence." In this form of proof, the accuser would claim to see the witch's spectre or shape at work tormenting her—such shapes being visible only to the victim. Witches were also accused of sending their spectres or shapes to witch meetings while their material bodies remained at home or in jail. Today this practice, called astral projection or out-of-body experience, forms one of the cornerstones of New Age doctrine.

While judicial torture of all kinds was the rule in Continental witch trials, in America, the Puritans proudly proclaimed that no torture was ever employed in the examination of suspected witches.[21] Confessions, which were believed to be the most reliable form of evidence, were obtained publicly and given freely. This claim has been disputed by the victims themselves. For example, one petition for damages during the Salem outbreak alleged that two suspects had been tied hand to foot till the blood ran from their mouths (*SWP* 2: 689–90). From the trial records, later historians have discerned that examiners applied psychological pressures similar to modern brainwashing techniques that leave no outward damages yet are as coercive as the rack. It is true, however, that in New England, more exonerated witches returned to their communities and lived on for many years than was ever the case in the Old World.

While recent scholarship has begun to reveal the great extent to which European systems of magic, popular and learned, were brought to America, data is still lacking on how much English settlers knew and absorbed of Indian magical beliefs. As Whittier suggested in 1847, we may not ever know "how far the superstitions existing in New England have been modified, and if we may so speak, acclimated, by commingling with those of the original inhabitants" (*Supernaturalism* 32). A few bits of evidence can be found for cultural "commingling": one comes from the trial of Mary Webster of Hadley, Massachusetts in 1683. Among the charges brought against her at her indictment was that of covenanting with the devil, that she "had familiarity with him in the shape of a *warraneage*," which is the Indian word for a black cat (Hall, *Witch-hunting* 261). In a Connecticut case in New Haven, 1653, a widow, Mrs.

---

[21]Apologists for the Inquisition claim that the stereotype of their activities familiar to us from Gothic romances is inaccurate. See Tedeschi, who concludes that torture and the stake were "used less frequently, with greater moderation, and with a higher regard for human rights and life in the tribunals of the Holy Office than elsewhere" (115).

Godman, accused of witchcraft by her neighbors, filed a counter-complaint against them for slander. One of her charges was that when a neighbor woman accused her of being a witch, she had said "that Hobbamocke [the trickster god of the vision quest] was her husband" (Hall, *Witch-hunting* 62). This shows a familiarity with Indian religion long after the Pequot Wars had subdued the Indians in the Connecticut Colony. Though Godman was indicted for witchcraft in 1653 and again in 1655, the court found her innocent of capital crimes, while keeping her under suspicion.

New Englanders' extreme concern about animal familiars may result in part from Indian shamans who depended upon animal spirits for their powers.[22] The guardian spirits of Indian powwows, discussed in Chapter Three, were termed "familiars" by European chroniclers. The Apostle to the Indians, John Eliot, described one Massachusetts powwow's guardian spirit as a little hummingbird, who would peck at him to get his attention.[23] Another such shaman had a pigeon as guardian (Simmons, *Spirit* 42). Letters of the Reverend Samuel Lee of Rhode Island, written in 1690, note that shamans might have crows and hawks as familiar spirits (Simmons, *Spirit* 91). It is not surprising that familiars in bird form, relatively rare in European witchlore, were commonly seen at Salem, where the afflicted girls claimed they saw the likeness of Goody Corey with a "Yellow-Bird, that used to suck betwixt her Fingers" (Trask 38). This bird had already been suggested to them by the testimony of Tituba (as recorded by Ezekiel Cheever) that the tall man of Boston who forced her to hurt the children "had a yellow bird that keept with him" (Trask 11).

One form of divination that may have been practiced by Tituba and the afflicted girls was that of scrying with an egg white in water to see who they would marry. During the trials, Sarah Cole of Lynn admitted to using an egg and a "Venus glass" to see what profession her future husband would follow (*SWP* 1: 228; Dailey). This same "project" or love-magic technique was collected from Gay

---

[22]Russell raises the possibility that the demon in animal form identified with the European sorcerers derives ultimately from Europe's Paleolithic hunting cults (188), as pictured in the Caves of Lascaux.

[23]The hummingbird "poohegan" or guardian spirit appears in a folktale collected by Alger, *In Indian Tents* 20.

Head Indians in 1928 (Simmons, *Spirit* 109) who might have learned it from the English—or perhaps it was the other way around.

Indian herbalists or "yarb doctors" were sought out by Europeans from the earliest times into the twentieth century. In the seventeenth century, their cures with roots and herbs were at least as efficacious as anything a university-trained physician might prescribe. Indian fortune-tellers were consulted by New Englanders: Eckstorm, writing in 1945, describes an old Indian woman who travelled through Maine, "with her bag of baskets to sell, her grimy pack of cards for fortune-telling" (28). When Eckstorm mentioned the word for witch, "*M'teoulin*" or "*medeowlin*," her informant provided her with folklore previously unshared with whites that became the book *Old John Neptune and Other Maine Indian Shamans*.

We have seen in Chapter Three how the Indians' religion had been equated by the Puritans with diabolism, and their shamans or powwows with witches. This misidentification had tragic consequences earlier in the century, yet in the drama of the witchcraft trials, Indians played almost no role. Surprisingly, no *American* Indians were implicated in the Salem outbreak, perhaps because few were left in the immediate vicinity (Tituba's husband, John Indian, was, like her, from the West Indies). This did not stop Mather from speculating that the whole affair might have been a plot of the few remaining Indian sagamores, who were "horrid Sorcerers, and hellish Conjurers, and such as conversed with Daemons" (qtd. in Silverman 239). Based on the reports of early English and French explorers and the lore preserved for hundreds of years by New England Indians, however, in these tribes shamanism was used for healing, rather than for harming; perhaps the average Puritan was aware of this and so refrained from accusing individual Indians of malefic witchcraft. As Alfred Cave notes, in a recent article on "Indian Shamans and English Witches in Seventeenth-Century New England," "it may well be that the indigenous inhabitants of New England first learned about *maleficium* from the English" (254).

3. "All Made up of Wonders": Poltergeists and Possession Prior to Salem

Crowded into their tiny ships, the English colonists on their way to the New World still found room for the Devil and his legions. Demonic possession had been well-documented from the New Testament onward, and no one was more familiar with that literature than the Puritan divines.

Possessions and exorcisms had taken place in New England long before Salem. In Connecticut, the case of Ann Cole, reported by Increase Mather in *Remarkable Providences*, led to the first Hartford witch hunt and several hangings. Cole, like many other energumens, was given the ability to speak foreign languages, or at least "Dutch-toned English." During her foreign-accented discourse, she named neighbors as agents of her torment. After these witches had been convicted or had fled into exile in Rhode Island, she recovered and became a good Christian once again (Burr 19–20; Tomlinson 27–40). Increase Mather's book containing the account of this incident became a best-seller. Demos claims that works like his served two purposes: they showed forth the power of "providence" in everyday life, and by demonstrating that good could triumph over the Devil, they helped to reduce his influence (98–99). In addition to these worthy motives, as we have seen, Gothic narratives have always made for the most popular reading. Accounts of showers of stone and demonic possessions had long been hawked in the streets of Old and New England in the form of ballads and chapbooks.

Of the many cases of what we today call poltergeists and possessions, those of the Morse family of Newbury, Massachusetts, in 1679,[24] and the Goodwin family of Boston in 1688[25] stand out. Though the afflicted members of both families were originally viewed as examples of direct diabolical possession, they eventually placed the blame on human witches, resulting in trials and deaths. Parapsychologists today believe that the physical phenomena characteristic of the poltergeist originate somehow in the energy of adolescent boys and girls. Significantly, there was a rebellious child at the center of each of these cases.[26]

---

[24]The Morse case is reported by Increase Mather in *Remarkable Providences* Chapter V; the documents are also reprinted in Hall, *Witch-hunting* 230-259.

[25]The Goodwin case is reported in Cotton Mather *Memorable Providences Relating to Witchcrafts and Possessions*, repr. in Burr 99-131. The documents are also reprinted in Hall, *Witch-hunting* 265-279.

[26]Demos gives a detailed psychoanalytic (and non-supernatural) reading of these cases and that of Elizabeth Knapp.

The focus of the Morse poltergeist seems to be a pre-adolescent grandson, John Stiles. If it was his energy that guided the attacks, he was swift to accuse others, including his grandmother, of witchcraft. The boy was much tortured yet lived on unscathed. He was thrown into the fire, his tongue was pulled from his mouth to a great length, a spirit fist was found beating him. Others in the house were also targets: they were pelted with cow-dung, showers of stones, sticks and fire came down the chimney, the family hogs invaded, furniture moved incessantly. The Morses testified at Goody Morse's trial: "I saw the andiron leap into the pot and dance, and leap out, ...and leap on a table and there abide ...the woolen wheel turned upside down and stood upon its end, and a spade set on it" (Hall, *Witch-hunting* 234). Suspicion fell upon a self-appointed exorcist, Caleb Powell (see above); he was exonerated. Elizabeth Morse stood trial for witchcraft and was condemned, although the sentence was not carried out.

The Goodwin family, especially the oldest daughter Martha, presented in 1688 a sort of dress rehearsal for the horrors to come in Salem four years later. They were minutely studied by Cotton Mather, who enjoyed having such dramatic proof of the Devil's power before his eyes. Today we might call Martha Goodwin's case possession, and Mather an over-proud exorcist who loved wrestling hand to hand with Satan. Cotton Mather recorded his long conversations with the possessed girl, Martha, and those inhabiting her which read much like those in Blatty's novel *The Exorcist*. Unfortunately for Mather, Puritans were not supposed to believe that their own powers or the reciting of any particular prayers or rituals would suffice to drive the Adversary forth—that would be too much like Roman Catholic practice. Mather's tone throughout his account is a fascinating combination of the righteous horror appropriate to a godly Puritan with the glee of an anthropologist allowed to witness a primitive ceremony that proved his pet theory. As he notes at the end of his account,

> But all my Library never afforded me any Commentary on those Paragraphs of the Gospels, which speak of Demoniacs, equal to that which the passions of this Child have given me.
> This is the Story of Goodwins Children, a Story all made up of Wonders! (Burr 131)

When the case began, all four children of the Goodwins were tormented by invisible hands, but Martha was taken with unusually odd fits. Their torments worsened; "they would make most pitteous out-cries, that they were cut with Knives and struck with Blows;" as in *The Exorcist*, the children's limbs were contorted and "their Heads would be twisted almost round" (Burr 102). They were sickened and made deaf by prayers and holy words, though all could hear joke books and Quaker tracts with no trouble. Finally Martha laid the blame on the mother of their laundress. Mrs. Mary Glover was a natural scapegoat, an old woman and an alien, who probably spoke Gaelic better than she did English. Arraigned at Boston, she was condemned and executed in 1688. A committee of doctors confirmed that she was "Compos Mentis," even though she was a "Roman Catholick." The court's proof of her guilt was the discovery in her home of several "small Images, or Puppets," instruments of sympathetic magic, "stuff't with Goat's hair." "When these were produced, the vile Woman acknowledged, that her way to torment ... was by wetting of her Finger with her Spittle, and stroking of these little Images." (Burr 104–5). The belief in the efficacy of image magic is one place where popular and learned belief coincided. According to Kieckhefer, such practices, called *invultuatio*, had been condemned in penitentials from the earliest Christian centuries (50–1). Though the materials from which the image is constructed may vary in different times and places, the practice remains universal, forming one of Frazer's laws of magic.

Though Mary Glover's images were confiscated and the accused witch executed, the torments of the Goodwin children continued, requiring further measures. Mather notes that this must be the result of direct intervention by the Devil. Eventually, Martha Goodwin was taken into the Mather household, where her behavior scandalized everyone, even after her exorcism was supposedly complete. She became a living symbol of "how ready the Devils are to catch us, and torment our Bodies" (Burr 131). [27]

Among the works inspired by the Salem witch trials' bicentennial in 1892 was one by John Nevius, who had studied occult phenomena and demonic possession while a missionary in China. His experiences there confirmed for him

---

[27]See Silverman's excellent and formidably researched analysis of Mather's role in these events in Chap. 4 "Letters of Thanks from Hell," *The Life and Times of Cotton Mather* (83-137).

the reality of Satan and the prevalence of possession by demons as detailed in the Bible. He believed that Salem's afflicted girls really had been possessed by Satan:

> It is the theory which was held by some of the accused, Not a few of them when under trial evinced a consistency, truthfulness, and conscientiousness worthy of Christian martyrs, preferring to die rather than falsify themselves. ...when asked in court how the tortures and abnormal conditions of the "afflicted" were to be accounted for, if they were not "bewitched," their answer in several instances was that they were *caused by the devil*; and I am strongly inclined to agree with them. What reason is there to prevent us from supposing that the "afflicted" were controlled by demons directly and immediately without the intervention of a human instrument, the so-called "witch"? (307–308).

The testimony of the slave Tituba may provide support for Nevius's hypothesis. There are four versions of the examination of Tituba on March 1, 1692, at the opening of the Salem witch outbreak. While she eventually admits to hurting the afflicted children herself, together with a large cast of human witches, the four recorders agree that when she was *first* asked "who hurts the children," her answer was "the Devill for ought I know" (Trask 12,13,14). Tragically, the examiners refused to believe her claim that the Devil could act in this way with no human agent as intermediary. Job Tuckey's testimony, cited above, also supports this theory of the Devil's direct involvement. Nevius believes that the girls' later contrition was consistent with the behavior of those from whom demons have been exorcised: "these girls declaring, when in their normal condition, that they had no ill-will towards the accused, and did not know what they had said when accusing them...entirely harmonizes with this theory" (308). This is far from the strangest theory attempting to account for Salem, that crux of American history. Only the assassination of John F. Kennedy has provided such fertile ground for those who see conspiracy everywhere. The events of 1692, enshrined in literature and legend, have come to define the dark side of New England's heritage.

Chapter Five
The Essex County Witchcraft Outbreak of 1692 and its Aftermath

> The whole business is so snarled.
> --Cotton Mather

The minister of a stern sect in Salem, Massachusetts, weekly preaches against witches who worship the Devil, while members of his congregation come forward to accuse their neighbors. Young women are stricken into hysterics as they recall being abused by their own relatives at Satanic rituals. The year? 1992. While official monuments to the executed witches were dedicated in Salem and Danvers, the Victory Chapel, a fundamentalist church, was protesting the presence at these ceremonies of modern witches. While tourists bought love-spells in the occult shops of Salem, the media reported accusations of Satanic ritual abuse of young children. The witch trials of seventeenth-century Salem horrify and fascinate Americans, but the obsessions and fears that made the trials possible remain in the consciousness of late twentieth-century America.

The year 1692 saw the last great witchcraft outbreak, (though not the last executions for witchcraft), in America, England, or the Continent. Historians since Salem have written libraries on the subject. The injustices of the trials have haunted the judges and their descendants, including Nathaniel Hawthorne, who added the "w" to his name in part because he was conscious of his ancestor Judge Hathorne's guilt. Many of those accused and executed at Salem had not previously been tainted with the crime of witchcraft. Unlike some earlier New England cases, little prior evidence was brought forward to claim preternatural powers for any of the persons executed as witches, except perhaps for Bridget Bishop and Wilmot Reed. Tituba, who was not executed, may have been familiar with the African traditions as brought to the West Indies, though exactly what she did or believed will never be determined. As we have seen, under pressure of interrogation and fear of death, she told the magistrates just what they wanted to hear, validating the learned witchcraft doctrines of pact and conspiracy.

Complicating analysis of the "Salem Hysteria" was the way it quickly spread far beyond the Gothic traditions of witchcraft described above. Every secular quarrel over land, rights, and boundaries, disagreements with ministers, with magistrates, all were tossed into the cauldron. In Andover, testimony reveals years of slights and grudges, yet somehow these resentments had been kept under control prior to 1692, and accusations were made only when the now-famous afflicted girls were brought to town. Perhaps the fear of revenge by an accused but freed witch had kept neighbors from complaining earlier, but in 1692, residents of Salem Village, Beverly, and Andover could see that the courts were arresting and hanging witches, not letting them go free to retaliate upon their accusers.

In Salem Village, the *accusers* who were the focus of bewitchment, including what we might term poltergeist activity, were decidedly in control, more so than in the Goodwin or the Morse cases discussed in the previous chapter. Unlike earlier (and subsequent) cases of possession, the afflicted girls of Salem Village were not all members of one family. Also setting them apart was the fact that their ministers, unlike later writers such as Nevius, seemed never to consider the hypothesis that the girls had been possessed by Satan without the intermediary of a human agency, the witch.[1] That so many victims had been attacked at once could only confirm the learned suspicion that Satan's agent was not one spiteful, familiar witch, but a grand conspiracy of them. Not a lone old woman, but whole congregations of witches, led by powerful men, even ministers.

1. The Disturbances in Salem Village

---

[1]The *Malleus Maleficarum* treats the nice distinctions involved here in Part II, Question 1, Chapter 10 "Of the Method by which Devils through the Operations of Witches sometimes actually possess Men" (128-134). Of the many who have tried to solve this puzzle since Nevius, see Boyer and Nissenbaum, *SWP* 23; McMillen 238.

Chroniclers from Mather and Hale to Arthur Miller to the creators of the "Salem Witch Museum" have speculated upon what may have occurred during the winter of 1691–92 to set in motion the tragedy in Salem Village, but there is no hard evidence. All we know are the results: the daughter and niece of Salem Village's minister, the Reverend Samuel Parris, began to act strangely, throwing peculiar fits and laughing or otherwise behaving inappropriately even during divine service. By the end of February, these two girls, aged nine and eleven, were joined in their fits and torments by other girls—daughters of prosperous farmers and bound servants—who, according to tradition, apparently used to gather at the home of Reverend Parris. Had they been learning voodoo and fortune-telling from Tituba? Had they been dancing naked in the woods? Was this "circle" of adolescent and pre-adolescent girls the only real coven in Salem? We will never know. Eventually there were twelve main accusers, including Tituba's husband John Indian and twenty-year-old Sarah Churchill, but history knows them as "the afflicted girls."

By the end of February, stories of their behavior and torments began to spread. When the local doctor ruled that there could be no natural explanation for their troubles, ministers who were expert in dealing with the Invisible World were consulted. On February 29, after long examination, the girls named Sarah Good, Sarah Osburn, and Tituba, the Parris's West Indian slave, as the witches responsible for their torments. Only a month later, too soon, one would think, for the news to have reached Connecticut, a servant girl in Fairfield also fell into strange fits. She, too, accused neighbor women, including one whom she described as "a black woman with thick lips" (Tomlinson 54). Unlike the girls of Salem Village, however, Fairfield's Kate Branch was not joined in her afflictions by any other victims. Salem Village was different: there, the hysteria was just beginning. The arrests and examination of three accused witches did not quiet the afflicted girls. Instead, their fits worsened, and they made other accusations, this time not against senile, friendless or powerless women, but against covenant members of the church, "gospel women" like Martha Corey and Rebecca Nurse.

Unlike some of the earlier New England witchcraft cases, we have extensive transcripts of the court proceedings at Salem. In some cases, we have three or four versions, taken down by different hands. Arthur Miller has made these trials as familiar to American high-school students as that of Joan of Arc is to students in France. The records of Tituba's examination, for example, reveal her initial bravery, her halting English, and her flair for improvising what the questioners longed to hear, while increasingly deflecting suspicion from herself and onto others. After initially disclaiming any involvement, and, as shown above, blaming direct demonic possession, she admits that the Devil may be hurting the children, but she has no dealings with Him. Finally, after much badgering, she admits to knowledge of the supernatural.

> Q. wth wht shape, or what is he like that hurts ym? A. like a man, I think yesterday, I being in ye Lentoe Chamber I saw a thing like a man that tould me Searve him & I tould him noe I would nott doe Such thing.   (Trask 13)

She eventually assents to everything her questioners suggested, often going them one better; when they asked if she had seen apparitions such as "Catts," she said she had seen phantom dogs—and hogs too. She may have determined the further course of the Salem outbreak when she testified not only to attending witch meetings, but to the identity of their leader, a tall white man with white hair. His black apparel sent the examiners on a quest for a minister, who would be the appropriate leader for this Satanic anti-church. George Burroughs, a former minister of Salem Village, was brought back from Wells, Maine, and accused of presiding over the coven.

Soon the previously obscure Reverend Parris, his family, and his supporters such as the Putnams, who counted two of the afflicted, mother and daughter, were more feared than Spanish Grand Inquisitors. But without the actions and proceedings of the Court of Oyer and Terminer, appointed by Governor Phips and presided over by Justices Corwin, Hathorne, and Gedney, the witch hysteria would have been confined to Salem Village. Instead, it spread throughout Essex County. By the time the trials ended, 19 condemned witches were hanged on Gallows Hill in Salem, in July and September of 1692. No witch was ever burned in America, though this remains a common misconception.

The mysteries of where the actual ladders stood (seventeenth-century culprits were "turned off a ladder," the trap-door gallows not having been invented yet), as well as what happened to the witches' bodies remain unsolved. Tradition says that the Nurse family recovered the body of Rebecca Nurse, though apparently not that of her sister Mary Esty, and buried it on their property, where a monument now stands. When the hysteria abated, the family made their actions public.

Less public were the actions of the Jacobs family, who somehow recovered the corpse of George Jacobs. The location of his burial site on the family homestead remained pretty much a Danvers secret. In 1860, a local historian wrote that the grave had been opened a few years previously, and they found "the bones of an old person with locket enclosing hair" (L. Stone 56). Writing in the *Historical Collections* published by the Essex Institute, Stone asks "Would it not be well for the Institute to erect some tablet to mark the spot?" (L. Stone 57). Nothing was done. It was obviously still too soon to honor a condemned wizard. In the 1950s, the Jacobs's ancestral farm was sold to new owners who planned to sub-divide the land. The bones were excavated, but at that time, (perhaps worrying about the anti-Communist witch-hunts), the family did not wish to risk a public re-burial. Still in secrecy, the bones made their way to the Danvers Historical Society, which hid them in their vault until the summer of 1992, when during the tercentenary of the trials George Jacobs was finally laid to rest in the Nurse family graveyard.[2]

Why such secrecy, why go to such lengths to hide these bodies? Though the medieval Church denied Christian burial to heretics and witches, consigning them, along with suicides to crossroads, the Puritans did not hold the same concept of hallowed ground. The earliest New England cemeteries were not laid out next to the meetinghouses; that would have been too much like Catholic practice. Perhaps the witches' bodies were hidden for a more pagan reason: fear of retribution from beyond the grave. But those who feared the witches' curses would not be protected regardless of where their material bodies ended up. A possibility that has not been considered is that there may have been a fear of necromancy on the part of the survivors, since no one really believed that all the witches had been discovered.

Supporting this theory are the ancient, medieval, and Elizabethan traditions regarding the powers of corpses after death. Necromancy was the crime of the Witch of Endor who raised the spirit of the prophet Samuel at the command of Saul, who had previously made such consultations illegal. Early councils of the

---

[2]This information comes from Richard Trask, who chaired the Salem Village Witchcraft Tercentennial Committee in Danvers; the "official version" can be found in "A Final Resting Place" 6.

Christian church warned "against allowing women to watch in cemeteries for fear of the crimes they might commit there" (Flint, *The Rise of Magic* 215). More than the relics of ordinary corpses, the remains of hanged criminals were especially sought after for all sorts of uses. In 1335, the Inquisition accused a woman in Carcassonne, in southern France, of learning witchcraft from Satan. Among the arts he taught her was that of poison ointments, "whose ingredients she obtained by ...going to gallows to obtain clothing, hair, nails, and fat from the bodies of hanged criminals" (Russell 183). Such accusations surface in witchcraft trials in Scotland and England in the sixteenth century as well. Kittredge publishes an English statute of 1604, explicitly invoking the death penalty against those who "'take up any dead man, woman, or child out of his, her, or theire grave, or any other place where the dead bodie resteth, or the skin, bone, or any other parte of any dead person, to be imployed or used in any manner of Witchcrafte, Sorcerie, Charme, or Inchantment'" (312). In the seventeenth century, people who stole pieces of the dead, preferably those who had been hanged or murdered, might not always be professional witches. Kittredge lists folkloric remedies that require ordinary folk to procure such unhallowed parts for themselves. Even the gallows itself was useful, as chips from it could cure toothache and the ague; the hangman's rope could cure the headache or bring luck in gambling (Kittredge 141–143). Little is said in the original Salem sources about the witches' bodies. Calef does note that the hastily-dug graves of Burroughs, Willard, and Carrier, who were hanged at the same time as Jacobs, were only about two feet deep, so that Burroughs' hands and his chin protruded. While this would have made it easier for the Jacobs' family to recover his body, it would also have facilitated the necromantic activities of those who followed the English folk traditions described above.

In the early summer of 1692, the scope of the witch hysteria widened beyond Salem Town and Village. Several of the afflicted girls were taken to Andover at the request of Joseph Ballard, whose wife was deathly ill: he feared she had been bewitched. A nineteenth-century local historian, Sarah Loring Bailey, notes that in Andover the accusations began with the friendless or the eccentric, but eventually, as in Salem Village, the process reached into all households, even the highest and most respectable. By this time, those accused of witchcraft in Andover had learned that the court was, at least temporarily, sparing the lives of those who confessed to practicing witchcraft—not exonerating them, but presumably reserving them to discover more witches in future rounds of questioning. If confession would save their lives, confessions there were in Andover in quantity and quality. As it turned out, in one of the great ironies of the events, the trials ended before the "confessors" could be brought back; therefore, only those who either never confessed or who bravely recanted forced confessions were executed in 1692. The Rev. Hale marvels at the amazing unity of detail in the stories told by the confessing witches in Andover, "their exact agreement with the accusations of the afflicted; their punctual agreement with their fellow confessors" (45). This phenomenon is not at all amazing. Confessions were often public, and the accused swiftly learned that the only way to save their necks was to tell their ministers the story religious leaders wanted to hear.

In Andover, the examiners found detailed evidence for the conspiracy they had feared and suspected so long. The surviving transcripts are not presented in question and answer form, nor are they as detailed as those in Salem Village. Still, it seems clear that the examiners went beyond leading the witnesses to the point of dictating their confessions in the manner familiar to us from hostage-taking and prisoner-of-war show trials. Bailey is one the very few to notice that the witchcraft examiners "in their zeal *almost* [my emphasis] put words into the mouths of reluctant confessors and faltering witnesses, and they placed implicit faith in every statement corroborative of their preconceived opinion" (195). Enders Robinson, a descendant of one of those executed, in his *Salem Witchcraft and Hawthorne's House of the Seven Gables* blames the extent of the Andover accusations on their new minister, Thomas Barnard, a friend and classmate of Cotton Mather, who shared the latter's views on conspiracy and witchcraft (79).

A local justice of the peace, Dudley Bradstreet, son of the poet Ann Bradstreet, at first went along with the procedures, but eventually he rebelled. "Dudley Bradstreet, Esq., having granted thirty or forty warrants for commitments, at length refused to grant any more." He and his wife were immediately accused; he was said to have killed nine persons by witchcraft. (A. Abbot 154; Robinson 160). Bradstreet went into hiding until it was safe to come out, at which time his and his wife's names begin appearing on petitions for the release of prisoners. Bradstreet provides indirect evidence for the way in which the learned magistrates conducted their examinations—that is, asking questions from scholarly sources about witchcraft and diabolism, and rejecting answers that did not fit the vision expounded in those sources. In a letter to magistrates Corwin, Hathorne, and Gedney, Bradstreet apologizes that his actions against the witches might not be following in the right tradition:

> I am wholly unacquainted with affairs of this nature neither have the benefit of books for forms &c., but being unadvisedly entered upon service I am wholly unfit for beg that my ignorance and failings may be as much covered as conveniently may be. (Mass. Hist. Soc. Coll; repr. in Bailey 224).

What were these "books for forms?" Perhaps Perkins, the *Malleus Maleficarum*, Glanville, or perhaps some other Inquisitor's manual yet to be found. In the European witch trials, inquisitors asked leading questions from a prepared list, so it was not surprising that the accused witches gave answers that corroborated pre-existing definitions of conspiracy, pact, and diabolism.[3] Comparing the transcripts of the Andover confessions, it seems likely that the same thing happened there.

Of the scores of accused who were imprisoned from Andover, only Martha Carrier, Samuel Wardwell, and Mary Parker were hanged. Ann Foster, an old woman whose daughter and granddaughter were also accused, died in prison. Carrier, celebrated as the "Queen of Hell" by Cotton Mather, based on the confessions of other Andover residents, never confessed. Bailey relays the local stories of her husband, of Welsh birth, who despite having his wife hanged and his family under suspicions, lived to be 109 and walked six miles a few days before his death. It seems strange that *he* was not suspected of having preternatural connections!

Though more people were accused of and confessed to witchcraft in Andover than in any other town, the Andover witchcraft remains largely an untold story (Hansen, "Andover"; Dailey). Writing in 1880, Bailey says that ever since the events of 1692–3, Andover "has been remarkably free from delusions and slow to be carried away by excitements" (237), whether because of the influence of the enlightened yet stern Andover Theological Seminary or because the author is unwilling to repeat folklore. The same trope comes up in Beverly, another Essex

---

[3]The *Malleus* gives numerous samples of proper forms for interrogation of witnesses and the accused. Nearly every one of the suggested questions would today be disallowed as "leading questions." (Part III, Questions 6 and 7; 210-214). See also Kieckhefer 28; 90ff.

County town drawn into the hysteria. Another local historian, Edwin Stone, says that in 1843, search as he would, he could find no supernatural legends in Beverly, no "gloomy caverns nor murderous-looking glens," no ghosts, witches, or even fortune-tellers (306). While Beverly has begun to honor John Hale's role in the events of 1692, Andover took little part in the tercentenary commemorations, and makes no attempt to exploit the witch trials in order to attract tourists.

On September 19, 1692, the last and most famous of the executions took place at Salem. Giles Corey, an iron man more than eighty years old, pleaded too strongly and with too arrogant a tongue for his wife Martha's life. He was himself brought to trial for being a wizard, but he stood mute three times, and would not plead "guilty" or "not guilty." By old English custom, the court was entitled to torture a plea from him, by first starving him and then "pressing"—piling heavy weights—on him. According to the best-known version of the legend, Corey was taken to an open field in Salem, stripped and pressed. Still he shouted "more weight!" No other plea was heard from him until he died, buried under the rocks. This story has been celebrated by writers ever since. Its accuracy is denied by some scholars, and during the summer celebrations of 1992, guides at the Essex Institute were at some pains to call it groundless folklore, unattested in the records. Samuel Adams Drake, writing at the end of the nineteenth century, says that the ghost of Wizard Corey was wont to appear in Salem, "the precursor of some calamity that was impending over the community," but, Drake adds, the ghost had long since ceased to appear, regardless of calamities (*New England Legends* 196). Robert Ellis Cahill, a retired Sheriff of Essex County, claims that Corey's ghost continued to appear long after Drake's time, that indeed his own father was frightened by the spectre. He also avers that Corey cursed George Corwin, the Sheriff who pressed him to death. Cahill alleges that "all the High Sheriffs of Essex County since Corwin, headquartered at the Salem Jail located in the field where Giles Corey was crushed to death, died in office from heart attack or were forced to retire because of heart conditions or blood ailments" (*Haunted Happenings* 20).[4] This curse has its literary counterpart in Wizard Maule's curse on the Pyncheon family in *The House of the Seven Gables*.

---

[4]Cahill has published innumerable pamphlets which transmit and keep alive the lore of hauntings and exorcisms and their effects upon local history.

Soon after the final round of executions in September of 1692, the fever began to die down. Reverend Hale of Beverly, at first a supporter of the trials, saw his own wife accused of witchcraft. This incited him to open others' eyes to the misdeeds of the "afflicted children." Accusations had been moving steadily higher in the social scale, until they reached the son of John Alden, the hero of the Plymouth Colony, and then the wife of Governor Phips. Suddenly, officials began to question the shaky basis of spectral evidence as sole proof of witchcraft. Other ministers joined Hale in calling for a re-evaluation. This pattern of accusations is typical of what Midelfort calls large-scale panics such as those he studied in Southwest Germany during the seventeenth century, when accusations would similarly move from friendless old women to the magistrates themselves, at which point the German trials would end.

When the trials in Essex County resumed in January, 1693, judges were as quick to exonerate as the earlier court had been to condemn. By spring there was a general "jail delivery," too late for some who had died of the cold and hunger over the winter, but the hysteria was over. The girls fade from history, which records a few ballads and legends of the condemned witches but few tales about their accusers. Only one, the younger Ann Putnam, was so haunted by guilt that she made a public act of repentance in order to be received as a covenanted church member in 1706. The Reverend Samuel Parris, after lawsuits, and charges of misconduct, was removed by his church in Salem Village. The congregation's successful petition of 1697 went so far as to accuse him of consorting with witches: "That Mr. Parris's going to Mary Walcott or Abigail Williams and directing others to them to know who afflicted the people in their illnesses;—we understand this to be a dealing with them that have a familiar spirit" (qtd. in McMillen 541).

In the rest of Essex County, even less was done to mark the passing of the witchcraft outbreak. We have little or no information on the years following 1692, as New England recovered from an excess of the Gothic. Few writers of history or fiction have asked the questions that the Andover Historical Society posed in 1992: "how did the townspeople feel about this tragedy that had robbed them of their loved ones, their livelihood and their well-being? How did they feel about their neighbors who had played major roles in the frenzy?" ("How Did Andover" 1).

There are no answers. After searching town archives, the Historical Society could respond to their questions only by saying "If private or public confrontations occurred they were never recorded. The subject of witchcraft, evidently too painful or shameful, was not acknowledged in town or church records" ("How Did Andover" 2). Though anthropological theory holds that witchcraft persecution can serve a helpful function in society, a kind of catharsis, such is hardly the case in New England. As Demos notes, the Salem outbreak was a divisive trauma (300–1). Any possible societal benefits from these trials, or from earlier ones, are extremely difficult to discern.

2. Explaining the Salem Witchcraft Outbreak

Ever since Cotton Mather conceded in the usually self-exculpating *Wonders of the Invisible World* (1693) that even *he* was unable to decide whether the judges at Salem had acted aright, historians have been attempting to account for the witchcraft outbreak. Many theories have been advanced to solve this conundrum in American Studies. Three hundred years have only fulfilled Mather's prediction that human minds cannot wholly fathom the deeds of darkness. While we may not agree that "the Devil improves the Darkness of this Affair," sorting out what happened and why it happened can seem like a "Blind mans Buffet," with historians and sociologists of all persuasions "mauling one another in the dark" (400).

Some explanations are flawed precisely because they look at the Salem outbreak as an isolated phenomenon, unrelated to witch trials in Connecticut and, more especially, to earlier witch persecutions in England and on the Continent. Some theories can be characterized by the desire of rationalist scholars to discover a single natural cause for events that all the participants believed to be supernatural. Kittredge had to insist in 1929 that the Salem outbreak must be studied in the context of the universality of the witch belief, particularly the long English tradition in folklore and common law (372–3). Judging by the widespread credence given to the ergot theory and other single effect hypotheses in our time, Kittredge's warning deserves to be reiterated.

The ergot theory, propounded by Linda Caporael in *Science* (April, 1976), claiming that hallucinations and seizures caused by this rye fungus account for the behavior of the afflicted girls at Salem, was discredited in the same journal by Spanos and Gottlieb (December, 1976), but has continued to live in the popular imagination. It is still propounded on television programs and by guides in Salem. Contemporary sources do condemn the baking of a "witch cake" in Rev. Parris's house, made of rye meal and the urine of the possessed children, as a form of diabolical counter-magic, as discussed above in Chapter Three. Even if the rye meal had somehow been tainted by the fungus, Calef makes it clear that the cake was concocted *after* the girls had begun to throw their strange fits, and furthermore, the cake was fed not to the girls but to the dog (224–225). Also, if ergot had contaminated any part of the village's rye crop, why were the hallucinatory effects confined to a few members of certain households?

For many years, most historians of the Salem outbreak tended to blame the girls, Cotton Mather, or both, while noting that such a thing could never recur in their own more enlightened times. During the heyday of spiritualism, Salem's afflicted girls were compared to the Fox sisters and other young mediums. With the advent of Freudian psychology, they were labelled repressed hysterics. Only when World War II had revealed the horrors that could be perpetrated by enlightened nations did more balanced treatments of the Salem witchcraft begin to emerge. Marion Starkey's *The Devil in Massachusetts* (1949) remains a model for readable history based on careful research. Soon after its publication, the McCarthy investigations of American Communists began, giving new immediacy to the term "witch-hunt." In this climate, Arthur Miller produced his drama *The Crucible*. Miller downplays the devices of Gothic horror, while favoring "social/historical" explanations for the events, which has resulted in his drama being taught as history in American schools. It is obvious from the beginning of the play that the girls, led by Abigail Williams (whose age he raises to sixteen, and whose character he conflates with Mary Warren's), were deliberately faking their fits. In his notes for *The Crucible* (1953), Miller draws parallels with the McCarthy hearings. In 1692, in the 1950s, and perhaps again during the 1980s, these words seem to hold true:

> The witch-hunt was a perverse manifestation of the panic which set in among all classes when the balance began to turn toward greater individual freedom...It is still impossible for man to organize his social life without repressions, and the balance has yet to be struck between order and freedom. (229)

From Puritan New England to the Iraq of Saddam Hussein and the America of George Bush, a similar progression holds true: "a political policy is equated with moral right, and opposition to it with diabolical malevolence ...society becomes a congerie of plots and counterplots, and the main role of government changes from that of the arbiter to that of the scourge of God" (A. Miller 249).

The rise of the discipline of social history has resulted in renewed interest in the witchcraft persecutions of early modern Europe and North America. In *Salem Possessed*, Paul Boyer and Stephen Nissenbaum demonstrated the extent of the factional feuding that divided Salem Village, as well as the larger divisions between Salem Village and Town. Their work is a model of its type; it is very convincing, except that at times it approaches a kind of euhemerization of the supernatural events, making them subordinate to more earthly motivations—the very opposite of Cotton Mather's view.[5]

Mather's defender, Chadwick Hansen, in *Witchcraft at Salem* (1969) attempted to restore the primacy of the Invisible World. He was the first—and others have followed—to emphasize that some real practitioners of healing and malefic arts were caught in the wide net cast by the afflicted girls. John Demos's formidable scholarship in *Entertaining Satan* goes beyond any of these theorists, since he covers all of the New England accusations for witchcraft, instead of focusing on Salem. Far from seeking a single cause, he instead applies the perspectives of many different social sciences—biography, psychology, sociology, anthropology—to the history of the period, making a solid case for each explanation.

Perhaps the girls *were* attacking others to avoid being named as witches themselves. As targets of demonic possession, they were in an ambiguous position. They might attract the attention of the great divines, but they might equally be called sinners and excommunicated. Pretending to be possessed was not the safest way to win attention, unless they could deflect the blame onto others. The surest way after all, then as now, to avoid suspicion is to accuse another of the same crime! Some of the accusers were at times suspected of being witches—especially Mary Warren, who attempted to recant, claiming that it had all been a

---

[5]Local historians and descendants of hanged witches, Robinson and McMillen applied Boyer and Nissenbaum's methods of social history to their own analyses of the Andover accusations and the Towne family connections, respectively.

fraud.[6]   As Boyer and Nissenbaum have confirmed, the accusers Ann Putnam Junior and Senior had the most to gain from implicating certain families in Salem Village, particularly the Nurses and their connections. But nothing accounts for their later accusations, first of strangers in Andover, and then of highly-placed people throughout Massachusetts Bay.

Whatever motivated the accusers, the official reaction to their accusations was inevitable, given Puritan fears of conspiracy and their dread of the Fall. Every time a witch, invariably pictured as female in the original woodcuts, signed the Devil's book, she was recapitulating the Fall of Mankind. The prints are designed to mirror the primal scene in Eden—the Devil, sometimes in the guise of a serpent, in the act of holding out temptation, the woman in the act of accepting it. According to the *Malleus Maleficarum*, the existence of witchcraft illustrates the two Divine Permissions: God permitted witches to afflict the innocent just as He had permitted Lucifer and then Adam and Eve to Fall (Part I, Question 13, p. 71). It is hardly necessary to elaborate on the inordinate number of women who were victims of witchcraft accusations, in the New World as in the Old.[7]

Cotton Mather's role in the Salem outbreak remains ambiguous. In popular literature, he is often pictured as urging on the accusers, or leading the tribunal. While neither of these is true, he did applaud their actions. Unlike many others in Massachusetts Bay, he never changed his stand on the trials or recanted his judgments. Certainly his theories of Satanic conspiracy were known and followed by those who questioned the witches. Yet he was divided in his heart and mind as to whether wholesale executions were necessary—at least until the Andover confessions, which convinced him of the extent of the Devil's penetration of New England. Writing to a parishioner, John Richards, on May 31, 1692, he urges that all measures be taken to seek out witches, from severe questioning to elicit

---

[6] See *The Crucible* for Miller's reconstruction of Warren's recantation; see also McMillen 334-5; Weisman 144.

[7] The *Malleus Maleficarum* devotes much space to proving the particular susceptibility of women to witchcraft because of the nature of Eve. Only recently, however, have feminist scholars begun to analyze the persecution of witches as an assault against women who were in some way threatening to the male Establishment, whether as midwives, property owners, inheritors of wealth, or simply self-supporting members of the community. See the excellent work of Carol Karlsen in *The Devil in the Shape of a Woman: Witchcraft in Colonial New England* and the earlier, less exhaustively researched, *Riding the Nightmare* by Williams and Adelman. See also Demos for feminist, Freudian, and Jungian perspectives on the New England witch-hunts.

confessions, to searches for witchmarks, even the water ordeal once condemned by his father, Increase. All this having been done, he closes his letter by wondering whether these "wretched creatures" had to be executed: "What if some of the lesser criminals be only scourged with lesser punishments, and also put upon some solemn, open, public, and explicit renunciation of the devil? I am apt to think that the devils would then cease afflicting the neighborhood..." (*Selected Letters* 40). The Rev. John Hale, whose *Modest Enquiry into the Nature of Witchcraft* upholds the learned view of witchcraft as pact and diabolic conspiracy, nevertheless came to question the application of those views during the Salem outbreak. In the final chapter of his 1697 work, he wonders whether all the proceedings against witches in the colonies, and particularly those of 1692, might not have been based "upon insufficient presumptions" and slender evidence, resulting "in the apprehending too many we may believe were innocent, and executing of some" (130–1).

Yet in the end, for Mather and for many other Puritans, the corruption of Salem could only be purged in blood. For the divines, the timing of the witchcraft outbreak in 1692 was no coincidence. All the signs and wonders in the divine and the human worlds pointed to a backsliding among New Englanders. Having abandoned the holy mission that drove them to Massachusetts Bay, they were like the Jews in the Old Testament, no longer a kingdom of priests and a holy people.[8] And like the Jews, who after being saved from Egypt went whoring after false gods, the Puritans were ripe for punishment. Instead of forty years in the desert or a Babylonian exile, the agents were to be the Indians and the Devil—the usual combination. Victory in King Philip's War did not end fears of Indian aggression: Andover and nearby Billerica had been attacked, and in 1691–92 Indians destroyed settlements in Maine. Fears of Indian attacks must have been very much on the minds of those in Salem Village and Andover. According to Andover historian Abiel Abbot, from that town alone "In August 1689, John Peters and Andrew Peters were killed by the Indians; and in the same year, Lt. John Stevens, Benjamin Lovejoy, Eleazar Streaton and Robert Russell died in the war at the eastward" [in Maine] (43).[9]

---

[8]See Kittredge 371-2.

[9]Demos compares witch-hunts with other disturbing historical events and discovers many significant correlations, in Chapter Twelve, "Communities: Witchcraft over Time."

120

Small wonder that one of the Andover witches confessed that the Devil had promised to keep her safe from Indians! The climate of the times was unsettled. Perhaps it was the "end time"? Not merely the end of a century, but the advent of the Second Coming?[10] Mather hints as much in a letter written at the height of the epidemic, saying that just as at Christ's first appearance Israel was plagued with devils, so it would be "just before our Lord's coming again" (To John Richards, 31 May 1692; *Selected Letters* 37). Elie Wiesel made some of these same connections in his keynote address at the dedication of the Salem Witch Trials Tercentenary Memorial. He linked the Salem occurrences with a kind of end-of-the century madness, and compared it to the amazing changes we are experiencing as we near the end of our millennium and century. He said that "when a century nears its decline, its end, history itself is shaking up...history hurries to its end, as if in a hurry to get rid of the phantasms; and so for a few months ...everything was possible in Salem." He did not add, though he might have, that the horrifying results of this orgy of possibilities made possible a swifter overturning of the old beliefs, so that the tide of skepticism about witchcraft could sweep in, and witch beliefs could be relegated to unlearned folk.

Early in 1692, however, Mather could see to the full the contentiousness and slipping away from the Church manifested in the quarrels of Salem Village documented by Boyer and Nissenbaum. It would certainly seem that human quarreling was giving the Devil easier entree into the world. In *Wonders of the Invisible World*, Mather advances this theory: "...the *wrath* which we have had against one another, has had more than a little Influence upon the coming down of the Devil in that *wrath* which now amazes us. Have not many of us been Devils one unto another for Slanderings, for Back-bitings, for Animosities?" (406). This connection of Satan with disharmony in the human community is a feature of the European witch trials as well. In the 1504 trials in the northern Italian Val di Fiemi, accused witches told the magistrates that Satan favored those of his disciples who fomented quarrels among the villagers: he particularly appreciated it when these quarrels broke out in church (Eisenach).

In Europe and America, scholars have found that witchcraft accusations and persecutions have tended to increase during unsettled times. The year 1692

[10]See Weisman 129-131.

admirably fulfills that function in the New England colonies. While England celebrated a "Glorious Revolution," the colonies' fate remained unclear. For the Puritan utopia, losing the original charter was an emblem of the Fall. Massachusetts would cease to be a special theocracy, a City on A Hill, and become an ordinary colony, or worse, a royal colony under the direct control of a non-Puritan king. Connecticut, too, was undergoing anxieties about its charter, which Sir Edmund Andros had revoked in the name of James II. Connecticut's citizens refused to surrender their charter, hiding it in the famous Charter Oak. The event, enshrined in state history, has its legendary aspects: the tree was located near the mansion of the Wyllys family, ardent opponents of witchcraft and preservers of the records of the Connecticut witch trials. In addition, the date ascribed to hiding the Charter is Halloween, October 31, 1687. Accusations of witchcraft, quiescent in Connecticut for two decades, increased in the years immediately following the Charter controversy.

3. Since Salem: History, Folklore, Fiction

Though after Salem no witches were executed in New England, belief in their powers did not die an immediate death. There were accusations and trials after 1692, learned occultists studied ancient sciences, and folk beliefs in witchcraft have continued, in one form or another, to the present day.

Cotton Mather believed that he was a particular target of the remaining witches of Massachusetts Bay because of his unceasing opposition to their activities. Immediately after the Salem trials, he was called upon to exorcize another young woman, more afflicted even than Martha Goodwin. Mather recorded Mercy Short's history in "A Brand Pluck'd Out of the Burning," which he circulated among his friends, not for publication. It was edited and published for the first time by Burr in 1914. Mercy Short's life was a mirror of the Gothic in New England, since she was an Indian captive, ran afoul of the condemned Salem witch Sarah Good, became possessed by the Devil, and was exorcized by Cotton Mather—all before her eighteenth birthday! Mather did not call upon her to accuse others of witchcraft; instead, he allowed pious folk to sing psalms in her Haunted Chamber, which vexed the evil spirits possessing her (Burr 276). Mercy confirmed Mather's conspiracy theories, reporting what Spectres told her about witch-meetings, where they saw some of the Salem crew, as well as "French Canadiens and Indian Sagamores" (282). The manuscript ends with Mather's partial success in driving out her devils, but his diary records dire prophecies regarding Satan's further plans.

Mercy's prediction that the Devil would revenge on the Mathers the defeat of his troops seemed to come true when Cotton's wife Abigail in March, 1693, bore a son with closed intestines that prevented him from defecating. This dreadful punishment, Mather noted in his diary, resulted from Abigail seeing, a short while before giving birth, "an horrible Spectre, in our Porch, which Fright caused her Bowels to turn within her" (qtd. in Silverman 123).

Nor did the attacks of Satan end here; in September, 1693, "many months after the general storm of the late enchantments was over" (Mather in Calef, *More Wonders* 28) another energumen, Margaret Rule, required Mather's exorcism. The account of her "sufferings" was also circulated in manuscript, and first published by Robert Calef in 1700 in order to attack Cotton Mather, whom he accused of laying on hands too enthusiastically, including rubbing the young woman's bare stomach and breasts. Mather's response to this accusation was that he had rubbed them *over* the bed-clothes. Still, Mather seems to have profited from the events in Salem, for in Rule's case, as in Mercy Short's, even though all the signs of malefic witchcraft and possession were present—levitation, fits, the Devil's book—he did not urge Rule to name her tormentor. Indeed, Mather says that the neighbors were suspicious of a local cunning woman, "who had frequently cured very painful hurts, by muttering over them certain charms," (Mather in Calef, *More Wonders* 30), and who had allegedly threatened Margaret Rule. Despite the presence of such a likely culprit, Mather prescribes prayer and supplication to God, which win out in the end. This case, unlike those of the Goodwins and the Morses, did not end in accusations of witchcraft and executions. Mather seems proud of his victories over Satan in the exorcisms of Mercy Short and Margaret Rule. He concludes his account with the following scorecard, showing that as a result of his exertions: "the devil got just nothing—but God got praises, Christ got subjects, the Holy Spirit got temples, the church got addition, and the souls of men got everlasting benefits" (50).

Witch trials continued in Connecticut after Salem, though there were no further executions. According to the New Haven County Court Records, in Nov.

1692, after the suspension of the trials in Salem, Winfred Benham of Wallingford, Connecticut was charged with witchcraft. Once again, according to New Haven Court Records, "her general answer was that she knew nothing of the matters testified, and was not concerned therein." With the fever having abated in Salem, the Connecticut case is also dismissed:

> The court ...not finding sufficient grounds of conviction for further prosecution ...do therefore at this time dismiss the business...told her if further grounds of suspicion of witchcraft, or fuller evidences shoud appear against her by reason of mischief done to the bodies or estate of any by any preternatural acts proved against her she might justly fear and expect to be brought to her trial for it. (1: 202 in Jacobs)

She was accused and brought to trial, for the second time, along with her daughter of the same name, five years later. Calef recounts the case (spelling her name Benom) in *More Wonders of the Invisible World*. According to New Haven County Court Records,

> A Special County Court ...held at New haven the 31st of August 1697
> Complaint being made...that Sarah Clark,....Elizabeth Lathrop, and Joh Moss ...were frequently and sorely afflicted in their bodies by the said Benhams, mother and daughter, or their apparitions...(1: 252 in Jacobs)

Although by this time Massachusetts justices had denied credence to spectral evidence, the Connecticut court still found this type of evidence sufficient to bind the accused over to a Court of Assistants in October. There are no further court records of a decision in this case. Calef says that they fled to "New-York government" (336; Tomlinson 65). The Benham case seems to be the last capital trial for witchcraft in New England.

By 1785, at least among lawyers in Connecticut, belief in witchcraft could be considered among the proofs of insanity. In a trial in Litchfield in that year, Thomas Goss was accused of murdering his wife, a charge he did not deny, claiming that she had proven to be a witch. His defense attorney argued that such an attitude proved his client was not guilty by reason of insanity, but Goss declared in court that his attorney had no right to make such an argument, that "his heavenly

Father had forbidden all such proceedings." The court found him guilty of murder: Goss went to the gallows declaring he had only followed the dictates of the Bible in killing his witch-wife (repr. in J. Barber 459).

In the eighteenth century, witchcraft appears in trial records most often in the form of suits for slander or damages by those accused of being witches. Such counter-suits were not unknown in the seventeenth century, but too often those trial records show that complaints of slander were taken as evidence of witchcraft, and the complainant could be condemned. In the later cases, the verdicts were more equivocal. A case in Colchester, Connecticut in 1724 ended with the accused witch receiving only a shilling for her trouble, while her accusers were assured by the court that they were not crazy for fearing her powers (Leventhal 86). By the end of the eighteenth century, the gulf between popular and learned views of witchcraft had opened so wide that people ceased to turn to the courts for relief from witchcraft in any form.

Folktales concerning the Salem witches and many others circulated in oral and written tradition in New England. Whittier reports a number of stories in his *Supernaturalism of New England*, claiming that in his day (the 1820s and 1830s), "the evil brood is not entirely extirpated." The tales he relates include both fortune-telling wise women and even the malefic witch, accused of killing children.

One of the most ancient witch beliefs, that witches rode their victims until they dropped from exhaustion—an explanation of the nightmare or night-hag—lingered long in folk tradition.[11] The tale is told of Betty Booker of Kittery, Maine, who rode Skipper Perkins down to York using a witch bridle, as well as some witches of the Old Colony of Plymouth, who transformed a boy into a pony with a similar witch bridle (Botkin 225–227). In a story fraught with racial significance, one Mohegan Indian witch was accused of night-riding her black hired man, "bridled and saddled like a saddle horse. That was how they found out that she was a witch" (Simmons, *Spirit* 99).[12] The witch-bridle tale is also told of a nineteenth-century witch, Rebecca Sims of Westerly, Rhode Island (Bourgaize 42).

---

[11]Demos tells of such an "enchanted bridle" in the accusations against Rachel Fuller of New Hampshire in 1680 (331).

[12]See Kittredge 220–222 for the ancient origins of these beliefs in "hag-riding."

New Englanders continued to believe in and invoke counter-magic against witches long after they ceased to bring suit in court. An ancient method for killing supernatural animals, whether werewolves or other witches' familiars, was the silver bullet. Meg Wesson, the Gloucester witch whose legendary powers haunted Cape Ann, was supposed to have been killed in this manner at the siege of Louisburg in 1745. Several Gloucester natives were pestered there by an uncanny crow. Believing it to be Old Meg in animal form, they loaded their guns with silver buttons from their tunics and shot the crow, breaking its leg with the first button and killing it with the second. Meanwhile, back in Gloucester, Meg Wesson fell down with a broken leg and died, with silver buttons in her wounds.[13] A similar remedy prevailed against Westerly, Rhode Island's witch Granny Mott, supposed to have lived around 1740. She had transformed herself into the leader of a flock of heath hens to attack some children who had attempted to use counter-magic against her. Their father loaded his rifle with a silver coin and shot the hen; instantly, Granny Mott was found dead with a silver coin in her forehead (Bolté 21–2; Simmons 98; Bourgaize 41–2). Another unnamed Rhode Island witch in Exeter was destroyed by a silver bullet while in cat-shape (Bourgaize 41). The Mohegan Indians tell about one of their witches taking the form of a goose in order to bewitch cattle; while in this shape, she was wounded with a silver bullet which shattered her human arm (Simmons 98–9).

The witch beliefs that so surprised the Vermont author of *Locke Amsden* in 1847 were current in Grafton County, New Hampshire throughout the nineteenth century, according to folklore collector John McNab Currier. He relates tales of witch-riding, counter-magic for the detection of witches, and even witch-meetings, with astral bodies of witches flying overhead to engage in youthful frolics that belied their cronish appearance in everyday life ("Contributions to the Folk-Lore" 292–3; "Contributions to New England" 254–6). Folklorist Richard Dorson collected living witch beliefs on Beal Island, Maine in the 1950s. These tales of Mother Hicks sound all the traditional notes—bewitched cattle, curses, counter-

---

[13] This is an unusually common witch legend, with much circumstantial detail. For some print versions, see Garrett 198–99; Bolté 17; Drake, *New England Legends* 259–60; Leventhal 101.

magic. The islanders would evoke her spirit when they met for spiritualist table-tipping evenings (*Buying the Wind* 55–63).[14]

By the nineteenth century, proving descent from a Salem witch victim had become the genealogical pastime it remains today. A few legends persisted in claiming that there was something strange about these families, especially the descendants of the Towne sisters Rebecca Nurse, Mary Esty, and Sarah Cloyse (who survived the outbreak, though condemned). The most accurate film version of the events of 1692, *Three Sovereigns for Sarah*, focuses on the attempts of Sarah Cloyse to clear the names of her martyred sisters. Mary Esty, one of the last witches to be hanged, has been the subject of numerous legends, most likely because her ghost figured in a strange footnote to the Salem outbreak. The Rev. Joseph Gerrish of Wenham took down the account of Mary Herrick, a 17-year-old member of his congregation, of her visitation by the "Ghost of Goody Easty," who brought with her the "shape of Mrs. Hayle" to afflict poor Mary. This accusation against his wife probably led to Rev. Hale's change of heart described above, and thus to the end of the witch-hunt. (Burr 369, 369n; McMillen 492–3). If this chain of events, set out by Calef in *More Wonders of the Invisible World*, was really accurate, it may be one of the few attested cases of a ghost achieving the vengeance and vindication for which reasons legend has them return from the grave.

Lovecraft wrote to Clark Ashton Smith (22 March, 1929) that he had heard from a descendant of Mary Esty:

> She hints at strange gifts & traditions handed down in her family, & asks me if I have access to any antient secret witch-lore of New England. Also, she wants to know if Dunwich & Arkham are real places! I shall answer the letter, & see if I can get the good old soul to relate some of the whispered witch-traditions! A story of Salem horror based on actual "inside dope" from a witch-blooded crone would surely be a striking novelty! (*SL* 2: 327)

By 1934, he is writing to Robert H. Barlow that the old lady died a year ago, and he does not reveal whether he ever received any secret knowledge from her (19 March 1934; *SL* 4: 392). Another descendant of Mary Esty, Persis McMillen, claimed in the prologue to her book on the witchcraft, *Currents of Malice*, that she

---

[14]Lengthy taped interviews with Dorson's informants and other residents of Beal Island and Jonesport, preserved in the Northeast Archives, confirm the accuracy of Dorson's accounts.

knew nothing about her ancestress until she had named her daughter Molly Esty
after her mother. An aunt informed her that her mother had been named for the
Salem witch (ix).[15]

Local histories and collections of New England folklore make it clear that
every village and town has its witch legends.[16] As these tales and those excerpted
above show, witches gradually lost their power to freeze the blood as their human
opponents' powers grew. As Demos notes, "the figure of the witch was effectively
scaled down, so as to shrink the elements of death-dealing power, and to emphasize
those of sheer eccentricity" (389–90). In one typical account, the Old
Saybrook/Killingworth region of Connecticut was home to Goody Wee and her
daughter Betty, famed as witches in the eighteenth century and reputed still to haunt
the valley where they once lived. These two and other witches would meet in a
cave guarded by a witch tree, sometimes called the "Cedar Sentinel." Stage coaches
on the Post Road tried to avoid the area at night, when witches in a nest high up in
the cedar were alleged to throw down burning brands onto the coach roofs. This
lore was still in active circulation in 1928, when the "Cedar Sentinel" was set afire
by school children and destroyed (White 1: 37; Holman 456-7). Folktales about
these witches remained in the oral tradition in the late 1970s, when they were
collected by one of my students.

Before and after the advent of spiritualism in the 1850s, fortune-tellers were
active in New England who in earlier times would probably have been denounced
as witches. On Block Island lived Dutch Kattern, who claimed to be a survivor of
the destruction of the *Palatine*, the emigrant ship set afire by wreckers that became
New England's most renowned phantom ship (Bourgaize 50). "Shepherd Tom"
Hazard recounts in his *Jonny-Cake Papers* a visit with two friends to the "old black
sibyl" Silvy Tory of Kingston, Rhode Island. She refuses to prognosticate for one
of the boys, saying "that young fellow has no fortune to tell," finally warning him
"Don't you by no means go east!" "Shepherd Tom" adds that her prophesies came
true when the boy died two weeks later in New Bedford, which lies well east of the
sibyl's home in South County (247-8).

---

[15]She knows nothing, however, about any of the "family secrets" described above by
Lovecraft (McMillen letter).

[16]Leventhal 95-107 recounts a number of other eighteenth-century witch tales from New
England town histories and family manuscripts. Demos (388-391) does the same.

While fear of malefic witchcraft lessened in New England as the years went on, becoming confined to rural backwaters, some functions of the professional witch were transferred to the medium, and eventually to the psychic, where they are revered today. Belief in the efficacy of astrology continued, as it continues today. Farmers guided their planting by the "natural astrology" of almanacs, while merchants consulted astrologers, sometimes referred to as "conjurers," to determine propitious sailing times. Leventhal documents the especial prevalence of these customs in Rhode Island (58–59); Bourgaize notes that Rhode Islanders engaged in the slave trade were particularly dependent on such otherworldly guidance (52). Some of the functions performed by astrologers, conjurers, white witches, and mediums included fortune-telling, locating hidden treasure, and solving crimes through consultation with the dead. Whittier celebrated the "Pythoness of Lynn, Massachusetts"—Moll Pitcher. This fortune-teller, who died in 1813, was never proven to be a fraud, perhaps because she refused to guide treasure-seekers. Prophecy ran in her family. Her grandfather, John Dimond, was reputed to be a weather-wizard. Standing on the highest point in Lynn, the old burying-ground, he could guide ships into port—or dash them on the rocks (Drake, *New England Legends* 144; Garrett 99–100). His ghost is still reported to be haunting that hill.

While Drake, Garrett and others created literary folktales from the witch tradition, and Whittier enshrined the witchcraft in verse, in the novel, the New England witch belief has been the inspiration more often for historical romance than for Gothic horror. Surveys of fictional treatments of the theme include hundreds of now-forgotten historical novels. Even Hawthorne shied away from focusing on the trial transcripts in his two great New England romances. Both *The Scarlet Letter* and *The House of the Seven Gables* reflect the excesses and secret sins of Puritan Massachusetts, but neither makes witchcraft the center of the narrative. Only in the short stories, especially "Young Goodman Brown," does Hawthorne unleash all the horrors implicit in the witchcraft belief, epitomizing Puritan hysteria and paranoia in one brief, brilliant piece.

Indeed, it is primarily in the short story that the witch belief has been treated as reality, not merely as a plot device or a deliberate hoax. The local colorist Mary Wilkins Freeman wrote both an historical drama, *Giles Corey, Yeoman* and several Gothic short stories that accept the witch belief as real. Her stories "Silence" and

"The Little Maid at the Door" (1898) remain effective in their understated, chilling accounts of folk traditions. "The Little Maid at the Door" skillfully combines the history of the Proctor family of Salem, victims of the witch-hunt, with a subtle ghost story, while "Silence" retells a lesser-known legend of the Deerfield massacre and a local seeress. Howard Pyle's "The Salem Wolf" (1909) is a chilling werewolf story whose horrific happenings are not rationalized.

More often, however, fictional treatments of the witch belief have been of the "fair Puritans charged with witchcraft" sort (Orians 71), where a noble, rational suitor, standing in for the presumably enlightened reader, proves the innocence of his falsely accused beloved. Criticism of the witch belief in fiction tends to focus on how historically accurate or credible (i.e. not Gothic) the authors are in their use of the trials (J.Clark; D. Levin). Arthur Miller, for example, in his well-researched *The Crucible* nevertheless invented an unhistorical love-affair between Abigail Williams and the condemned witch John Proctor to motivate the tragic plot. With adultery as his secret sin, and a desire to protect his own good name by not confessing or implicating his friends, Proctor becomes, like Willy Loman, the tragic hero as common man. The invisible world plays a very small part in *The Crucible*; it is a proletarian tragedy, not a Greek one.

As we will see, twentieth-century male horror writers have for the most part avoided the witch belief, except for the theme of the witch's curse on a place or a family, used so effectively by Hawthorne in *The House of the Seven Gables*. In this century it has fallen to women, among them Ann Petry, Marion Starkey, Norma Farber, Shirley Jackson, and Esther Forbes, to transform the Colonial witching times into romance and allegory. Ann Petry, an African-American, was the first to treat Tituba as a strong and sympathetic character in *Tituba of Salem Village* (1964). This novel, like those of Farber and Starkey, and the non-fictional account by Jackson, was intended for a "Young Adult" audience, yet these treatments of the witchcraft, based on meticulous research, have stood up to the passage of time and can profitably be read by adults. Farber's *Mercy Short: A Winter Journal, North Boston, 1692-3* is an account of her possession from a different perspective than Mather's. Starkey's *The Tall Man from Boston* and *The Visionary Girls* are lightly fictionalized accounts that translate her pioneering research for *The Devil in Massachusetts* into terms comprehensible to children and teenagers. Shirley Jackson's *The Witchcraft of Salem Village* (1956) was my own introduction to the subject. Its argument remains as accurate, its treatment of the evidence as careful, and its prose as beautiful as I remembered.

While Esther Forbes is better known today for "Young Adult" historical novels such as *Johnny Tremain*, her *A Mirror for Witches* (1928) is decidedly aimed at an adult audience. Narrated in the voice of a Puritan divine, with Gothic intent, accepting the supernatural, the novel delineates the damnation that awaited both witches and victims of witchcraft. No one has surpassed her in recreating the tone of those times: no one has summed up the paranoia implicit in Puritanism better than her narrator's concluding words:

> ...in those days there were sights and wonders that will not come again.. In those days God was nearer to man than He is to-day, and where God is there also must be His Evil Opponent—the Prince of Lies, for show me Paradise, and there, around a corner, I will show you Hell.   (214)

A contemporary novelist who also refuses to dismiss the supernatural is Maryse Condé, a francophone Afro-Caribbean, who envisioned an entire life for Tituba, in *I, Tituba, Black Witch of Salem*, based on the slender evidence of the trial transcripts. Condé's theory is that Tituba was a black Barbadian, trained in the African traditions of *obeah* that would later become voodoo and *santería*. This post-modern novel has Tituba encounter Hawthorne's Hester Prynne while in jail awaiting trial. Hester instructs her in what New England judges expect to hear from a witch, thus accounting for Tituba's knowledge of the Satanic bargain and other facets of the learned tradition of European witchcraft.

The Connecticut witch-hunts have received almost no fictional attention, one exception being Elizabeth George Speare's young adult novel *The Witch of Blackbird Pond* (1958). While the setting is historically accurate, the plot follows the typical nineteenth-century "innocent victim/ rational suitor" design; it does not begin to tap the Gothic wellsprings of the real incidents.

In the twentieth century, tales of witchcraft are by no means confined to the pages of historical romance or popular horror novels. In one town alone, New London, Connecticut, indeed on one street, people have been following the guidance of fortune-tellers for nearly three centuries.[17] In 1827, the local-color poet J.G.C. Brainard wrote of "The Money Diggers," treasure-seekers he said were at that time "working by the side of one of the wharves in New-London,...by the advice and recommendation of an old woman. . .who assured them she could distinctly see a box of dollars packed edge-wise" (Brainard 66).[18] Her vision could have been true: in 1752–3, New Londoners had despoiled a Spanish treasure ship of forty such chests. The disabled ship had entrusted the bullion to New London customs officials. When the Spanish captain sought the return of his cargo, not a trace of the bullion could be found. The mystery of the gold's "magical disappearance" was never solved, and treasure-hunters soon began to dig for it, and to seek supernatural assistance in the quest.

The seeress in 1827 used a scrying-stone to find the right place:

> And where the Thames' bright billows gently lave,
> The grass-grown piles that flank the ruin'd wharf,
> She sent *them* forth, those two adventurers brave,
> Where greasy citizens their bev'rage quaff   (Brainard 67)

On that same street, now called Bank Street, some forty years after Brainard's treasure-seekers failed to locate the Spanish gold, lived two brothers named Smith who were whaling captains. Local legend says that they consulted a seeress, or witch, supposed to be of Black and Indian descent[19], as to whether they would have "greasy luck" on their next voyage. Instead, the seeress said, in her crystal she could see no luck at all; all she could see was a "damned black snake." History records the return of only one of the brothers. Legend says that the other, while fighting a storm at sea somewhere in the Pacific, was seized around the neck by one of the lines and strangled to death. Since all ropes on board ship were tarred to prevent rotting, it seemed to the horrified crew that Captain Smith was being choked by a black snake.

---

[17] Demos traces a similar persistence in Hampton, New Hampshire in Chapter Ten, "From Generation to Generation," focused on the figure of Goody Cole.

[18] cf. Whittier 108. Whittier also recounts two similar treasure-quests motivated by wise women in New Hampshire in the 1830s (*Supernaturalism* 99-100).

[19] As demonstrated by Hazard's story of Silvy Tory, the black seeress must have been something of a stock figure in nineteenth-century New England. Whittier writes of "an old colored woman" who was a respected prophetess in his home town; he puns on the irony of his bigoted countrymen "looking at Futurity through a black medium" (*Supernaturalism* 102).

Bank Street today remains a place where citizens quaff brews, and many of its wharves lie once more in ruins. In the early 1980s, on the very spot where the "Money-Diggers" worked—now called City Pier—a modern seeress, psychic Pat Gagliardo of neighboring Norwich, Connecticut, led police to the body of a murder victim. Her scrying-stone was the man's credit-card; using the technique of "psychometry," she was vouchsafed a vision of the man dead in his submerged car, which is where police found him the next day. Though the names by which we know them may change, claims of paranormal powers and the urge to seek out the Invisible World remain the same.

4. Salem Re-possessed

To the horror of the Mathers, were they to return, and the chagrin of the rationalists, Salem at the end of the second millennium is a veritable nest of witches. During the planning for the tercentenary of the trials, representatives of modern witches' covens protested that the festivities were purveying negative images of witches. Actually, the official ceremonies and publications were models of sensitivity: the condemned witches were treated as heroes and victims of religious persecution, while pagan priestesses were invited to speak on public platforms along with other clergy.

The question of the continuity of the witch belief in New England, as in Old, is a vexed one. Most scholars scoff at Gerald Gardner, founder of the modern revival of the witch cult, who claimed to have discovered covens hidden in the British countryside whose activities had continued unbroken from the Middle Ages, or indeed from Neolithic times. Yet social scientists from all over the industrialized world continue to report witch beliefs: to cite just one example, the social historian Muchembled discovered that in his enlightened France,

> on 29 February 1976 Jean Camus, *rebouteux* (bone-setter, country doctor) was found assassinated in his own house...Two brothers admitted to having committed the crime, following the death of their older brother and the disappearance of several of their farm animals and a dog. Their mother accused Jean Camus of being a sorcerer. He 'was the Devil. He gave cancer to all who laughed at him.' (*Popular Culture* 276)

In New England, while there is plenty of evidence, as we have seen, for the survival of folk beliefs in healing and cursing as well as for the technology used by "cunning folk" for discovering and countering such cursing, the only evidence for organized worship of other than Christian gods comes from confessions dictated or produced under torture.[20] Current worshippers of the Mother Goddess generally came to their faith quite recently. Still, serious occultism is by its very nature secret. In the past, families with any such traditions would be highly unlikely to write them down or to broadcast them to their neighbors. With the resurgence of Neo-Paganism since the 1960s, more and more non-scholars are aware of their theories about witchcraft. Regardless of what scholars have written about what happened in Salem, the "nature religion" theory of witchcraft has taken firm hold on the popular imagination. In 1993, the supermarket tabloid *Sun* profiled Levi Thornton, descendant of [unnamed] Salem witches, who claimed that "my ancestors were persecuted because they practiced witchcraft ...it was their religion" (N. Miller 26).

The claim that Salem is the home of over 2500 practicing witches has been disputed by local historians such as Richard Trask, Director of the Danvers Historical Society who scoffed "There aren't twenty-five hundred practicing *Christians* in Salem!" He believes the correct figure is closer to 60.[21] Laurie Cabot, the Official Witch of Salem, would differ with Trask—at least over the number of would-be witches who seek her out in classes and lectures. Her shop, Crow Haven Corner, flourishes in the very shadow of the Essex Institute, repository of the trial transcripts.

Today, Salem capitalizes on its reputation as the "Witch City;" Salem's Halloween celebrations, Haunted Happenings, draw over 50,000 tourists a year. Every hotel room for miles around is occupied, and the Witch House, Witch Dungeon, Witch Museum and Wax Museum are overflowing with customers. Halloween in the 1990s is a billion-dollar industry, and Salem is its capitol. Though tourism in Salem had always emphasized the witchcraft motif, the city's

---

[20]It is interesting to note that in Muchembled's 1976 case, one of the brothers who killed the sorcerer claimed preternatural powers for himself, in the tradition of the professional unbewitcher. He had "attempted to cure a well-known victim [of Camus's] by his 'fortunate gifts. .. but the other one was too strong. So he had to kill him'" (Muchembled, *Popular Culture* 276).

[21] *Yankee*, in March 1994, put the "estimated number" of modern Salem witches at 3,000.

official tourist agencies began "selling witchcraft" in earnest beginning only in the depressed 1970s. Despite their dependence on tourist dollars, there is still a certain ambivalence in official circles about selling the city's Gothic heritage: Salem's most recent advertising slogan reads "Sea more than witches," referring to maritime history. As they were for Hawthorne, however, the faded glories of Salem's Custom House and her China Trade remain for modern tourists merely a preface to the main narrative: that of Puritan sin, paranoia, and diabolism.

Strangely, illogically, the Old Religion has emerged once again in New England: Neo-Pagans join a fascination with medievalism to a reverence for Native American mysteries. The *Sun* can safely print detailed instructions for "The Salem Witches' Magic Money Spell." But despite this seeming acceptance, shadows hung over the interviews I did in 1992 with Neo-Pagans. Though 1992 marked the Columbus Quincentenary, modern witches as well as Jews remember that 1492 saw the triumph of the Inquisition in Spain. The tercentenary of the trials produced remarkably tasteless souvenirs (including T-shirts that read "just hanging around in Salem"), but the monument to victims of the Hysteria was dedicated by Elie Wiesel, who noted parallels with the Nazi Holocaust as well as with the "Culture Wars" declared at the Republican convention that same August week. Earlier that summer, Salem's Heritage Day parade saw open clashes between communicants of the fundamentalist Victory Chapel and representatives of the Wiccan community. The Chapel's minister has made clear in sermons that New Age Wiccans are agents of a diabolical conspiracy in a different guise.

In another eerie parallel with the events of 1692, some converts to this fundamentalist group have suddenly remembered that they were victims of "ritual abuse" and have come forward to accuse their abusers. Their behavior is explained by the theory that women who have been subjected to sexual abuse, by parents or by Satanic cults, repress these memories completely until, as adults, therapists help them to "recover" the memories under hypnosis. Investigators skeptical of this assumption have noticed that the methods therapists use to evoke repressed memories are similar to those used by the examiners of suspected witches. Both have tended to suggest answers through leading questions: "Why did Satan tell you to hurt these children?" "When you met Satan, what did he offer you?" or "When were you abused by your father?" "What would he do when he came to your room?" Lawrence Wright, chronicling this disturbing trend in the *New Yorker*, concludes that psychotherapists who believe in the absolute reliability of "recovered memories" play the same role today as did the Puritan divines in 1692 who believed in the "scientific" view of witchcraft as demonic conspiracy: "One idea is modern and the other an artifact of what we like to think of as a credulous age, but the consequences, depressingly, are the same" (24 May; 76). In another recent child-molestation case, therapists also followed the methods of witch-trial examiners. Just as the magistrates in the Andover witch-hunt were accused of dictating confessions for illiterate witches to sign, so the therapist of one seven-year old boy "reads from the notes I already told her" to provide evidence of Satanic practices in court (Mydans).

In the 1950s, the term "witch-hunt" came to be synonymous with the persecution of suspected Communists by McCarthy and the House Un-American Activities Committee. Today it often signifies the accusations of child abuse brought against day-care workers or parents in custody cases. At the same time, currently practicing witches—Neo-Pagans—fear that "witch hunting" may not remain a metaphor. There are those living in Salem in addition to the congregants of the Victory Chapel who believe that the Puritan authorities were justified in their actions. If belief in the learned and popular traditions of witchcraft remains alive, however transmuted, we should not be surprised that fear and hatred of those who control supernatural powers remains alive as well. With Neo-Pagan covens meeting in the woods and fields of Essex County, police officers lecturing worried parents on how to recognize the coded symbols of Satanic cults, and preachers calling for a new crusade against an ancient evil, the witch belief seems to be flourishing in New England.

Not all Gothic traditions are so tenacious. Another example of the survival of medieval superstition on New World soil is much less well known today. For about one hundred years, for many reasons, New England was home to its own version of the world-wide fear of the reanimated dead.

Chapter Six
The New England Vampire Belief

...that consumption is not a physical but
a spiritual disease, obsession, or visitation
--George Stetson

Tuberculosis "a disease of the lungs is, metaphorically, a disease of the soul," according to Susan Sontag's *Illness as Metaphor* (18). In the nineteenth century, this "white plague" "consumed" the young and healthy. It was especially prevalent in the backwoods farmhouses and teeming industrial slums that were associated with the decline of New England. Fear of tuberculosis seems to be responsible for the tradition native to New England of a vampire-like revenant or hungry ghost, attested in folklore and in newspaper accounts from the late eighteenth and nineteenth centuries. Popular belief defined the New England vampire as a member of the community, often female, unable to rest in the grave, who would return to drain the life force—though not always the blood—of other members of the family. These narratives can be considered as an objective correlative for economic decline and as a warning for us now in a time of resurgent, drug-resistant TB, when images of the Fall have become frighteningly real.

Reports of the exhumation and destruction of vampire-like revenants in Rhode Island, Connecticut, and Vermont until recently have been treated as fiction more often than as history. Recently, startling archaeological evidence has been uncovered that supports at least some of these attempts to regain power over the hungry dead. In this case, burial customs can be seen as an icon for survival of an older stratum of superstition in rural New England. As little known as the witch belief is famous, the native vampire belief may remind us of the Gothic novel which popularized the figure of the vampire in literature, but it is more akin to the folklore underlying those novels—the ancient fear of the blood-drinking spirit or reanimated corpse.[1]

The fine line between history and folklore is crossed continually in this chapter, whose sources are not those associated with scientific history, but rather with the oral transmission of tale and legend. As Mary Bolté notes in her introduction to the folktale collection *Haunted New England*, "the stories are old, weathered and warped much like timeworn barn doors" (7). For most of my sources, the horses escaped long ago, and there can be no possibility of verification. But the recent discovery in eastern Connecticut of a corpse mutilated somewhat in accordance with the practices reported in these accounts takes this study out of the realm of Gothic fiction and returns it to that of archaeology and local history.[2]

Many explanations are possible for the particular shape of the vampire belief in New England: always there is a close connection to morbid fears of tuberculosis, a disease that could run through whole families yet leave neighbors untouched. As with European vampire beliefs, young female vampires frequently appear as sexual victims turned victimizers. Finally, as with other manifestations of the supernatural in New England, the vampire superstition can stand for backwoods degeneracy, secret sins, and the region's fall from economic and political pre-eminence.

1. History and Definition of the Vampire

"Vampire" is probably the wrong word to describe the native bogey, but our language does not provide another. Most functional definitions of the term, after all, begin "vampires suck blood." Yet blood-sucking is not usually mentioned explicitly in the New England vampire cases: instead, we may hear about "draining the vitality" or just "fading away and dying." Stories collected in Vermont,

---

[1]The earliest Gothic novels did not feature vampires, but during the Romantic period, following the publication of *Varney the Vampyre or, The Feast of Blood*, vampires became appropriate subjects for serious literature-poetry, drama, and fiction. In the process, the vampire was removed from his folkloric origins (not until Bram Stoker was he re-connected to the Balkans) and, in turn, from the folk culture. See Twitchell, *The Living Dead*, for a detailed survey of the origins and permutations of the Romantic vampire.

[2]See Section Three of this chapter for a discussion of these recent discoveries.

Connecticut, and southern Rhode Island follow the same pattern: someone dies of a wasting disease—consumption. When other members of the same family sicken and die, suspicion falls on the first victim, whose hungry ghost is assumed to be afflicting the remaining relatives. The family or townspeople exhume the body of the suspected revenant, cut out the heart and burn it in order to lay the hungry ghost and perhaps cure any remaining victims.

The most authoritative source for the native New England vampire belief appeared in 1896, when *The American Anthropologist* published "The Animistic Vampire in New England," detailing the strange indigenous superstition thriving in rural backwaters of Rhode Island and Connecticut.[3] Stetson believed that his backwoods informants were sincere in their beliefs and were telling the truth, however outlandish it sounded. "In New England," he said, "the vampire superstition is unknown by its proper name" (3). This fact, in Stetson's analysis, proved the uncorrupted native origin of the New England vampire belief. It is true that, according to the *OED*, the word "vampire" entered the English language only in 1734, from a document reporting the depredations in Serbia and Greece by "the bodies of deceased persons ...which suck the blood of many of the living." The *Hartford Courant*, (21 Jan. 1765), reprinted the same definition of a "vampyre," with the comment that "such a notion will probably be look'd upon as fabulous but it is related and maintained by authors of great authority." The word did not enter non-scholarly American usage, however, until well into the nineteenth century.

The concept of a blood-drinking revenant seems to have existed in the English-speaking world at least as far back as the eleventh century. One account in Walter Map's *De Nugis Curialium (Courtiers' Trifles)* comes from the twelfth century; as in later European folklore, a dead man is transformed into what we would call a vampire because in life he had been a sorcerer and a non-believer. The story resembles the New England belief only in that the *"maleficus,"* a Welsh wizard, calls the names of his former neighbors and friends, "As soon as they are summoned, they grow ill and die within three days, so that now only a few survive." A brave English soldier takes on the role of vampire slayer, pursues the

---

[3]Stetson's article has been the basis for most studies of the vampire in America. Sociologist Norine Dresser's recent *American Vampires: Fans Victims, Practitioners* borrows heavily--occasionally without adequate attribution--from Stetson. She believes that vampirism is real, with many present-day practitioners.

140

reanimated corpse back to its grave, where—though he does not remove the heart—he "clave its head to the neck" (Map Chap. 27.125–6)..[4]

Beowulf's foe Grendel may have been this type of blood-drinking revenant; certainly the analogous figures in Old Norse legend were dead, yet reanimated with more than natural strength. Glam in *Grettir's Saga*, "endowed with more power for evil than any other revenant," (79) had been killed by a similar spirit, and, as in the Eastern European folktales, his body was infected by the vampire disease and could not lie still in the grave. Glam outdid his predecessor in frightfulness until vanquished by Grettir, who wrestled with him as Beowulf did with Grendel (Fox and Palsson Chaps. 33–35).

In Britain, burials from Roman and early Christian times have yielded bodies decapitated or with the leg bones rearranged. Merrifield, in *The Archaeology of Ritual and Magic*, sees the need to "distinguish between mere apparitions and the walking dead, who in some cultures and at certain periods seem to have been particularly dreaded" (75). Among other English examples, he mentions the "partial dismemberment" of a corpse at Dunstable (Bedfordshire) and Helmingham (Suffolk) which "may also have been a precaution against its re-animation" (75). Grettir, after killing the re-animated Glam, cuts off his head and places it against his buttocks, a precaution he had observed earlier with a re-animated barrow-dweller (Fox and Palsson Chaps. 35.79;18.37). Merrifield states that some corpses in England have been found buried face down, as if to indicate the direction that they should travel. He claims that the custom continued into the nineteenth century, when some undertakers would turn over the bodies of notorious witches or other sinners, as though to show them the way they should go.

For the most part, however, Merrifield believes that in England, Christianity at first lessened fears of the walking dead by providing protection in the form of the cross and Latin prayers. Perhaps in nineteenth-century New England the ritual protections of Christianity had worn down, as had the Puritan faith, not given to ritual in any case. Or perhaps the comforts of religion were insufficient against the mystery of TB, making it easier for people to believe once again that the dead could walk and kill.

---

[4]Cf. Kittredge 43.

2. New England's Abandoned Farms and Declining Cities

The period in which the native vampire belief flourished (ca. 1790–1890) coincides with the gradual decay of rural New England, as farms were abandoned for more easily cultivated land to the west. Eastern Connecticut, one locus of the belief, was exporting settlers to Vermont and New York State even before the Revolution. The Rev. Levi Hart's 1801 "Sketch of North Preston" [later known as Griswold and a center of the vampire belief] notes that the parish's population had been slowly declining. "The emigrations to New Settlements have been numerous.... the number of children in families is generally less than in the more early stages of society" (qtd.in Phillips, *Griswold—A History* 316). By the 1830s, parts of the New England countryside that had once been plowed field were reverting to woodlands, a process that continues to this day. To nineteenth-century observers, emigration from unprofitable farmland seemed designed to drain rural New England of its most enterprising young citizens, leaving the old and unfit behind. The results were appalling to contemporary observers. In 1869, the *Nation* asserted that "Puritan stock is diminishing, ...such of it as.remains is no longer what it should be." Indeed, the editors note, "we are forever felicitating ourselves that the West is being peopled in great measure by the hardy citizens of Maine, but we are continually forgetting what sort of an effect this is likely to have upon Maine" ("The Decay of New England" 411).

And not only the farming villages were decaying or being abandoned. Hawthorne's "Custom-House" sketch shows the decline of New England's traditional shipping trade. As Van Wyck Brooks notes, in Hawthorne's time, "Salem was still Gothic, in a measure...in its isolation from the currents of world-thought and feeling, it seemed to be only a step removed from the age of the Dance of Death" (218). The fall of Salem from its pre-eminence in the early China trade was only part of the decline in the New England sea trades. By the 1850s, the New England ports had been supplanted by New York in international shipping. Whaling, so important to New Bedford and New London, began to decline following the Civil War. Sarah Orne Jewett's *Deephaven* and *The Country of the Pointed Firs* vividly portray the once-prosperous Maine coast whose decay, already beginning after the War of 1812, was complete by the 1880s. To the slow decline of inland New England could be added the rapid rise and fall of many port cities.

Not everyone accepted the abandonment of rural New England as inevitable. Dorothy Canfield's story "Adeste Fideles!" (1915) portrays an indomitable Vermont spinster, Miss Abigail, who refuses to let her village die, even when all its inhabitants leave for jobs in the cities. Her solution is to sell family land and an unspoiled river to provide water-power for a new factory. In an early version of today's conflict between jobs and the environment, a visitor misunderstands her motivation, complaining "That bespeaks the materialistic Yankee, doesn't it?—to want to spoil a quiet little Paradise like this village with a lot of greasy millhands" (345). Canfield did not share other New Englanders' pessimism over foreign admixture to the native stock. In her collection *Hillsboro People*, a poem entitled "Salem Hills to Ellis Island" welcomes immigrants "brave homestead-seekers come from afar," who will fill the dying villages and work the abandoned farms.

In the latter half of the nineteenth century, however, most observers agreed that New England's Paradise had been lost to outsiders. Racialist theories of that day foresaw decay, pollution, and disaster when Irish, French Canadian, and then Polish immigrants replaced first the Puritan farmers and later the Yankee millhands whose blood had produced the patriots and founders of democracy in our land. As Charles Nott, a descendant of the Puritans, lamented in the pages of the *Nation* in 1889, "it is very sad that the highest, purest, noblest agricultural population that this world has ever possessed, is being dissipated, and, as a race, merged and lost" (408).

In the notorious articles concerning "A New England Hill Town" which ran in *The Atlantic Monthly* in 1899, the inbred inhabitants of the decayed hill towns of western Massachusetts are described in terms that recall similar Social Darwinist studies of the Appalachians and the Ozarks. The articles picture New England towns inhabited by dwarfs, giants, and idiots, all mutated from the ancient noble stock by what Rollin Hartt calls "natural selection the other end to—the survival of the unfittest"(572). He is shocked to think that the drunken rabble he meets at the Belchertown Agricultural Fair can possibly be "descended from the Puritans...the upland has reduced them to barbarism: they do but bespeak the future of rural New England"(573). In such a climate of opinion, audiences of scholarly journals or of scandal-sheet newspapers such as *The World* were ready to believe anything about the inbred folk of backwoods New England. Any superstition or survival of ancient beliefs might linger in those benighted areas left behind by the westward march of American civilization.

3. The Extent of the Vampire Superstition in New England

Stetson himself links the vampire superstition explicitly to the rate of abandoned farms. He notes that though Rhode Island is the most densely-populated state in the Union, nevertheless the South County towns had been depopulated in the nineteenth century, and that "The town of *Exeter*, ...had but 17 persons to the square mile in 1890, and in 1893 had 63 abandoned farms, or one-fifth of the whole number within its limits" (8n).

Stetson's fieldwork was inspired by the accounts in *The Providence Journal* of the 1892 exhumation of the Brown family of Exeter. Much of the background material on vampirism in Stetson's article follows closely an authoritative unsigned *Journal* piece "The Search for Spectral Ghoul in the Exeter Graves/ Not a Rhode Island Tradition but Settled Here." Stetson's article did not inspire a rush of vampire scholarship: the journal in which it appeared never published another article by him, nor did *The Journal of American Folklore*. In the twenty years following 1896, neither of these journals returned to the subject of vampirism in the United States. One explanation may be that, as Stetson's article was going to press, Bram Stoker, was finishing *Dracula*, which through its stage and screen versions so re-defined the vampire archetype that within 30 years, when H.P. Lovecraft was doing his antiquarian research, he could find no trace of the native belief in Rhode Island; he was forced to reconstruct it for his fiction with the aid of an offprint of the *American Anthropologist* in the John Hay Library.

The popular press, on the other hand, swiftly publicized the lurid aspects of Stetson's research, causing him to shun all further interviews with what he called the "vulgar newspapers."[5] A copy of one of these newspaper accounts may even have influenced the writing of *Dracula*. According to Raymond T. McNally, expert on "the real Dracula," the Romanian prince Vlad Tepes, the only contemporary newspaper clipping found among Bram Stoker's papers is from the *New York World*, February 2, 1896, which paraphrases and quotes the Stetson article. Its

---

[5]In a manuscript letter to Sidney Rider deposited in the John Hay Library.

144

scare headline reads "VAMPIRES IN NEW ENGLAND—Dead Bodies Dug Up and
Their Hearts Burned to Prevent Disease—STRANGE SUPERSTITION OF LONG
AGO—The Old Belief Was that Ghostly Monsters Sucked the Blood of Their Living
Relatives" (qtd. in McNally 163).

Stetson seems to have been the first to identify the New England vampire
belief with the dread disease of consumption:

> It is there believed that consumption is not a physical but a spiritual
> disease, obsession, or visitation; that as long as the body of a dead
> consumptive relative has blood in the heart it is proof that an occult
> influence steals from it for death and is at work draining the blood of
> the living into the heart of the dead and causing his rapid decline.
> (3)

Such a depiction contrasts sharply with the romantic trappings associated with the
vampire in Gothic literature and art. There are no cloaked noblemen, metamorphosis
into wolves or bats, crucifixes, or strings of garlic. The only seeming commonality
is in the victims' red blood. Yet the New England revenants, like their
Transylvanian cousins, are not mere powerless shades: they are actively dangerous
to the living. The New England belief can be linked to Eastern European vampire
traditions because both respond to the same underlying need to explain the
unexplainable mysteries of death, decay and survival. It seems likely, however, that
the vampire belief originated spontaneously in New England, in response to the
increased incidence of and dread of consumption in the late eighteenth and nineteenth
centuries.

Although the hill towns of Vermont and western Massachusetts provided the
first published evidence for the decay of rural New England, the remoter parts of
Connecticut and Rhode Island soon joined them as symbols of decline after the
publication of the Stetson article. The native vampire belief held sway in that part of
eastern Connecticut nearest in language, customs and ethnic origins to Rhode
Island's South County. The town of Griswold, indeed, was partly settled by
emigrants from western Rhode Island. Local tradition characterized these Rhode
Islanders as profane and uneducated. According to local historian Daniel Phillips,
"their clownish manners and their lack of schools were all objects of ridicule and
contempt. They were accounted ignorant and vicious" (*Griswold—A History* 135).

Perhaps among the other vices they brought with them was the native vampire belief. In the 1840s and 50s, an outbreak and exorcism was recorded in the borough of Jewett City, part of Griswold. Dudley Wright in his *Book of Vampires* quotes a contemporary account (1854) from *The Norwich Courier*:

> About eight years previously, Horace Ray of Griswold had died of consumption. Afterwards, two of his children—grown-up sons— died of the same disease, the last one dying about 1852. ...the same fatal disease had seized another son, whereupon it was determined to exhume the bodies of the two brothers and burn them, because the dead were supposed to feed upon the living; and so long as the dead body in the grave remains undecomposed, either wholly or in part, the surviving members of the family must continue to furnish substance on which the dead body could feed. Acting under the influence of this strange superstition, the family and friends of the deceased proceeded to the burial-ground on June 8th, 1854, dug up the bodies of the deceased brothers, and burned them on the spot. (155–6)

Atypically, in this story suspicion fell not upon the father who was the first to die of consumption, but upon the two sons.[6]

The Ray family—and their suspected vampires—lie buried in a peaceful cemetery in Griswold. In 1990, the accidental discovery of the long-abandoned Walton family cemetery only a few miles away reopened the question of the truth behind the published accounts of the vampire belief. The discovery of the graveyard might have come from a weird tale: children sliding down a steep bank in a newly-opened gravel pit found skulls and bones sliding with them. A rainstorm had eroded the sides of the bank, exposing the graves. Authorities called in Connecticut's State Archaeologist, Dr. Nicholas Bellantoni, who quickly covered the site and began a dig. What he found there startled him.[7]

He soon was able to tell police that the boys had not found victims of a recent serial killer; instead, the graveyard belonged to the now-extinct Walton family, with burials dating from the eighteenth century through the 1840s. At the

---

[6]This story has not had the wide circulation in folk tradition or in print that the Rhode Island vampires have known: I have found it reprinted only in Wright and in David Philips' *Legendary Connecticut*, who gives as *his* unique source a 1976 newspaper article from *The Norwich Bulletin*, the successor to *The Courier* which covered the original story.

[7]I wish to thank Dr. Bellantoni for his enthusiastic participation in an interview at his office at the University of Connecticut, 17 March 1992.

Walton site excavation, Dr. Bellantoni was to find several coffins in relatively good states of preservation. In a moment from a Gothic novel, the first one he exposed to light bore upon it his own initials, "N.B.," and his own birthdate, outlined in brass tacks.[8] This was only a minor shock: there were more to come. The coffin next to "N.B.," marked "J.B.—55" was enclosed within a fieldstone crypt, a unique construction never previously recorded in America. The diggers found that the crypt had been broken into *after* the time of the original burial, with one stone shattered to pieces just above the body's trunk. The skeletal remains within had been "purposefully disturbed," according to Dr. Bellantoni. The chest cavity had been "literally ripped into," most likely to allow the removal of the heart and other internal organs. The skull was found oriented toward the west and "sitting where the chest ought to be." The femur, the long bones of the leg, and the skull had been carefully placed to form an apparent skull and crossbones, while the bones of the lower leg and feet were still in their normal place. The dig also uncovered the foundation of a farmhouse nearby, making it necessary for these post-mortem activities to be sanctioned and "socially acceptable," according to Dr. Bellantoni.

Only *after* the discovery of this anomalous burial did a graduate student on the investigating team remember that he had read, in David Philips's *Legendary Connecticut*, about an outbreak of vampirism in nineteenth-century Jewett City, a borough of Griswold. At that time, the investigators knew nothing about the similar cases recorded in Rhode Island. None had ever heard of H.P. Lovecraft. They could not know how data from the dig would substantiate what Lovecraft in "The Shunned House" called "the Exeter superstition."

Many of the 29 bodies excavated from this site have undergone DNA and other types of testing at the National Museum of Health and Medicine in Washington. The mutilated corpse of "J.B." definitely died of consumption. He was determined to be about 55 at his death (as the brass tacks indicated), and "the man's ribs were marked with scars from a long-term battle with the disease, according to Paul S. Sledzik, curator of the anatomical collection at the National

---

[8]A number of the other coffin remnants were marked in this way, usually with initials and either age or date of death. This practice may be the origin of the expression "let's get down to brass tacks," synonymous with today's "the bottom line." Such a shift from the stark realities of death to the stark realities of profit is a fine emblem for the change from early nineteenth- to late twentieth-century attitudes.

Museum" (K.Johnson B7) Sledzik noted in a telephone interview that such scarred ribs meant that "J.B." must have showed dramatic symptoms of coughing and expectorating, making him an obvious sufferer from consumption. In addition, "J.B." had healed fractures of the collarbone and ribs that would have caused him to appear strangely hunched. All in all, a fine choice for a scapegoat. The other corpses from the graveyard showed no direct evidence of TB; however, some forms of TB, particularly what the nineteenth century called "galloping consumption," may leave no traces in the bones of the victims. Based on these results, Dr. Bellantoni affirms that the vampire belief is an acceptable hypothesis to explain mortuary practices unique both in his experience and in the previous literature on historic cemeteries. The bodies taken from the Walton graveyard, except for "J.B.," were re-buried September 9, 1992, with the minister of the First Congregational Church of Griswold, Rev. Michael Beynon, officiating. He shared with me his fears that any publicity about this ceremony might attract attention from modern occultists, and so the word "vampire" was never used in any of the newspaper or radio accounts of the reburial. Instead, those involved were careful to speak only of "superstitious practices" or "ritual mutilations." Fears of the powers of the dead are not ended!

The deliberate mutilation of the "J.B." corpse's bones took place at least ten years after the man's death from consumption, which could explain why the bones were rearranged—there may not have been a heart to burn! Since "J.B." is supposed to have died after 1800, the ceremony therefore occurred after 1812, when the Rhode Island emigrants had arrived. Transmission of the vampire belief from Rhode Island would also explain why no earlier mutilations were found in the Walton graveyard, where the majority of the bodies analyzed at the National Museum of Health and Medicine were judged to have died late in the eighteenth century. Tuberculosis had been common in Griswold before "J.B." succumbed, as attested by Rev. Levi Hart's 1801 narrative of local history which claims that "in the last *twenty-five years consumptions* have proved mortal to a number." (qtd. in Phillips, *Griswold—A History* 319; emphasis mine).

The full significance of these discoveries is yet to emerge; still, since the Walton family is not among the known cases reported in contemporary newspapers, it would seem that the folk remedy for consumption was applied more often than the few documented outbreaks would indicate. Just as belief in witchcraft was widespread even where no official accusations, trials, or executions are recorded, so the people of backwoods New England may have used their folk remedy against TB on occasions when they did not announce it to the courts, apply for permission for exhumation, consult learned physicians, or even tell stories about it, thus accidentally preserving the episode for posterity. Rather than a small number of aberrant, unconnected events, the discoveries in Griswold may support the existence of a serious folk belief, underground except when the chances of written history preserved it, which died out of its own accord and also because of the penetration of the Transylvanian vampire into the world's popular culture. Still, the Walton site discovery, while fascinating, is unlikely to lead to wholesale excavations in historic burial grounds. Descendants of Colonial families, many still "first citizens" of their towns, would rather that this particular side of their New England heritage remain securely buried.

While I have found no Connecticut vampire accounts after the 1840s, the belief apparently lingered longer in Rhode Island, especially in the area called "South County." Stetson, in the *American Anthropologist*, claims that

> By some mysterious survival, occult transmission, or remarkable atavism, this region, including within its radius the towns of Exeter, Foster, Kingstown, East Greenwich, and others, with their scattered hamlets and more pretentious villages, is distinguished by the prevalence of this remarkable superstition ....in the closing years of what we are pleased to call the enlightened nineteenth century. (7)

He cites informants from what must be Narragansett or East Greenwich—"a small seashore village possessing a summer hotel and a few cottages of summer residents not far from Newport" (8)—who had "lost children by consumption, and by common report claimed to have saved those surviving by exhumation and cremation of the dead" (8).

Another "living witness" informed Stetson that he had been part of a consumption-attacked family, who had been advised to exhume and burn the body of the first son to die: not believing the superstition, the family delayed, losing yet another son. The narrator, falling ill from consumption, finally exhumed and burned the first body, "'living' blood being found in the heart and in circulation"(9). The narrator recovered from his illness, and no more members of the family were attacked. The article also reports the prevalence of the belief in what must be the town of Exeter, where "there have been made within fifty years a half dozen or more exhumations" (9). One presumably more reliable informant, a doctor, told the investigating anthropologist that the most recent case had been within two years, involving the exhumation of a child. This doctor "declares the superstition to be prevalent in all the isolated districts of southern Rhode Island, and that many instances of its survival can be found in the large centers of population" (10).

Despite Stetson's claims for such a wide acceptance of the vampire belief, standard histories of Rhode Island omit all mention of these supernatural visitations. None of these vampire reports from Connecticut or Rhode Island made their way into the great nineteenth-century collections of folklore. They do not appear, for example, in Whittier's *Supernaturalism of New England* or Samuel Adams Drake's compilations. Perhaps these legends were insufficiently colorful, or, more likely, too close to "medical belief" to take a firm hold on the imagination of story-tellers. This in turn accounts for their neglect by the great writers such as Hawthorne and Melville who drew upon New England folk beliefs. As noted above, printed accounts may exist only because the afflicted families applied for medical or legal permission before carrying out their traditional remedies.

The commemorative Bicentennial history of the town of Exeter, apparently the very center of the vampire belief, consigns the darker side of the town's past to a few pages. Florence Parker Simister, Rhode Island's best-known popularizer of local history, does admit that "legends about Exeter must include the one about vampires" (96). She does not, however, name her informants, nor does she cite newspaper sources for the stories she retells.[9]

The earliest known account of vampirism in Rhode Island first saw print in a version collected by the antiquarian Sidney Rider. Rider corresponded with Stetson after the publication of the *American Anthropologist* article. In a letter dated August 13, 1897, Stetson thanks Rider for sending him "a remarkable instance in the last century" which must be the "Snuffy Stukeley" case. This unique narrative is dated only "at the time of the Revolution." A family of fourteen children was attacked by consumption. The father, identified only as "Snuffy Stukeley,...a young

[9]She may have found the information in Clauson's *These Plantations*. Barton St. Armand, Brown's resident New England Decadent, directed me to these sources. Clauson states that he [Rider] "had heard of a similar case at Wakefield, perhaps in a past too remote to obtain details inasmuch as he doesn't give them"(68).

farmer"(Clauson 68), dreamed that half his orchard had died. The oldest daughter, Sarah, died first of the disease. As the consumption took each family member in turn, she complained that "Sarah,...came and sat with her at night and caused her pain." The family decided to exhume all the bodies, finding that "only Sarah's heart had blood in it and only her eyes were open and fixed. Her heart was cut out and her body and the other six were re-interred. Then the heart was burned in the cemetery behind the Chestnut Hill Baptist Church" (Simister 96).

This cemetery, now so idyllic, is also the abode, though apparently not the resting place, of Mercy Brown. Les Daniels, a contemporary Rhode Island critic and writer of horror, calls her "the state's star bloodsucker...whose gruesome fate is rehashed every Oct. 31...a minor local industry in Exeter." Her grave in the Chestnut Hill Baptist Church Cemetery has attracted Satanist pilgrimage and ritual desecrations. The Brown family's vampire infestation, mentioned pseudonymously by Stetson, is documented in the *Providence Journal* articles. Mercy died in 1892, following a mother and sister who had died nearly a decade before, apparently of consumption. When her brother, Edwin, also fell ill, the remaining family and neighbors decided to exhume the three earlier victims. The case came to public attention because, seeking sanction, they called upon a Dr. Harold Metcalf, "the Medical Examiner of the District...a young and intelligent graduate of Bellevue" who "discouraged the suggestion," but eventually agreed to examine the bodies ("The Search"). They found the two-months-dead Mercy in near-living state, her heart still engorged with blood, while the other two victims were decayed. Dr. Metcalf told the *Providence Journal* that though such evidence of vampirism may have satisfied the ignorant locals, he believed that it "was just what might be expected from a similar examination of almost any person after the same length of time from decease" ("Exhumed the Bodies"). As in the eighteenth-century accounts, the 1890s vampire hunters removed Mercy's heart and burned it on a rock in the cemetery. Going beyond this preventive measure, they prepared a potion from the ashes of the burned heart and fed it to the ailing Edwin, who nonetheless died.

Another suspected Rhode Island vampire left nameless in the Stetson article could be Nellie Vaughn, on whose grave in West Greenwich, near Exeter, "no grass will grow" (Daniels). The inscription on her tombstone reads "I am Waiting and Watching for You." Another South County case reported by Dudley Wright is that of a William Rose, of "Placedale[*sic*][10], Rhode Island, Mr William Rose dug up the body of his own daughter and burned her heart, under the belief that she was draining the vitality of other members of the family"(156).

The vampire belief also held sway in parts of Vermont, apparently from the eighteenth century onward. It seems significant that the two towns from which cases have been collected, Woodstock and Manchester, were both settled from eastern Connecticut and named after towns in that region. Contrary to the idyllic picture now conveyed by Vermont villages, Vermont in the 1790s was still very much a frontier region (Smith 27).[11]

Rockwell Stephens, writing in *Vermont Life*, reprints a story from the October 9, 1890 *Vermont Standard* entitled "Vampirism in Woodstock." Stephens was apparently unaware of the analogous incidents in other parts of New England. The date of the original article can be no coincidence, as this is the very period of national media interest in the decline of Vermont hill farms and the resulting decadence of the old New England stock. Unlike the Rhode Island cases, the earlier exhumation and burning in Woodstock were carried out with the sponsorship and enthusiastic participation of the doctors from the local college of medicine.

The first case alluded to in the *Vermont Standard* article occurred in June 1830, when the Corwin family suffered the usual epidemic of consumption. One brother died of it and, six months later, another brother fell ill. There was some disagreement among the attending doctors "as to the exact time that the brother of the deceased was taken with consumption. Dr. Gallup asserted that the vampire began his work before the brother died. Dr. Powers was positively sure that it was directly after" (qtd. in Stephens 73). The body being exhumed, the expected blood-filled heart was boiled in an iron pot on Woodstock Green. In this case, heart, ashes, pot and all were lowered into a huge hole in the center of the green, and, in a ceremony reminiscent of Eastern European folk vampire beliefs, "the blood of a bullock was

---

[10]This is most likely a typographical error for Peacedale, a village within the township of North Kingstown.

[11]See also the story "In New New England," in which Dorothy Canfield [later Fisher] has to remind her readers in 1915 that conditions in the Vermont of 1762 were "more as they had been in Connecticut and Massachusetts a hundred and forty years before" that date.

sprinkled on the fresh earth, and the [town] fathers then felt that vampirism was extinguished forever in Woodstock" (qtd. in Stephens 73).

The reporter in 1890 claims that some years after the exhumation, searchers for the pot were unable to find a trace of it, but that in the course of excavations "they heard a roaring noise...and a smell of sulphur began to fill the cavity...considerable disturbance took place on the surface of the ground for several days, where the hole had been dug, some rumblings and shaking of the earth, and some smoke was emitted" (qtd. in Stephens 73–74). It is almost impossible now to imagine such hellish conflagrations taking place on and under the surface of the peaceful Woodstock Green.

Rockwell Stephens also cites an unpublished memoir of Daniel Ransom, found in the Norman Williams Public Library on the Green—the very same Williams who is listed as one of the instigators of the Corwin heart-boiling. The Ransom family, too, was decimated by consumption, though the memorialist was writing in 1894 when he was over 80 years old. Daniel Ransom states that his father shared the common superstition "that if the heart of one of the family who died of consumption was taken out and burned, others would be free from it" (qtd. in Stephens 79). Accordingly, about 1817, "the heart of Frederick [Ransom was] taken out after he had been buried, and it was burned in Captain Pearson's blacksmith forge" (qtd. in Stephens 79). The folk remedy did not work, however, for Ransom's mother died in 1821, his sister in 1828 and two more brothers a few years after the burning of the heart on Woodstock Green.[12]

A strikingly similar case occurred in Manchester, Vermont, in the 1790s. Gerald McFarland, in his book The "Counterfeit" Man, retells a story from the Proceedings of the Vermont Historical Society. Both McFarland and the original reporter seem unaware of the Woodstock cases, though they do treat the Manchester occurrences as history rather than fiction. According to these accounts, in 1793, Captain Isaac Burton's second wife fell ill of the consumption that had killed his first

---

[12]Though Stephens presents his story as fact, the editors of the Vermont Life volume do not agree: they note that his account is "apparently entirely fictitious," but concede that it "illustrates considerable narrative skill in that its tracing is purposely obscured by framing it as a story within a story . . . and the interjection of the names of attesting witnesses who were prominent citizens"(170). In general, Yankee, Connecticut and other New England popular magazines have represented and continue to represent folkloric accounts of the vampire belief as fiction.

wife three years previously. "The first wife's body was dug up and what was left of her heart, liver, and lungs were removed.... the first wife's organs were burned in a blacksmith's forge," (53) a fate that parallels the second Woodstock occurrence. John Pettibone, the local historian transmitting the account in 1930, somewhat misinterprets the native belief. In his explanation, the townsfolk believe that a "Demon Vampire" who killed the first wife might be killing the second; thus, they are making a kind of ritual sacrifice, using the blacksmith's forge as an "'altar,' in hopes that this would propitiate the Demon and 'effect a cure of the sick second wife'" (qtd. in McFarland 53). Based on the other accounts of the New England belief, however, it seems clear that the villagers were merely following prophylactic folk medical practice, and that Captain Burton's first wife was assumed to be the vampire, though it is extremely unlikely that the 1790s Vermonters would have employed that word.

While I have not found records of any outbreak of the vampire belief in New Hampshire, folklorist John McNab Currier reported the following from Grafton County, NH in his 1891 "Contributions to New England Folk-Lore": "If the lungs of a brother or sister who has died of consumption be burned, the ashes will cure the living members of the family affected with that disease" (253). This seems like a remnant of the full animistic vampire story, recorded at the same time by Stetson in Rhode Island.

4. Some Explanations of the Vampire Belief

It is difficult if not impossible to ascertain whether the New England superstition arose only in the late eighteenth century, or whether the belief existed but earlier cases were simply not documented. In 1892, for example, informants in Exeter, Rhode Island told the *Providence Journal* that it "is a tradition of the Indians" ("The Search"). But no evidence exists to support these practices in any Native American cultures from the contact period until today. We can safely agree with the 1892 editorial writer who said that grave desecration and making medicines from the ashes of the dead was a tradition so "horrible to contemplate" that the locals could "hardly be blamed for attributing it to the Indians" ("The Search").

If the native New England belief is truly a creation of the late eighteenth and nineteenth centuries, one possible explanation may lie in the incidence, suspected or actual, of premature burial—Edgar Allan Poe was not the only one in America obsessed with this particular horror. Asa Snow, who lived in one of the western Massachusetts hill towns condemned by Rollin Hartt in the *Atlantic Monthly*, in 1872 took elaborate precautions against premature burial. He commissioned a coffin with a plate-glass viewing window, and arranged with the undertaker to visit the tomb for a week after his burial, all to make certain he was truly dead. Snow's plans backfired: after his death, his widow excused the undertaker from his charge, while the notorious windowed coffin drew curiosity-seekers who despoiled the tomb. They also spread tales that the tomb's occupant lay in a vampire-like state of preservation, so perhaps his fears were justified. Snow's tomb became a legendary haunted site until the Quabbin Reservoir covered it (Greene 114–115). Such legends notwithstanding, some scholars claim that premature burial was no fiction. According to Anthony Masters' *The Natural History of the Vampire* "American statistics in the early 1900's show that not less than one case a week of premature burial was discovered" (17). The incidence of death-like trance was called "epidemic." Thus, it is not strange that an exhumed corpse could be found in the grave weeks after burial, seemingly engorged with its victims' blood. The horrified struggles to escape could account for the disordered limbs, the staring eyes; and the subsequent rise in blood pressure would explain the flushed cheeks and even, perhaps, the blood-filled heart.

But the practice of burning, staking, or eating the revenant's heart responds to a more ancient imperative: the need to exert power over the unknown. The dead must remain dead, and their memory should strengthen, not destroy, those left behind. An explanation drawing on this ancient imperative is advanced by Paul Barber, whose *Vampires, Burial, and Death* has recently collated all extant European vampire accounts. Barber ascribes these traditional beliefs and practices to the misunderstanding of natural phenomena, resulting in the widespread fear of the powers of a corpse after death. In his explanation of mythopoeic reasoning, blaming a corpse for an epidemic makes perfect sense. In Europe, as in the New England cases, "a person may become a vampire simply by being the first person to die of an epidemic, and the epidemic is interpreted as the effect of his depredations" (34).

Yet another possible explanation takes into account the fact that the New England vampire is not usually an overt blood-sucker: the victims of these accounts may complain of weakness, choking or smothering. Barber views these latter two effects as folkloric explanations for apnea and other sleep disturbances: "knowing that some people awaken and report that they were choked or smothered (which is a common dream-phenomenon associated with apnea), they assume that, if a person dies suddenly during sleep, the choking must not have been interrupted in time" (187). The nocturnal visitation of a familial vampire can thus be linked to older legends of nightmares as the sendings of witches or demons who also cause choking or smothering sensations.

Above all, the New England vampire belief in life and as interpreted in literature is most intimately connected with the prevalence and horror of tuberculosis. Consumption, Susan Sontag argues in *Illness as Metaphor,* was an appropriate name for the disease. TB for the nineteenth century played the demonic role of AIDS in our time: mysterious, fatal, and somehow linked to sexual abnormality or excess. Tuberculosis was a major cause of death in otherwise healthy adults. In the first half of the century, some authorities estimated that "one fourth...of all deaths...in the Northern and Middle States" could be laid to the account of consumption (Larkin 79). Until the isolation of the tuberculosis bacillus at the end of the century, the best theories medical science could produce, those of "miasma" or bad air, were no closer to accuracy than the folk belief in depredations of a familial vampire. In addition, the very idea of "contagion" was denied by educated physicians until late in the nineteenth century. During the first period of anti-vampire activity, 1790–1840, Larkin notes in *The Reshaping of Everyday Life,* "Contagion was almost a folk belief, widely held by ordinary people but frequently dismissed as superstition" by medical authorities. (77). Just as with the AIDS virus, even when the cause of TB became clear, the cure had to wait for many years, until the development of antibiotic agents during World War II.

As Sontag notes, "any important disease, whose causality is murky, and for which treatment is ineffectual, tends to be awash in significance" (58). Accounts of the New England vampire belief accord well with Sontag's paradigm of TB as a romanticized disease. Although TB was thought to be inherited, at the same time it was viewed as "a seemingly arbitrary, uncommunicable taint" (38). Vampirism in Eastern Europe was often described in terms of an "epidemic": such imagery recurs in Stoker's *Dracula.* As in that novel, the vector of the disease in the New England accounts was often a young girl. Even today, doctors have by no means dispelled all the mystery surrounding the disease. Because of a combination of nineteenth-century problems like homelessness and poor sanitation, together with immune-deficiency diseases, the incidence of TB is on the rise, signifying for believers in scientific progress a "glaring social failure" (Cowley 53).[13] Not only does the disease remain, but scientists have identified new drug-resistant strains. As Lawrence Altman reported in the *New York Times* (25 January 1992), even today the exact mechanisms of contagion remain a mystery: "for reasons doctors do not understand, some people seem to spread the tuberculosis bacillus more easily than others do ...some people seem to escape infection even when other people living in the same household become infected" (1). Such a seeming immunity within a single household could account for the occasional efficacy of folk remedies against consumption. After the destruction of the suspected vampire, one or two family members might indeed survive the epidemic.

How appropriate then, at a time when the body of New England was seen as falling into a decline, with the woods reclaiming what the Colonial pioneers had conquered at such a cost, and the remaining descendants of the Puritans sinking into inbred barbarism, that the souls of New England's rural inhabitants should be gripped by a disease that reflected their weakness and decadence. Vampirism is indeed a fitting metaphor for tuberculosis and, even more, for the decline of rural New England. Along with some of the older skeletons in New England's closet, the persecution of witches, the practice of necromancy, as well as a more modern one, the exploitation of immigrants in crowded city slums, the New England vampire belief would soon find literary expression in the fiction of H.P. Lovecraft. A living archetype of the Gothic, Lovecraft transformed the region's supernatural folklore and history into an art filled with images of the decline of New England—and of humanity.

---

[13]Cowley's article was *Newsweek*'s cover story on 16 March 1992. For other articles covering the epidemic and the ancient fears it has aroused, see Winerip, Altman.

Chapter Seven
The Local Color is Black—H.P. Lovecraft

> Loathsomeness waits and dreams in the deep,
> and decay spreads over the tottering cities of men.
> --H.P. Lovecraft, "The Call of Cthulhu"

Of the many artists who have made their home in New England, none so
exemplifies the region's darker side in his life and art as Howard Phillips Lovecraft.
So much did he identify with the city in which he spent his life that he was given to
saying "I am Providence."[1] His imagination soared through unknown gulfs of
space and time, while his body remained firmly anchored to Providence's College
Hill and his heart to eighteenth-century New England. Nor did he find his self-
imposed limits confining: as he wrote of his alter ego, Charles Dexter Ward, "It
was this place and the mysterious forces of its long, continuous history which had
brought him into being, and which had drawn him back toward marvels and secrets
whose boundaries no prophet might fix" (*AMM* 165).

H.P. Lovecraft (1890–1937) wrote horror fiction for pulp magazines and
served as a ghost writer for Houdini, among other clients. He never saw his works
between commercially-printed hard covers.[2] Yet since his death, he has become

---

[1]The statement can be found in several letters (16 May 1926 (*SL* 2: 51); 10 February
1927 (*SL* 2: 102). These were the words chosen to be engraved on the monument belatedly erected
to him in the Phillips family plot in Swan Point cemetery with funds raised at the World Fantasy
Convention in Providence in 1975.

[2]Friends in amateur journalism attempted publication of several books: none was
commercially distributed. "The Shunned House" had a weird history of its own. W. Paul Cook
printed a slim volume which was never bound or sold; according to the John Hay Library, Robert
Barlow bound and put under copyright in 1936 a few copies of the unbound earlier sheets. A

the object of cult adoration. His collected works remain in print, and Borges once called him one of America's three greatest science-fiction writers. French critics have judged Lovecraft greater than Poe in the realm of the weird tale. Less often acknowledged, however, is his kinship to Hawthorne in the tradition that gazed into New England's soul and found only blackness within.

Early in his career, in a vignette of cannibalism and New England antiquarian lore called "The Picture in the House," Lovecraft declared that "the true epicure in the terrible ...esteems most of all the ancient, lonely farmhouses of backwoods New England; for there the dark elements of strength, solitude, grotesqueness, and ignorance combine to form the perfection of the hideous" (*DH* 116). Lovecraft followed his own dictum: in his fiction, he replaced the haunted castle of European Gothic with the backwoods farmhouse, the Inquisition with the Puritan divines, and Europe's decadent aristocracy with the degenerate descendants of New England's old stock. The horrors he inflicted upon his neurasthenic heroes, however, went far beyond those that menaced the heroines of traditional Gothic novels, nor were they confined to the shapes inherited from the European Middle Ages—ghost, werewolf, vampire, witch. Instead, Lovecraft devised a new cosmology in which human evil and traditional monsters were made to seem almost comforting in comparison to the infinite spaces of a profoundly unknowable, inimical universe.

1. Lovecraft's Life: His Own Greatest Creation

Because he chronicled his fears in such great detail in letters as well as stories, more critical attention has been devoted to analyzing Lovecraft's life than to his art. Many critics have echoed Vincent Starrett in proclaiming Lovecraft "his own most fantastic creation—a Roderick Usher...born a century too late." At first glance, there seems to be nothing in his life that would support such a characterization. Lovecraft spent his entire life in Providence, residing first with his mother and then with his aunts, with the exception of a brief marriage. He never held a "day job." He wrote no best-sellers. He died almost penniless,

---

version of *Supernatural Horror in Literature* and one of "The Shadow Over Innsmouth" also existed as amateur rarities.

unrecognized for the most part by the Providence he immortalized in his stories. He was not a drunk, a womanizer, an opium eater, or syphilitic. He left no children. He spent most of his time writing.

In vivid contrast to the dull facts of his life, Lovecraft re-created himself through letters. So prolific a correspondent was he that five volumes of over 2000 pages represent only "Selected Letters." Publishing the rest of the extant letters could require another 40 or 50 volumes! From those letters, an unforgettable picture emerges of a tall, gaunt man with a prominent nose and haunted eyes who avoided the light of the sun but walked miles by moonlight, sleeping by day and writing by night. He chronicled his aversions (the cold, fish); his enthusiasms (fanlights, cats) in exhausting detail. He established fiercely loyal friendships that were wholly epistolary. In addition to the endless letters, Lovecraft devoted much time to amateur journalism. He wrote and edited amateur periodicals, wrote lengthy travelogues, and a great deal of verse, light and serious. He published over fifty stories, ranging from short sketches to novellas, and it is on these that his reputation is based.

Lovecraft's life mirrored the regional decline reflected in New England Gothic. Indeed, his own fortunes declined even more dramatically than those of the region he called home. His maternal grandfather Whipple Phillips, a factory owner and connection of many prominent Rhode Island families, represented the apex of the family's rise to fortune: everything after his death in 1904 represented a fall. The money that was supposed to have kept Lovecraft and his aunts in comfortable affluence vanished. His grandfather's estate (by some reports, no more than $20,000 to begin with) disappeared in a series of bank failures and, eventually, the Crash. Lovecraft could not seem to earn enough money from writing. Most of his tiny income came from ghost-writing (he called it "revision"). Occasionally, commercial publishers expressed some interest in reprinting his fiction, which appeared in pulp magazines such as *Weird Tales* for a cent a word or less—but each time he was rejected. These rejections threw him into profound depression: though he was producing hundreds of pages of letters a week, he told his correspondents that he was utterly blocked from creative work. In 1932, he told his young disciple August Derleth, "what depressed me in the Putnam incident [an editor at G.P.Putnam had asked to see a collection of his stories] was not the nonappearance of the volume but the logical analysis which convinced me of the permanent inferiority of my efforts" (31 March 1932; *SL* 4: 34). He was to write only a few more weird tales before his death in 1937.

In his life as in his art, entropy ruled. St. Armand notes that Lovecraft identifies the fall of the physical house with the fall of the mind, just as Poe does in "The Fall of the House of Usher" (*Roots of Horror in the Fiction* 16–18). The repeated motif of "skewed structures, like the Witch House in Arkham" represent, according to St. Armand, Lovecraft's "psychic allegories of decadent and tumbled-down minds, twisted to exquisite and picturesque degrees of insanity by the forces of age and heredity" (*Roots of Horror in the Fiction* 19). It is true that insanity haunted his family: Lovecraft's father died mad, most likely of the paresis that characterized the last stages of syphilis. Lovecraft's mother was confined to the same mental hospital after 1919. The psychiatrist's diagnosis blamed her collapse on physical circumstances: "a traumatic psychosis, an awareness of approaching bankruptcy" (qtd. in Scott 59). For her son, however, the fall of his own house was inseparable from the fall of New England and, indeed, of Western civilization before the forces of barbarism and entropy. Lovecraft was not alone in these beliefs. The feminist Charlotte Perkins Gilman, who had lived in Providence and eastern Connecticut only a few years earlier, chronicled her own descent into madness and dependency in "The Yellow Wallpaper." Less well known is that after years of winning fame for her writing and economic theories, Gilman returned to Norwich, Connecticut only to find her time had passed, along with that of her home region. Living in obscurity from 1922 to 1930, she remarked in her autobiography that "no one with a sense of historical perspective can live in a New England town and not suffer to see its gradual extinction" (326). How much more did Lovecraft grieve to see the decline of his beloved Providence, with which he identified so completely.

The fictional objective correlative for all this emotional angst, turmoil, and decay is the physical and moral degeneration of his characters. Those who worship the forbidden gods degenerate from human to less-than-animal. The sad state of New England's "last Puritans" is reflected in the ghouls who undermine modern Boston in "Pickman's Model." In this story, a "Bohemian" artist has found the ultimate way to shock the bourgeois: he paints ghouls from life. I have never felt completely comfortable riding the Red Line of Boston's "T" after reading Lovecraft's description of Pickman's painting "'Subway Accident,' in which a flock of the vile things were clambering up from some unknown catacomb through a crack in the floor of the Boylston Street subway and attacking a crowd of people on the platform" (*DH* 20). Like their creator, Lovecraft's characters delight in digging up the underside of the past, when "there were witches and what their spells summoned; pirates and what they brought in from the sea; smugglers; privateers—I tell you, people knew how to live, and how to enlarge the bounds of life, in the old times!" (16). Above all, the decline of the formerly hardy New England stock is mirrored in the enervated, passive protagonists of his stories. Lovecraft once asked Clark Ashton Smith, a fellow chronicler of the outré for *Weird Tales*, to "write a tale of somebody who lived down the ages and saw the little details of familiar life crumble around him whilst alien powers and unfamiliar ways engulfed his land and left him an exile from an earlier and forgotten world" (18 Nov. 1933; *SL* 4: 320). This wistful request is strange, for it constitutes the allegorical reading of every story Lovecraft ever wrote; indeed, it is how he read his own life, an exile in a world he never made.

This feeling of being an outsider was a constant in Lovecraft's life and art: one of his most famous stories is titled "The Outsider." Sometimes he expressed the feeling in terms of an existential dread at the ineffable strangeness of the universe. His credo was the reverse of the anthropic principle: in his cosmos, the Earth, its non-human inhabitants (except for cats), and the rest of the universe are equally indifferent to man. Humanity has no escape and no recourse from the alien Outsiders.

In life and art, Lovecraft also projected his dread of such Outsiders and his own alienation upon the members of non-Aryan races, "that new and heterogeneous alien stock which lies outside the charmed circle of New England life and traditions" ("The Terrible Old Man," *DH* 273). In this brief sketch, an Italian, a Portuguese and a Slav set out to rob an ancient sea captain who turns out to be a necromancer who keeps the souls of his former piratical colleagues in bottles. This time, the "charmed circle" of old New Englanders easily overcome the representatives of the "alien stock." In life, Lovecraft could see no similar triumph. Instead he roamed the slums of Providence, seeing strange buildings and stranger inhabitants, alien and multiform. The overwrought prose of this letter of 23 April, 1926 typifies his reactions to non-Aryans, this time Jewish:

162

> Oozing out of various apertures and dragging themselves along the narrow lanes are shapeless forms of organic entity whose dead faces hint fiendishly of the rites and orgies and incantations in the hideous leaning synagogue whose wormy, unpainted boards hold strange Eastern signs and unholy marks taken from the cabbala and the *Necronomicon.* (*SL* 2: 44)

He adds, "I shall weave all this into a tale some day," a promise he does not seem to have kept, although defiled *churches* figure in several stories. In essays, letters, and stories, Lovecraft projected his lifelong feeling of deracination, of being an outsider, upon the changes he found in Providence and all over the Northeast:

> Within the lifetime of people now middle-aged, the general tone of our northern cities has so changed that they no longer seem like home to their own inhabitants..... Italian & Portuguese faces everywhere. One has to get down to Richmond to find a town which really *feels like home*—where the average person one meets looks like one, has the same type of feelings & recollections, & reacts approximately the same to the same stimuli. (8 Nov. 1933; *SL* 4: 308).

Of course, when Lovecraft did remain in the South for more than a day at a time, he discovered that while the "average persons" may have been good Nordic types, they were no more "like him" than were the Yankees of Providence, whose narrow-minded Victorian attitudes he used to lampoon to correspondents. According to St. Armand, who is familiar with the East Side milieu, "the best that most of his more affluent Providence connections could say of Howard was that he was indeed 'queer' or 'crazy as a bed-bug' (*The Roots of Horror in the Fiction* 78). He was an alien in any company except that of a few like-minded men, thus explaining the paradox of a reputed recluse whose friends worshipped him to the point of idolatry.

All the elements of New England Gothic come together in Lovecraft, who so identified with the Eighteenth Century's view of the Gothick past[3]. His love of New England's past warred with his observations of its degenerate present. Like the great Gothic artists of the nineteenth century, he applied his own nightmares and neuroses to the landscape; ironically, the New England climate itself inspired him to

---

[3]Lovecraft always spelled the word this way, one of his eighteenth-century mannerisms. See 11 Jan. 1923 letter to Reinhardt Kleiner, for example, which describes the "Gothick" town of Marblehead, Mass. (*SL* 1: 204).

horror. Because Lovecraft was made physically ill by cold weather—unable to leave the house at all when the temperature dropped below 20 degrees—he automatically associated cold with feelings of dread. As he told fellow *Weird Tales* writer Catherine L. Moore, "I can't feel the same deep, Gothic horror in any mild and genial region that I can in the rock-strewn, ice-bound, elm-shaded hillsides of my own New England. To me, whatever is *cold* is sinister, and whatever is warm is wholesome and life-giving" (2 July 1935; *SL* 5: 180–1).

H.P. Lovecraft dipped deep into the pool of local color and found it black as Usher's tarn. He collected and transformed New England folklore, shaping it according to his own preoccupations, until the results may seem far removed from the original folktales. In addition to reading all the printed sources from Mather to Whittier to Drake, he diligently sought out living informants who knew local legends of the supernatural. In his excursions around New England, he delighted in collecting folklore at the source. He describes one such excursion, shared with Clifford M. Eddy, in a letter (8 Nov. 1923) to his protegé, writer Frank Belknap Long. He and Eddy had searched Chepachet, in western Rhode Island, for a Dark Swamp, so mysterious that "there are but two men who ever heard of it." Eddy had learned of its existence in a scene that seems familiar to us through many horror films, yet which Lovecraft represents as factual:

> One very antient man with a flintlock said that IT had mov'd in Dark Swamp, and had cran'd ITS neck out of the abysmal pothole beneath which IT has ITS immemorial lair. And he said his grandfather had told him in 1849, when he was a very little boy, that IT had been there when the first settlers came; and that the Indians believed IT had always been there. (*SL* 1: 264)

Lovecraft travelled tirelessly through New England, to every ancient burial ground and crumbling slum, searching for local legends and secrets. He took great delight in the survival of old customs and practices in forgotten backwaters; there he found, as he says in "The Whisperer in Darkness," "the continuous native life which keeps alive strange ancient memories, and fertilises the soil for shadowy, marvellous, and seldom-mentioned beliefs" (*DH* 244–45).

Like his character who insists on sleeping in the most haunted room of Salem's Witch House, Lovecraft sought out the very places that most haunted his nightmares. This is a basic theme of the Gothic: for every forbidden room, there is always someone (usually a woman) who is compelled to open that door.[4] But Lovecraft needed no Gothic castle to feel threatened: he was capable of seeing undercurrents of horror in the most mundane and modern scenes. This series of three dreams seems to make explicit the connection between his medieval Gothic fears and the New England of his own time:

> ...my dreams (1) of the ancient house in the marsh, and the staircase that had no end, (2) of the mediaeval castle with the sleeping men-at-arms, and the battle on the plain between the archers of England and the *things* with yellow tabards over their armour, who vanished when their leader was unhelmeted and found to have *no head inside the empty helm*, and (3) of the street car that went by night over a route that had been dismantled for six years, and that lost five hours in climbing College Hill, finally plunging off the earth into a star-strown abyss and ending up in the sand-heaped streets of a ruined city *which had been under the sea*? (21 May 1920; *SL* 1: 114)

The first two dreams may have resulted from reading too much Horace Walpole, whose name he had used as a signature in a 3 Dec. 1919 letter to the same correspondent.[5] The third dream, however, proves Lovecraft's contention that he could find horrors in Providence that would surpass any of Walpole's. Wandering through the "old west side of Providence," (an area now mostly obliterated now by Interstate 95), Lovecraft found Hogarth-like scenes that reminded him of the undesirable side of eighteenth-century London. He described one such ramble:

> ...the strange streets stretching down silent and sinister to the unknown elder mysteries that gave them birth ...grotesque lines of gambrel roofs with drunken eaves and idiotick tottering chimneys, and rows of Georgian doorways with shatter'd pillars and worm-eaten pediments. (24 Nov. 1923; *SL* 1: 270).

Such relatively realistic descriptions rapidly give way to horrors that only he could experience. Describing the same neighborhood, Lovecraft claimed to have seen

> . . .a fog, and out of it and into it again mov'd dark monstrous diseas'd shapes. They may have been people, or what once were, or might have been, people....claws of gargoyles obscurely

---

[4]See Aguirre 93.

[5]Lovecraft rarely signed his letters with his given name: he would either employ one of a series of Latinate pseudonyms based on translations or anagrams of his name, or else that of an 18th-century personage such as Walpole.

beckoning to witch-sabbaths of cannibal horror in shadow'd alleys
that are black at noon ...long, long hills up which daemon winds
sweep and daemon riders clatter over cobblestones ... (*SL* 1: 270)

It is no wonder that the lucid dreamer who could see such horror while open-eyed
in the city continues to haunt our imagination, or that the "old gent from
Providence" is better known today than any character he created in his weird tales.

2. Sea Monsters, Strange Creatures, Stranger People

When Lovecraft invented the most commonly-invoked god of his pantheon,
he turned to New England's original nemesis, the sea serpent. This is not
surprising, as he had a life-long horror of all that dwelled in deep waters, expressed
in his absolute refusal to consume any form of seafood. [6] Yet he loved to gaze out
at the sea, and once took a brief sea-voyage to Nantucket. At times, like the
narrator of "The Shadow Over Innsmouth," Lovecraft felt "queerly drawn toward
the unknown sea-deeps instead of fearing them" (*DH* 367). In this ambiguity he
was carrying on New England's love-hate relationship with the sea. In the oldest
seaports, the houses of fishermen and ships' captains turn their backs to the sea,
safe on higher ground. Only in the late nineteenth century, among those who were
not dependent on the sea for their livelihood, did the vogue for building on the
littoral or on the sea-cliffs begin.

Lovecraft introduced his sea monster-god in the 1926 story "The Call of
Cthulhu." He also shows us its worshippers, who are nearly as monstrous as their
god: "degenerate Esquimaux," Louisiana swamp-dwellers, and Pacific islanders.
His descriptions of their rites resemble the impressions of the earliest English
explorers who were convinced that the Indians were devils in the forest, employed
in worshipping a greater Devil. Lovecraft's vision of alien races is embued with the
same fear and loathing of the unexplainable Other. In this description of the cult's
graven image, we can see Cthulhu's hybrid nature: a sea monster grafted on to a

---

[6]For example, he would consent to bring his friends to Rhode Island's famous shore
dinner halls, but could not bear to stay with them. In a memoir, E. Hoffman Price remembered
Lovecraft using profanity at the mere thought of eating seafood: "HPL's plain 'damns' were
reserved for state occasions. It was only in the face of that supreme horror, a man about to eat a
steamed clam, that he could achieve blasphemy" ("The Man Who Was Lovecraft," *Something
About Cats* 284). See also DeCamp, *Lovecraft* 78.

Doré demon, "with an octopus-like head whose face was a mass of feelers, a scaly, rubbery-looking body, prodigious claws on hind and fore feet, and long, narrow wings behind"(*DH* 134). When the reality behind the image is encountered, we discover that it is amorphous as a jellyfish. Most of Lovecraft's cosmic horrors share this quality: in addition to his loathing of fish, Lovecraft feared shapeless things; anything whose surface was soft and wiggly—like custard—would set off the horrors.[7]

In "The Call of Cthulhu," Lovecraft outlined the cosmology that would be extended and imitated by his admirers, and eventually inspire role-playing games and fringe cults. The degenerate cultists of his fiction, who could be found in the dying towns of New England as well as in Louisiana or Polynesia, carried the racial memory of Outside gods and monsters such as Cthulhu, and were ever poised to bring them back, though such an advent would mean the destruction of Earth and perhaps of the worshippers as well. (It is never clear whether they realize the latter.)

> They worshipped...the Great Old Ones who lived ages before there were any men, and who came to the young world out of the sky. Those Old Ones were gone now, inside the earth and under the sea; but their dead bodies had told their secrets in dreams to the first men, who formed a cult which had never died....hidden in distant wastes and dark places all over the world until the time when the great priest Cthulhu...should rise and bring the earth again beneath his sway. (139)

Later, in "The Dunwich Horror," Lovecraft makes the prospect of the evil cults' triumph even more frightful: the otherworld beings, it seems, plan to clean all human life off the earth, "to wipe out the human race and drag the earth off to some nameless place for some nameless purpose" (*DH* 198). Lovecraft's scholarly investigators are the only ones who can decipher the seemingly scattered and meaningless clues and see the dreadful conspiracy for what it is. Their method, "piecing together of dissociated knowledge" (*DH* 125), resembles that of the finders of ancient inscriptions in New England, who correlate previously unrelated pieces of evidence into a secret history hidden from more orthodox archaeologists. In Lovecraft's universe, however, the record of the rocks reveals invaders not from

---

[7]See St. Armand's *The Roots of Horror in the Fiction of H. P. Lovecraft* for a psychological evaluation of this "dread of the viscous."

ancient Phoenicia or even drowned Atlantis, but from beyond the sky. Setting the pattern for twentieth-century horror fiction and films, the monsters come from other planets or even other dimensions.

The catalyst for the action of "The Call of Cthulhu" is a subterranean earthquake that brings Cthulhu's ancient city of R'lyeh up from the bottom of the sea, causing an epidemic of nightmares and insanity in sensitive souls all over the world. A luckless vessel finds the island, leading to an encounter with Cthulhu. In a scene reminiscent of the narratives of Olaus Magnus[8], Lovecraft's fish-demon-god attacks a Norwegian captain's steam-vessel. Cthulhu differs from the "real" sea monsters because he is unkillable and viscous, made of no earthly flesh or blood:

> There was a mighty eddying and foaming in the noisome brine, and as the steam mounted higher and higher the brave Norwegian drove his vessel head on against the pursuing jelly which rose above the unclean froth like the stern of a daemon galleon. The awful squid-head with writhing feelers came nearly up to the bowsprit of the sturdy yacht, but Johansen drove on relentlessly. There was a bursting as of an exploding bladder, a slushy nastiness as of a cloven sunfish, a stench as of a thousand opened graves...then there was only a venomous seething astern; where...the scattered plasticity of that nameless sky-spawn was nebulously *recombining* in its hateful original form.... ("The Call of Cthulhu," *DH* 153).

The Norwegian mate Johansen, the only survivor, leaves a manuscript account which the narrator reads: from this point onward, he will dread the sea and all that dwells therein, and no wonder "when I think of the horrors that lurk ceaselessly behind life in time and in space, and of those unhallowed blasphemies from elder stars which dream beneath the sea, known and favoured by a nightmare cult ready and eager to loose them on the world" (*DH* 149). Lovecraft's narrators, like Poe's, are usually mad, dead, or barely clinging to sanity and life. "The Call of Cthulhu," told through manuscripts, interviews and letters, typifies Lovecraft's narrative technique, which draws on eighteenth and nineteenth-century models, as does his diction. The story explicitly invites sequels, for at the end, though R'lyeh has sunk once again, "Cthulhu still lives...Loathsomeness waits and dreams in the

---

[8]See Chapter One, pp. 1-2.

168

deep, and decay spreads over the tottering cities of men" (154).[9] This double decay, loathsomeness within expressed in outward decline, exemplifies Lovecraft's Gothic vision.

Two other stories focus on New Englanders' fascination with and horror of monsters from the deeps. "Dagon," one of his earliest stories, reads like a sketch for "The Call of Cthulhu," while "The Shadow Over Innsmouth" brings the Polynesian setting of the earlier story home to the decaying coastal towns of Massachusetts' Essex County. "Dagon," written in 1917, was Lovecraft's first sale to *Weird Tales*. It features a narrator who is both mad *and* (by story's end) dead; a land-upheaval in the Pacific; and "the ancient Philistine legend of Dagon, the Fish-God" (*Dagon* 19). Here, the narrator sees the monster come up from the deeps: "Vast, Polyphemus-like, and loathsome, it darted like a stupendous monster of nightmares to the monolith, about which it flung its gigantic scaly arms, the while it bowed its hideous head and gave vent to certain measured sounds. I think I went mad then" (18). In "The Call of Cthulhu," Lovecraft also makes an extended comparison to Odysseus's encounter with the Cyclops, Polyphemus. By the later story, as we have seen, the physical description of the monster has become more vividly detailed.

"The Shadow Over Innsmouth" (1931) takes a skewed look at New England's history of maritime commerce. Instead of bringing back tea or porcelain from the East Indian or China trades, the Marsh family of Innsmouth imports a cult that reveres the Deep Ones, monster-gods like Cthulhu and Dagon. Instead of marrying a Chinese woman or a Polynesian maiden, Captain Marsh marries an immortal undersea dweller, a kind of fish-frog, and brings her kin to dwell on Devil Reef outside the harbor of Innsmouth. Eventually, all the townspeople are either sacrificed to or bred with the fish-frogs. Their offspring have "the Innsmouth look," becoming more fish-like as the years pass, until they are completely transformed and hop down to live under the sea forever.

Lovecraft, an adherent of the racial theories propounded by Houston Stewart Chamberlain, projects his horror of miscegenation into the attitude of outsiders toward the strange people of Innsmouth: "simply race prejudice—and I

[9]It was Lovecraft's disciple, August Derleth, however, and not the master who coined the name "Cthulhu mythos" to codify his cosmology.

don't say I'm blaming those that hold it" (*DH* 307). Along with theories of Aryan supremacy, however, went an absolute faith in evolution and its opposite, "biological degeneration" (314). Races could fall into barbarism more swiftly than they had risen to civilization. The protagonist of "The Shadow Over Innsmouth" cannot connect the town's abnormalities—"queer narrow heads with flat noses and bulgy, stary eyes that never seem to shut" (308)—with any existing race of *humans*, however inferior. The real "shadow" over Lovecraft's universe is the prospect of reversed evolution, of man devolving back towards the viscous slime that was the ancestor of Aryan and non-Aryan alike. In this relentlessly pessimistic view, the most civilized Aryan may be only one generation removed from the ape— or the frog.[10]

Though the descriptions of decaying Innsmouth are vivid, and there is a frightening sequence set in the town's sinister hotel which must have been inspired by the crumbling rooms Lovecraft stayed in on his bargain-basement tours of haunted New England, those who do not share Lovecraft's horror of seafood will be more amused than terrified at the numerous references to the "insufferable" and "nauseous" fishy odor of the town. Still, it *is* horrifying to live in a dying town, not merely economically depressed, but, as the last fully-human inhabitant describes it: "...with everything a-rottin' an' a-dyin', an' boarded-up monsters crawlin' an' bleatin' an barkin' an hoppin' araoun black cellars an' attics every way ye turn' (339). Unlike Lovecraft's other degenerate cultists, these New Englanders have called in the Outside beings for recognizable motives: the promise of abundant fishing and gold. Human sacrifices to alien gods and forced breeding with fish-frogs can be read allegorically as stand-ins for the dark secrets of real New England merchant families. As we used to say on tours of historic Providence, "if you say your great-great-grandfather was in the China trade, it was opium; if he was in the West Indian trade, it was slaves."

3. Puritan Paranoia: The Witch Belief

---

[10]See St. Armand, *The Roots of Horror in the Fiction of H. P. Lovecraft* 78-81 and *passim*, for further discussions of this theme of reversed evolution.

Following the model of his Puritan ancestors, Lovecraft transforms the aborigines of his New England into veritable monsters and demons. His motives, unlike those of the Puritans, do not pretend to be redemptive. He lets all hell loose among the hills of Massachusetts and the alleys of Providence to provide readers with a frisson of horror, not to save their souls. As Barton St. Armand noted at the Centennial Commemoration, Lovecraft mythicizes the Puritans, replacing their reliance upon the Bible and other religious texts with his characters' dependence on blasphemous texts of his own invention, such as *The Necronomicon*. In Lovecraft's fictional universe, these invented texts represent survivals of medieval superstition that have been transmitted to the New World by Puritans who, like Hawthorne's Chillingworth, have mastered forbidden arts.

In his tale "The Unnamable," set in Puritan Salem, Lovecraft expresses his mixed feelings about his ancestors: though they were superior Aryans, he condemns them as thoroughly as he does their degenerate descendants. Here is his characterization of the seventeenth century:

> The witchcraft terror is a horrible ray of light on what was stewing in men's crushed brains, but even that is a trifle. There was no beauty; no freedom—we can see that from the architectural and household remains, and the poisonous sermons of the cramped divines. And inside that rusted iron strait-jacket lurked gibbering hideousness, perversion, and diabolism. (*Dagon* 203)

In this view, the Puritans are medieval in their architecture and their religion; therefore, he condemns them. At the same time, they are Anglo-Saxons and they are *his* ancestors; therefore, they must be superior beings. Lovecraft recoils from the Puritans' Gothic barbarism with the fervor of an eighteenth-century enlightened gentleman, while feeling the same attraction to hidden perversion and diabolism those gentlemen once felt.

Lovecraft is equalled only by Nathaniel Hawthorne in blending New England local color with supernatural horror, and in re-seeing the Puritans in this demoniac light. There are, as well, many parallels between Hawthorne's years of seclusion in Salem and Lovecraft's self-immolation in Providence. Just as Hawthorne based his *House of the Seven Gables* on Salem's history and legends, attaching them to an actual site, so Lovecraft projected his own fears of dissolution onto the very fibre of New England's land and people.[11]   There were also direct influences: besides having read all of Hawthorne's fiction, by 1919, Lovecraft had read Hawthorne's notebooks. According to scholar and enthusiast Don Burleson, one of Hawthorne's notes, "An old volume in a large library, every one to be afraid to unclasp and open it, because it was said to be a book of magic," may have inspired Lovecraft to invent the *Necronomicon* (267).   Philip Shreffler also designates Lovecraft as an heir of Hawthorne, but notes that Hawthorne saw the dark-light struggle within a person's soul, whereas "the evil experienced by Lovecraft's main characters is external to them and is pervasive in the world" (158). Unlike Hawthorne, Lovecraft esteemed above all else in literature the "cosmic terror," he constantly externalizes evil and objectifies it into monsters from Outside. Lovecraft's horrors from Outside are invoked by necromancers who are descendants of the Puritan divines and of Hawthorne's mad scientists.   It is Lovecraft's meticulous attention to details of the New England countryside and cityscape, however, that brings the cosmic horrors to gruesome life.   Winfield Townley Scott, the Rhode Island essayist who was one of the few to recognize Lovecraft's achievement soon after his death, links him to Hawthorne and to Mary Wilkins Freeman in a great tradition of "haunted regionalism" (52).

Despite his obsession with Puritan diabolism, Lovecraft never wrote an extended treatment of the witchcraft delusion.   He did tell correspondents of his wish to write a novel about the New England witch belief "in which some hideous threads of witchcraft trail down the centuries against the sombre & memory-haunted background of ancient Salem" (21 Jan. 1927; *SL* 2: 99).[12]   It is unfortunate that he never carried out this plan, for as we have seen, only a few novelists have treated the New England witch belief in the light of Gothic horror.   One reason he never finished such a novel is expressed in the same letter, where he affirms, as he did in *Supernatural Horror in Literature*, that the natural form for horror was the short story; like Poe, he believed that longer forms of fiction destroyed the single effect.

He did employ a Salem setting for "The Unnamable," as he explained in another letter. "The graveyard …is really the old Charter St. Burying Ground in

---

[11]See Burleson, "H.P. Lovecraft: The Hawthorne Influence" for more explicit parallels, especially between "The Shunned House" and *The House of the Seven Gables.*

[12]See DeCamp, *Lovecraft* 299.

Salem. There *is* an old house abutting on it (also mentioned by Hawthorne in *Dr. Grimshawe's Secret*) with a cracked tomb nearby; and there is also a huge willow engulfing an illegible slab near the centre of the cemetery" (13 Feb. 1934; *SL* 4: 386). This short story with its shocker ending, written in 1923, is unusual for its time and place of publication. In metafictional style, one character mocks the narrator's technique for writing pulp fiction. Joel Manton, the narrator's friend, claims that nothing can be beyond clear description: "constant talk about 'unnamable' and 'unmentionable' things was a very puerile device." The narrator admits that he may be "too fond of ending my stories with sights or sounds which paralysed my heroes' faculties" (*Dagon* 200). Lovecraft has often been attacked for employing these same "puerile devices." Critics have objected to his habit of constantly teasing the reader with the threat of revealing something too horrible to know and remain sane, since after all reader and writer alike remain uninstitutionalized at the story's end. This style may be an inevitable concomitant to the Gothic mode in fiction. Kiely defines the "Romantic novel" partly in terms of its reliance on the same "allusive, euphemistic" style of narrative. "Phrases like 'unspeakable horror' or 'indescribable transports of joy' may at first have been little more than trite literary evasions," he explains, but they are inevitable when the Romantic artist must deal with the numinous, the supernatural, or any supernal emotion. Kiely claims that the nineteenth-century Romantics were engaged in expanding their own minds and those of their readers to accommodate "feelings and dreams which seemed to defy--at least before Freud--a referential vocabulary" (11). To an antiquarian like Lovecraft, however, Freud had in no way increased the vocabulary with which to explain supernatural horror: it remained forever "unspeakable."

The literary discussion in "The Unnameable" unfolds as Manton and the narrator sit upon the strangely cracked tomb in the Charter Street Burial Ground in Salem. The nameless horror unleashed upon them comes straight from Cotton Mather's *Magnalia Christi Americana*, a tale Lovecraft calls "crazy country mutterings...so poorly authenticated that even he [Mather] had not ventured to name the locality where the horror occurred"(203). The narrator lays bare Lovecraft's own method of composition, which consisted of "amplif[ying] the bare jotting of the old mystic" (200). Lovecraft indeed found his "example" in the sixth book of

Mather's *Magnalia Christi Americana*, which Mather originally used to illustrate the horrors of buggery. Here is Mather's version of the tale:

> There have been *devilish filthinesses* committed among us ...At the southward there was a beast, which brought forth a creature, which might pretend to something of an humane shape. Now, the people minded that the *monster* had a blemish in one eye, much like what a profligate fellow in the town was known to have. This fellow was hereupon examined, and upon his examination, confess'd his infandous Bestialities; for which he was deservedly executed. (*Magnalia* 2: 344–5).

Lovecraft (through his narrator) congratulates himself for imagining the untold portion of Mather's horror story, saying that "nobody but a cheap sensationalist would think of having it [the monster with the blemished eye] grow up, look into people's windows at night, and be hidden in the attic of a house.... till someone saw it at the window centuries later and couldn't describe what it was that turned his hair grey" (203). Lovecraft does all these things. He transforms Mather's bestial hybrid into Dr. Grimshawe's secret, then hides it in the real seventeenth-century house overlooking Salem's ancient burial ground, resting place of the witch trial judges. He mixes into the brew the folk belief that windows may retain the impression of faces that have stared into them for many years and the habit of old New England families of locking shameful secrets away in the attic--and the charm is wound up.

While Lovecraft shared many of the Puritans' paranoid attitudes in more modern guise, he took delight in referring contemptuously to Mather, who had not plumbed the depths of the Invisible World so far as he had. In "Pickman's Model," the scornful artist-ghoul boasts of his own superior knowledge of the underworld of Colonial Boston: "'I can shew you a house he lived in, and I can shew you another one he was afraid to enter in spite of all his fine bold talk. He knew things he didn't dare put into that stupid *Magnalia* or that puerile *Wonders of the Invisible World*'" (*DH* 16). Despite his pose of contempt, Lovecraft had read and understood his sources (he owned an ancestral copy of the *Magnalia Christi*); unlike Lovecraft's characteristically purple prose, Mather's is fittingly described by the narrator of "The Unnamable" as "stern as a Jewish prophet, and laconically unamazed as none since his day could be" (*Dagon* 203).

174

Lovecraft's only completed excursion into the New England witch belief, "Dreams in the Witch House" (1932), is set in the invented town of Arkham, here clearly meant to be Salem.[13] This later and longer story merges science fiction and horror so thoroughly that we can agree with Lovecraft's recent editor James Turner who says "one can only marvel at Lovecraft's audacity in attempting so formidable a synthesis of New England black magic and Einsteinian physics!"("A Mythos in His Own Image," *AMM* xv). The narrator, Walter Gilman, attends Miskatonic University, the strange college Lovecraft created, where freshmen major in medieval metaphysics, whose library holds the *Necronomicon* among other forbidden tomes. Lovecraft weaves real detail from the witchcraft trials--belief in familiars, transcripts of the examinations by Judge Hathorne in the Court of Oyer and Terminer—into a single tapestry with 1920s science—fourth-dimensional mathematics and quantum physics, the names of Planck, Heisenberg, and Einstein. Authoritative as Lovecraft sounds in these esoteric realms, the occasional error of the auto-didact creeps in, such as the reference to "non-Euclidean calculus" [*all* calculus is post-Euclidean!]. Lovecraft also weaves in the strands of his invented mythos, as he identifies the demons and gods of the witches with his own deity Azathoth, and equates "the immemorial figure of the deputy or messenger of hidden and terrible powers—the 'Black Man' of the witch-cult" with his "'Nyarlathotep' of the *Necronomicon*" (*AMM* 286).

As noted above, the protagonist seeks out the haunted room once occupied by the notorious Keziah Mason, an accused witch who somehow escaped in 1692: as it turns out, she and her rat-like familiar Brown Jenkin had discovered the secret of fourth-dimensional travel. They also possess the secrets of immortality, and they have lived until the time of the story by stealing children at the seasons of the witches' sabbats, Walpurgis Night and Halloween. The fourth-dimensional secrets of immortality have something to do with unnatural angles and geometry and secret signs: "not even Cotton Mather could explain the curves and angles smeared on the grey stone walls" of the jail cell that Keziah escaped in 1692 (263). Gilman dreams in the old witch house that he accompanies the witch and the rat through fourth-dimensional space, where all "his physical organisation and faculties were

---

[13]In the earlier stories such as "The Picture in the House," Arkham seems to be located some miles inland. See Murray for discussion of the locales of Lovecraft's fiction.

somehow marvellously transmuted and obliquely projected" (267). Though he has moved into another dimension, the organic creatures he finds there are familiar pulp horrors: viscous, octopus-like or amorphous.

More vivid, however, than the trips into Einsteinian curved space are the evocations of ancient evil in the town of Arkham. "Brown Jenkin" is much more frightening than the vague monsters found in the other dimensions. Like the familiars described in less detail in the transcripts of the witchcraft trials, "it had long hair and the shape of a rat, but that its sharp-toothed, bearded face was evilly human while its paws were like tiny human hands. It took messages betwixt old Keziah and the devil, and was nursed on the witch's blood--which it sucked like a vampire" (266). The old crone Keziah haunts Gilman waking and sleeping: she is one of Lovecraft's best-realized horrors. The sounds of a low tittering and the scrabbling of rats in the walls of the Witch House will remain in the memory long after the "monstrous burst of Walpurgis-rhythm" and "space-time seethings" (291) from the other dimensions are forgotten.

Forming a kind of Greek chorus to the tragedy are the modern inheritors of Salem/Arkham, the Polish, Portuguese, and Black in-comers who had by the 1920s replaced the earlier immigrants condemned by Batchelor and Henry James. Salem was already "polluted" by foreigners in the late nineteenth century when the Rev. George Batchelor, a local historian, wrote that "the Irish brogue and the French language are heard now where pure English was once the rule" (17). These views echo those of George Marsh who in 1843 in *The Goths in New England* was already dismissing New England's industrial cities as places alien to descendants of the "real Goths"--the Puritan settlers. Henry James seems to have had an identical reaction of horror when in 1904 he went to look for the House of the Seven Gables and asked directions from a young man who had the effrontery to answer in Italian. Reporting in *The American Scene*, James employs an image Lovecraft might have used to report the obliteration of all he had held dear in his boyhood. Even James's childhood home had been razed to make room for the new Boston: "I had the vision ...of a huge applied sponge, a sponge saturated with the foreign mixture and passed over almost everything I remembered and might still have recovered" (qtd. in O'Connell 104). In James' imagination, the "foreign mixture" seems to stand for the Irish and Italian immigrants of Boston as well as the modern ideas of progress and commercial success that had infected his own Anglo-Saxon upper class.

Lovecraft was less likely to blame his own class for New England's decline; instead, he could deflect some of the blame onto cosmic monsters and cultists of degenerate races.

In Salem in 1888, Batchelor noted that foreigners occupied most of the historic houses, "the mansions built by merchants of English descent...inhabited by operatives in the mills or laborers, who have no interest in the old ways of the former inhabitants" (16–17). On the contrary, Lovecraft's immigrants *do* remember the "old ways." In "Dreams in the Witch House," they play the part of a superstitious peasantry who carry on the witch belief unwisely abandoned by their Anglo-Saxon betters. Though they may have little comprehension of what happened in their adopted home in 1692, their Old-World memories of Walpurgisnacht and remedies against vampires and witches enable them to survive when the Anglo-Saxon protagonist does not.

4. Necromancy: Digging Up The Past

Necromancy is a connecting theme or obsession in Lovecraft's work and life. His intense nostalgia for his own past and for New England's lost glories led to a desire to make the dead past speak. He would sometimes translate the *Necronomicon* as "The Book of Dead Names," or "Of the Law of the Dead," but as commentator Everett Bleiler has remarked, it "simply means HOW TO CONTROL THE DEAD" (322). The fear of the dead is ever-present in Lovecraft's works: necromancy is something more horrific than nostalgia, after all! In the letter discussed above recounting his ramble through the horrors of Providence's west side slums, Lovecraft notes that "there must be crime where so many dead things are ...the mass'd dead of Colonial decay ...the dead that draw shapes out of the night to feed and feast and fatten" (24 Nov. 1923; *SL* 1: 270).

Typical of the Gothic mode, Lovecraft's dead refuse to stay dead. As in Horace Walpole's *Castle of Otranto*, the "dead hand" of the past will always haunt the present. In New England Gothic, however, the haunted ancestral castle is replaced by the ancestral mansion, farmhouse, or church. A perfect emblem for Lovecraft's double vision of the Puritans can be seen in the austere, soaring white church--with ghoul-swarming crypts beneath. In his story "The Festival" (1923), a descendant of a very old family indeed returns to Kingsport to dig up his ancestor's secrets. He moves through time into a seventeenth-century city, modeled upon Marblehead, Mass. There he joins a Yule ritual kept "when festival was forbidden" (*Dagon* 208). The celebrants of the dreadful rite march into the church, "up the aisle between the high white pews to the trap-door of the vaults which yawned loathsomely open just before the pulpit. . .into the dank, suffocating crypt" (213). Though Lovecraft experienced an epiphany when he first sighted Marblehead at sunset,[14] and though he describes this sunset vision in loving detail early in the story, he transmutes all his delight into horror, until, like the narrator, we shiver at the thought "that a town should be so aged and maggoty with subterraneous evil" (213).

Despite his emphasis on unholy ritual and nightmares, Lovecraft as a *fantaisiste* was not merely an inspired dreamer any more than he was a believer in the supernatural. His letters make it clear that he approached his fiction with care, did research in person and in books, and made conscious artistic choices. He wrote to Clark Ashton Smith (9 Oct. 1925), admitting that up till then he had drawn his magical incantations from an old *Encyclopedia Britannica*, but would like to find some more appropriate sources. He asks "are there any good translations of any mediaeval necromancers with directions for raising spirits, invoking Lucifer, & all that sort of thing?" (*SL* 2: 28). Apparently he found what he was seeking, for by 1936 he shows a formidable erudition regarding these primary sources; he has read the works of the real necromancers. In a letter to the young fan Willis Conover, who had apparently inquired about the sources of forbidden knowledge, Lovecraft responds that "you will undoubtedly find all this stuff very disappointing. It is flat, childish, pompous and unconvincing ...Any good fiction-writer can think up 'records of primal horror' which surpass in imaginative force any occult production which has sprung from genuine credulousness" (29 July 1936; *SL* 5: 287).

Lovecraft succeeded in this task: nowhere more so than in the novella *The Case of Charles Dexter Ward*, which concerns a Colonial necromancer, Joseph Curwen, and his return to life in Providence of the 1920s. It is also a dark Valentine to his home town. In this story, composed in 1927 but printed only after

---

[14]See 17 Oct. 1933; *SL* 4: 275 and 11 Jan. 1923; *SL* 1: 203 for more details on this Marblehead epiphany.

his death, Lovecraft unites the Salem hysteria, Rhode Island history and the decline of New England as mirrored in the spiritual decline of its narrator, making it a perfect exemplar of these Gothic themes.[15] The horrors visited upon Charles Dexter Ward result from the type of antiquarian and genealogical pursuits sponsored by local historical societies. It is appropriate, therefore, that the strongest explication of the tale, Barton St. Armand's "The Facts in the Case of H.P. Lovecraft," was originally presented to the Rhode Island Historical Society. In this story, as in "The Shadow Over Innsmouth," Lovecraft warns us against too over-zealous an attempt to "dig up our ancestors": any "roots" we find may grow from forbidden ground.

The novella could be used to teach Rhode Island history. Lovecraft endows the title character with his own love of walks through historic Providence as well as his own earliest memory. Like Lovecraft,

> He had been wheeled, too, along sleepy Congdon Street...The nurse used to stop and sit on the benches of Prospect Terrace to chat with policemen; and one of the child's first memories was of the great westward sea of hazy roofs and domes and steeples and far hills which he saw one winter afternoon from that great railed embankment, all violet and mystic against a fevered, apocalyptic sunset.... (*AMM* 113)

The rest of Ward's youth, however, passes as Lovecraft wished his own life had, but did not: plenty of moneyed leisure and the opportunity to attend Brown University. We know that Ward is doomed to destruction when he "discovered a hitherto unknown great-great-great-grandfather" (116), Joseph Curwen, a sorcerer escaped from Salem, who eventually returns and possesses the younger scholar. Nothing could have averted this fate, for true genealogists are fanatics: as Lovecraft notes, perhaps with a touch of irony, "No spirited and imaginative genealogist could have done otherwise than begin forthwith an avid and systematic collection of Curwen data" (148). Ward's assiduous search for the hated sorcerer is reflected in reality by the number of people who are eager to prove descent from the witches

---

[15] The composition of "The Case of Charles Dexter Ward" is described in a letter to Frank Belknap Long (Feb. 1927; SL 2: 99-100). Characteristically, Lovecraft never put this manuscript into final form nor did he attempt to publish it. In a letter of 15 Feb.1933, he tells E. Hoffman Price, another *Weird Tales* writer, "I tried once to put my imaginative reactions to old Providence into a story . . . . but which I could never get the energy to type"(*SL* 4: 152).

hanged in Salem. Lovecraft warns in "The Shadow Over Innsmouth" against uncritical ancestor-worship. The protagonist, also a student genealogist, discovers that he is descended from the loathsome hybrids that had stalked him in the hotel: he would have been better off letting the dead past stay dead.

For Charles Dexter Ward, the "dead hand of the past" takes on literal meaning, for Curwen had devised a way to come back from the grave. A portrait of Curwen is found in the crumbling Colonial house now lived in by some of the few normal non-white characters in all of Lovecraft's works. The colonial-era Curwen looks exactly like his descendant, seeming "to confront the bewildered Charles Dexter Ward, dweller in the past, with his own living features in the countenance of his horrible great-great-great-grandfather" (155). The latter, along with several colleagues, had refined a new type of necromancy: through alchemy, they had learned to revive the intelligences of the dead from the "essential salts" of their corpses. For hundreds of years, these "nightmare ghouls" were engaged in "robbing the tombs of all the ages, including those of the world's wisest and greatest men" and they had "achieved a way of tapping the consciousness of the dead whom they gathered together." These sorcerers had gone far beyond the worst imaginings of the Salem witch trial judges: they had bargained not with Satan but with the Other Gods, "with a necromancy even older than the Salem witchcraft" (199).

In Colonial times, brave Rhode Islanders had succeeded in driving out the original Curwen; for his witch-hunters, Lovecraft employs the actual men who burned the British ship Gaspee in a confrontation antedating the Boston Tea Party. These included the founders of Brown University and his own ancestor Capt. Abraham Whipple. In Charles Dexter Ward's time, the heroic Dr. Willett finishes the job, with some help from the John Hay Library and one of the Otherworld demons. Curwen, like Faust, suffers from hubris, seeking for more knowledge than his masters had bargained for. Unlike the smart Yankees of the region's folktales, this New Englander does not defeat the Dark Forces. His "own evil magic" proves his undoing. Curwen is dissolved once again into dust--at least until the next ancestor-worshipper brings him back!

Another side to New England's obsession with dead ancestors was the fear that they might not be resting at peace in their graves. As we have seen, grave-robbing for nefarious purposes was an ancient custom in New England; so, apparently, was meddling with the bones of suspected revenants. Because the early Puritans preferred that graveyards not be located next to meetinghouses, New England is dotted with historic cemeteries, many of them abandoned like that of the Waltons in Griswold, Connecticut.[16]   When growing cities encroached upon family burial grounds, these ancient cemeteries would be excavated and the bodies relocated. Lovecraft knew Providence legends, however, warning that not all those buried had found new resting places: he employed this knowledge in "The Shunned House" and "The Case of Charles Dexter Ward." As Joseph Curwen warns his sorcerous colleagues, grave markers were not always accurate, and tombstones could be moved, destroyed, or replaced by others.

Lovecraft's dreams, like Poe's region of Weir, were ghoul-haunted. He personified fears of grave desecration in the form of a race of New England ghouls, who derive material sustenance from the dead past. In "Pickman's Model," Lovecraft's process of bringing nightmares into the light of day through fiction is mirrored in the paintings of Richard Pickman. The decadent artist is condemned for doing what Lovecraft, Hawthorne, and before them, the Mathers had done: Pickman "turned colonial New England into a kind of annex of Hell" (*DH* 20). Inspired by his rambles in Boston's North End, Lovecraft in "Pickman's Model" imagines that a subterranean race inhabits the network of tunnels reputed to underly the crumbling historic houses. The artist Pickman, descended from a witch hanged in Salem (justifiably executed, unlike the actual victims of the hysteria), reveals what he has learned by "digging around in the past" (16). In one of his macabre paintings of the ghouls at their work, he encapsulates the darkness at the root of the flowering of New England:

> where scores of the beasts crowded about one who held a well-known Boston guide-book and was evidently reading aloud. ...every face seemed so distorted with epileptic and reverberant laughter that I almost thought I heard the fiendish echoes. The title of the picture was "Holmes, Lowell, and Longfellow Lie Buried in Mount Auburn." (20–21)

Even the sacred Household Poets are not safe from the dark forces who symbolize New England's decline! Like all who inquire too deeply for forbidden knowledge,

---

[16] Discussed in Chapter Six, Section Three.

Pickman pays the price. He undergoes a reverse evolution and joins the subterranean race, though there are hints in his paintings that he had been a hybrid or changeling ghoul from birth—another Outsider. Lovecraft's nostalgia for New England's past is always a Gothic nostalgia, strongly tinged with horror.

5. Images of the Decline: New England and Beyond

Lovecraft's vision of decline and degeneracy extended far beyond New England. From boyhood he had deplored the fall of Greece and Rome; he may have been the only child in Rhode Island ever to mourn that great Pan was dead. As an adult he moved from Gibbon to Spengler, and mourned with that philosopher the decline of the West. This elegaic tone underlies his horror fiction, but even more so his letters and philosophical musings. While he could contemplate with some equanimity the approaching fall of Western civilization, he was moved to passion at the destruction of the physical remnants of that civilization's greatest achievement: eighteenth-century architecture.

Even as Lovecraft praised New England above all other parts of the world, he lamented her fall from glory. He distributed blame for this fall equally among the degenerate descendants of the old race and the "teeming masses" of newer immigrants. We have seen his rhetorical stance on alien races. An account of his first visit to Danvers, Massachusetts, the Salem Village of the witchcraft hysteria, provides an example of his equal disdain for those of Anglo-Saxon ancestry who have "let down the side." At the Capt. Samuel Fowler house, built in 1809, he met the two aged granddaughters of the builder. In a letter to Frank Belknap Long and Alfred Galpin (1 May 1923), he describes the experience: the two women, hideous as witches, live in a "degraded kennel," amid the rags of ancestral splendor. Lovecraft contrasts the glorious achievements of Colonial architecture with the degenerate state of the present curators of that splendor:

> 1809–1923—one hundred and fourteen years of slow, insidious decay. In the veins of those terrible wrecks—last of their line— flows the mingled blood of all that was proudest in the Salem region....Such is the dying New-England of today—a whole section's tragedy was epitomised when these unfortunate survivors paus'd beneath an oaken frame and amidst their tatters hoarsely

call'd attention to the coat-of-arms which bespoke the haughty
gentility of the Fowler blood.... (*SL* 1: 220)

It is clear that Lovecraft identified with the two old women, "last of their line," as
he was also the last of his family. Dying without issue, he may have been the last
male to bear the Lovecraft name in America.

Inspired by Gibbon and Spengler, Lovecraft was fundamentally pessimistic
about the state of the world and the cosmos. His own life had supplied the best of
reasons for pessimism.[17] Though he may have seemed self-absorbed, he watched
in horror as his city of Providence crumbled and lost its influence and its traditional
industries, as his New England came to be considered a stagnating backwater
instead of the nation's cultural arbiter, as his proud English lineage seemed to grow
weak while newer races of immigrants teemed and grew strong. These themes
haunt his letters: he harps on the subject, producing Aryan supremacist tracts that
horrify modern readers, who cannot conceive of a racist with so many admiring
friends, many of whom represented the very ethnic groups that he condemned in
the letters and amateur journal articles. The vexed question of Lovecraft's racism is
inextricably tied to his belief in the decline of the West, and to his practice of
blaming the decline upon anyone other than Nordic Aryans. As in so many aspects
of his life, he was anachronistic in his views on race and heredity. Rhetoric like
that of Lovecraft's racist diatribes can be found in the pages of *The Nation* or *The
Atlantic* from the 1880s and1890s. In his own time, writers such as Ezra Pound,
T.S. Eliot, and H.L.Mencken shared many of his views on racial matters. A
review in the *New York Times* defended Mencken's newly-published memoir—
"liberally salted with ethnic slurs, most of them about Jews and a few offensive in
the extreme"—with the admonition that intelligent, open-minded readers must
"make allowances for the commonly-held prejudices of turn-of-the-century authors"
(Teachout 10). Mencken, born ten years before Lovecraft, seems to have realized
by the time he suffered a stroke in 1948 that American attitudes on racial prejuice
were changing: this may explain why he asked that his diaries and memoirs be
withheld from publication until 1991. Lovecraft left no such instructions, though

---

[17]He was unlikely to use this word, however, instead ascribing his feelings to the cosmic
indifference of the universe. Two years before his death, he told a correspondent "I am not a
pessimist, but merely a realistic *indifferentist*. . . .the truth is that the cosmos is blind &
unconscious" (23 Sept. 1935; *SL* 5: 195).

he fervently wished in his later years that the pro-Aryan tracts he had published as a young amateur journalist might remain in obscurity. Unfortunately, Lovecraft's friends and disciples have put into print every scrap of his writing, so that the racism implied in his fiction is plain for all to see in early essays and letters. Lovecraft did not live long enough to see the dire results of Aryan supremacy theories, but he did find them more difficult to defend in the 1930s, when he engaged in tortuous attempts to justify Hitler to his correspondents. While he never praised Hitler's actions, Lovecraft continued to defend the discredited science behind Hitler's racialist doctrine.[18] S.T. Joshi argues that in Lovecraft's later years his Tory political views moderated into cautious approval of Franklin Roosevelt. and New Deal socialism. Even in Lovecraft's last letters, however, he clings to what we now call "racist beliefs."

While Lovecraft bemoaned the decline of New England, in New York he saw the realization of his worst fears, the obliteration of the "old stock" by the "mongrel races." He lived in New York only during his marriage, between 1924 and 1926, but in that time he transformed the city according to his moods, from Dunsanian fantasy of spires at sunset to the "pest zone," home of monstrous aliens, harbinger of the onrushing decline of the West. Lovecraft was not alone in such judgments. When Freud and Jung visited New York some fifteen years earlier, they noted similar phenomena. The two psychiatrists viewed with some alarm the city's mongrelization of culture, "including signs in the park in German, Italian and Yiddish as well as English." According to Jung, "they had talked about 'Jews and Aryans,' and how "one of my dreams clearly pointed up the difference." (Meisel 20). Although Meisel retells the anecdote to demonstrate Jung's Aryan bias, it actually illustrates how pervasive such ideas were in the culture—in 1912, Freud probably accepted them as fully as Jung did. Theories of race memory and the collective unconscious rest on assumptions about the evolutionary progression of the races, with blacks representing the childhood of the species. Jung in *Psychology of the Unconscious* several times refers to "lower races, like the negroes" (26) who are childlike in their minds and souls. Lovecraft's degenerate

---

[18]Further discussions of Lovecraft's racism can be found, among other places, in DeCamp; Lévy; Schweitzer; and Davis. See *SL* 4 and 5, *passim*, for the defenses of Hitler, esp. 29 May, 1933; *SL* 4: 191-200 and 12 June, 1933; *SL* 4: 205-212.

184

cultists, black and white, similarly represent the perverted childhood of the race, the
result of downward evolution.

"'Inbreeding?' Armitage muttered...'Shew them Arthur Machen's Great
God Pan and they'll think it a common Dunwich scandal!'" (*DH* 172). These
words sum up Lovecraft's technique of merging the perceived decline of New
England with fictional horrors from Outside in one of his best-known stories "The
Dunwich Horror" (1928). This story especially owes a debt to the articles from the
late nineteenth century that depicted the abandonment and degeneration of rural
New England.[19] Dunwich might have emerged from the pages of the 1899 *Atlantic*
article "A New England Hill Town" which warns of the consequences of
inbreeding. The "Glenns" of that town, which Hartt calls "Sweet Auburn," after
Goldsmith's deserted village, are so intermarried that their family tree has become a
jungle vine, "here and there quite hideous." According to Hartt, "It is not nice to
have six toes on each foot. It is worse to be hare-lipped. Cross-eyes are none the
less disagreeable ...One of our families is 'muffle-chopped.' Another whole family
is deaf and dumb'" (569). Hartt claims that inbreeding has caused mental decay as
well, but "the clan expects idiots, just as it expects midgets and giants and deaf-
mutes" (570).

Lovecraft's fiction derives from a worldview in which these late-nineteenth-
century articles are accepted as fact. The inhabitants of Dunwich, like those of
Sweet Auburn, are "repellently decadent, having gone far along that path of
retrogression so common in many New England backwaters. They have come to
form a race by themselves, with the well-defined mental and physical stigmata of
degeneracy and in-breeding" (*DH* 157). Their decaying village might have been
inspired by an 1889 article in the *Nation*, describing a derelict town north of
Williamstown, Mass., where "the church was abandoned, the academy dismantled"
and two farmers were the only inhabitants (Nott 406).[20] A traveler visiting
Lovecraft's Dunwich in the 1920s would notice "that most of the houses are
deserted and falling to ruin, and that the broken-steepled church now harbours the
one slovenly mercantile establishment of the hamlet" (156). Lovecraft notes that the

---

[19] See Chapter Six.
[20]Another coincidence is that the "good farm" mentioned in the *Nation* article's title is
said to be located on the "Cold Spring road," a name which also figures in "The Dunwich Horror."

decadence of this region came to public notice when the local draft board could not find soldiers fit for the Great War. It is true that this war brought on a renewed interest in eugenics and the study of in-breeding in the Appalachians and in backwater New England.

Some things about Dunwich and its inhabitants, however, go beyond even the most pessimistic predictions of journalists. Hartt in 1899 had noted with alarm that negroes had moved to Sweet Auburn, and its degenerate population was slowly "turning black" (573). Lavinia, the unmarried mother of the "Dunwich Horror" is an albino with negroid hair. But while the townspeople of Dunwich may assume that Lavinia has committed incest with her father, Wizard Whateley, she has actually had intercourse with Yog-Sothoth, an Outside being more dreadful than the Christian Devil, but apparently sharing the latter's appetite for mortal women. The motifs of incest and intercourse with demons are repeated in "The Thing on the Doorstep" (1933) and "The Shadow Over Innsmouth"; as in the learned witch belief, so in Lovecraft's work women are particularly suited to be vessels of the darker powers. Lovecraft's female characters, however, contrary to Puritan paranoia, are not especially active in seeking the intervention of Outside gods: that role is reserved for male necromancers and cultists.

While the dying town and deserted farmsteads of "The Dunwich Horror" come directly from New England reality, Lovecraft also places stone circles and sacrificial altars on the hilltops, landscape features that no one searching for the origins of Dunwich in the Connecticut River Valley around Wilbraham, Mass. is likely to find.[21] In "The Dunwich Horror," Lovecraft weaves together folklore from different parts of New England. He reported to one correspondent that he had learned from residents of western Massachusetts about a strange belief concerning whippoorwills: "It is vowed that the birds are psychopomps lying in wait for the souls of the dying, and that they time their eerie cries in unison with the sufferer's struggling breath" (158). This folk belief was also found in Rhode Island, according to "Shepherd Tom" Hazard, who calls the bird the "death angel." The

---

[21]There does exist, however, a lovely water tower on a hill overlooking Holyoke that once made me think I had found a Greek Temple. According to Burleson, Lovecraft knew about the stoneworks at Mystery Hill in New Hampshire, which could account for the "sacrificial altars" in "The Dunwich Horror." Lovecraft places Druid circles on hilltops in Vermont in the story "The Whisperer in Darkness" (*DH* 221).

night bird is not only a harbinger of death, but it seems to hasten that death with its ominous cries, though Hazard does not say anything about "counting breaths" while the victim is dying (*Recollections* 138).

At the same time, Lovecraft transforms the legends from eastern Connecticut about the Moodus Noises (related in Chapter Three) to fit their new setting in Dunwich. Lovecraft describes the mysterious hill noises in terms very close to those used to explain real geological phenomena in East Haddam. In "The Dunwich Horror," ". . .legends speak of unhallowed rites and conclaves of the Indians, amidst which they called forbidden shapes of shadow out of the great rounded hills, and made wild orgiastic prayers that were answered by loud crackings and rumblings from the ground below" (157–8). Lovecraft also mentions a "Devil's Hop Yard," in Dunwich, inspired, perhaps, by the witch-haunted site at Chapman's Falls on the Eight Mile River in East Haddam, Connecticut (discussed above in Chapter Three). In "The Dunwich Horror," heroic scholars from Miskatonic University are able to use formulas from the *Necronomicon* to put down the evil that the Whateleys had summoned by using the same text. One wonders why Miskatonic and Harvard retained copies of this blasphemous book in their libraries!

Other dying backwaters of Massachusetts form the settings for "The Shadow Over Innsmouth" and "The Colour Out of Space." The first story derives from Lovecraft's visits to Newburyport, then in severe decline. Like Newburyport, Innsmouth had been

> quite a port before the War of 1812—but all gone to pieces in the last hundred years or so....
> More empty houses than there are people, I guess, and no business to speak of except fishing and lobstering....Once they had quite a few mills, but nothing's left now. ("The Shadow Over Innsmouth," *DH* 306).

"The Colour Out of Space" was inspired by Lovecraft's visits in the 1920s to the countryside in western Massachusetts just before it was flooded to form the Quabbin Reservoir. Lovecraft learned legends of this area from his friend W. Paul Cook, an amateur journalist who lived in nearby Athol. One of the drowned towns was called Greenwich, which may have inspired the name "Dunwich." These towns of the Swift River Valley had been the subject of the 1899 *Atlantic Monthly* articles about "A New England Hill Town" whose inhabitants were apparently undergoing reverse evolution. Newspapers of late nineteenth century often featured stories of murder, prostitution, and incest in these isolated communities, leading the *Athol Transcript* in 1878 to declare that "the state of morals among the residents is ...something revolting" (qtd. in Greene 74). Believing that the hill towns were inhabited by dangerous, immoral throwbacks may have made it easier in the 1920s to justify evicting these monsters and drowning their homes to provide water for Boston's benefit. Some current residents, like activist historian J. R. Greene, feel that the attitudes of Bostonians toward "decadent" rural western Massachusetts have changed very little since the building of the reservoir.

"The Colour Out of Space," Lovecraft's favorite story, owes its chills to the devices of science fiction rather than to those from the medieval Gothic arsenal No human wizards or cultists summoned the horror that devastates the Gardner place: it simply fell from Outer Space in the form of a meteor. Similarly, no human agency defeats the horror: it leaves of its own accord to return to Outer Space, but enough remains behind that the narrator refuses to taste the water from the new reservoir that has drowned the "blasted heath" where the meteor fell.

The story opens with some of Lovecraft's most evocative prose, so admired by his disciples that very similar passages can be found opening their pastiches:

> West of Arkham the hills rise wild, and there are valleys with deep woods that no axe has ever cut....On the gentler slopes there are farms, ancient and rocky, with squat moss-coated cottages brooding eternally over old New England secrets in the lee of great ledges; but these are all vacant now, the wide chimneys crumbling and the shingled sides bulging perilously beneath low gambrel roofs.
> The old folk have gone away.... (*DH* 53).

In this story, the monsters are only suggested rather than shown: they take the form of a color not part of our spectrum. The effects on a New England farm after infestation from the meteor are eerily similar to the effects of atomic radiation—eerie because the story was composed in 1927, before the atomic bomb, and long before the mutations caused by radioactivity became a science fiction cliché. Visitors to the farm notice mutations in the animals and plants, and the luxuriant flora quickly decays into dust: where the meteor has fallen, "The aspect of the whole farm was shocking—greyish withered grass and leaves on the ground, vines falling in brittle wreckage from archaic walls and gables, and great bare trees clawing up at the grey November sky with a studied malevolence …from some subtle change in the tilt of the branches" (68–9). This does sound like a portrait of a post-nuclear world, but the meteor's effects on humans are closer to those found in traditional Gothic horror: "'Sucks an' burns…jest a cloud of colour…feeds on everything livin' an' gits stronger all the time…It's some'at from beyond'" (75). Once again, the blight on New England's rural landscape is not stony soil or better land out West; it is willed by an actively malevolent intelligence "from beyond" our control.

"The Whisperer in Darkness" (1930) combines the science-fictional elements of "The Colour out of Space" with the thorough grounding in local lore of "The Dunwich Horror." As "The Colour out of Space" was inspired by the building of the Quabbin Reservoir, so "The Whisperer in Darkness" finds its point of departure in the "historic and unprecedented Vermont floods of November 3, 1927" (*DH* 209). This story explains the decline of Vermont's isolated hill towns, and the reversion of these "haunted hills" back to forest, as the result of an Outsider race of crab-like starfarers, "whose ultimate source must lie far outside even the Einsteinian space-time continuum" (228) who visit those hills to mine for metal.

6. The Native Vampire Belief

The first fictional appearance of the native New England vampire belief is in "The Shunned House," written in 1924 though published only after Lovecraft's death. He created "The Shunned House" by attaching a wealth of Rhode Island history and superstition to a reputedly haunted house on Benefit Street in Providence.[22] The vampires who suck the lifeblood from the proud old family in "The Shunned House" march straight from Rhode Island history into symbolic life.

---

[22]There is some disagreement both over which house this is and what actual legends were attached to it. Beckwith says that Lovecraft's Shunned House is 133 Benefit and "it is not haunted. There is nothing out of the ordinary--nor was there ever--buried in the basement" (48). But a typescript by Virginia Doris in the John Hay Library claims that the Shunned House is the Stephen Harris Mansion at #135 Benefit Street; she states that "it is common knowledge that…Lovecraft superimposed the "cellar burial" and the "vampiric ghost" over the Rhode Island STEPHEN HARRIS MANSION, i.e. French couple who didn't make it to North Burial Ground." As documentation, she claims that the Providence Preservation Society in 1964 had folders on "all sorts of ECTOPLASM," including this case. To confuse the issue, Lovecraft refers only to "the Babbitt house" in his letters.

In a letter to his aunt, Lillian Clark, (6 Nov. 1924), Lovecraft describes the circumstances that inspired its composition. On a trip to Elizabeth, New Jersey he saw "a terrible old house…suffocatingly embowered in a tangle of ivy so dense that one cannot but imagine it accursed or corpse-fed. It reminded me of the Babbitt house in Benefit Street …causing me to write a new horror story with its scene in Providence and with the Babbitt house as its basis" (*SL* 1: 357).

Though physical and psychic vampirism and demonic possession are major themes in his other work, "The Shunned House" is Lovecraft's only specific account of the native belief.[23] He knew the anthropologist Stetson's "Animistic Vampire" article and referred to it directly in the short story: "As lately as 1892 an Exeter community exhumed a dead body and ceremoniously burnt its heart in order to prevent certain alleged visitations injurious to the public health and peace" (*AMM* 242). He even creates a character, the maid Ann White, as the mouthpiece for Stetson's account of "Exeter superstition." Because she was born in that part of Rhode Island's South County, she is the only one who recognizes the cause of the deaths in the "Shunned House": "alleging that there must lie buried beneath the house one of those vampires—the dead who retain their bodily form and live on the blood or breath of the living" (245).

The eponymous house is "shunned" because too many people die in it: the haunting does not take conventional forms, but instead, as in the native vampire belief, something like TB, more lingering and wasting, claims the victims.

> These persons were not all cut off suddenly by any one cause; rather did it seem that their vitality was insidiously sapped, so that each one died the sooner from whatever tendency to weakness he may have naturally had. And those who did not die displayed in varying degree a type of anaemia or consumption… (237).

Lovecraft's persona, like Lovecraft himself, is immersed in antiquarian research with his uncle, Dr. Whipple[24]. He learns that for 150 years after its building, no child was born alive in that house, and all its adult occupants either go mad or waste

---

[23] In "The Case of Charles Dexter Ward," the newly revived Joseph Curwen must drink blood for three months, leading to "revolting cases of vampirism which the press so sensationally reported" in the 1920s. (177). The implication is that such behavior was not unexpected in Rhode Island.

[24] Named, perhaps, after his grandfather Whipple Phillips.

away. These raw-boned healthy New Englanders become Romantic-looking consumptives: "Mercy Dexter's once robust frame had undergone a sad and curious decay, so that she was now a stooped and pathetic figure with hollow voice and disconcerting pallor" (243). As in the folk vampire beliefs, the victims of this house complain of being choked or having the breath sucked from their body.

The evil, as it turns out, is not a family curse on the hapless builders of the house, but something older. In a manner familiar to us from the Spielberg *Poltergeist* movies, the unfortunate house has been built on a graveyard, and thereby incurs a curse. As in Providence legend, not all the bodies in the family burial ground were moved to the new cemetery. Instead, the Shunned House lies over the grave of a French sorcerer and necromancer, who has contrived to live forever, swollen with the vital substance of his victims. This sorcerer is no pathetic "Mercy Brown" or other innocent victim of an Exeter delusion: this vampire is an active, hellish intelligence. Lovecraft's narrator watches the vampire wholly possess and annihilate his saintly uncle, until "He was at once a devil and a multitude, a charnel-house and a pageant" (258). While the story departs at this point from the folk beliefs, there are some similarities. The victims do not themselves become vampires; instead, the emphasis is on passive possession and the destruction of the possessed. Most of all, the healthy members of the community need to track down a single scapegoat and destroy it to end the infestation. Ann White reminds us that in the native belief, "To destroy a vampire one must, the grandmothers say, exhume it and burn its heart, or at least drive a stake through that organ" (245). Lovecraft's persona updates the method but echoes the intent. When the narrator digs down beneath the cellar, he discovers the infinite size and disgusting form of the vampiric Roulet; he discovers "how big it might have waxed through long ages of life-sucking" (260), and he pours four carboys of acid into the hole, creating toxic fumes and a literal and figurative catharsis for the house and the reader. While the sexual motivation never appears explicitly in the folklore narratives, Lovecraft transmutes the revenant sister or daughter reported in Rhode Island into the type of dangerous outsider more typical of vampire fiction. The sexual threat of such a character may be sublimated in "The Shunned House," but, as is typical of Lovecraft, phallic imagery is unmistakable even though the vampire entity's body part is identified as his "titan *elbow*." When the narrator digs into the cellar of his unconscious, he exposes something "like a mammoth soft blue-white stovepipe doubled in two, its largest part some two feet in diameter." (261). As is usual with Lovecraft's viscous horrors, its texture "was fishy and glassy—a kind of semi-putrid congealed jelly with suggestions of translucency" (260).

"The Shunned House" is somewhat of an anomaly in Lovecraft's *oeuvre* because of its relatively "happy ending." S.T. Joshi noted at the conference commemorating the Centennial of Lovecraft's birth that while the writer had no problem annihilating his fictional composite towns such as Innsmouth and Dunwich, he drew the line at destroying the "real" Providence. In "The Shunned House" and again in "The Haunter of the Dark," the evil powers claim a sacrificial victim, but the city is spared. Also, despite Lovecraft's pessimism about the fate of New England, he retained something of an Eighteenth-Century materialist's optimism about the power of science. He describes his philosophy in many letters as skeptic, materialist: for example, in a letter to Elizabeth Toldridge (4 May 1929), who seems to have accused him of being a member of the "Lost Generation," he responds that his inspiration is much more ancient. He claimed to belong to "the old line of sceptics beginning with the Greek atomists & Epicureans & linked to the present by such figures as Hobbes, Voltaire, Diderot, Hume, & the later groups centreing in Schopenhauer & Nietzsche" (*SL* 2: 335). Throughout his life, he retained a keen interest in relativity and other scientific developments: indeed, works such as "The Dreams in the Witch House" and "The Colour out of Space" are often identified as science fiction. In "The Shunned House," enlightened science defeats the dark forces. Science may be perverted into magic by those who summon the Elder Gods, but uncorrupted investigative scientists may yet undo the harm done by the atavistic wizards. The necromantic vampire must be destroyed because it is an unnatural survival and a danger to the living. It is "an anomaly and an intruder, whose extirpation forms a primary duty with every man not an enemy to the world's life, health, and sanity" (252).

The ending of "The Shunned House" represents another kind of allegory, one less comfortable for the modern reader. As we have seen, Lovecraft longed to cleanse all of New England with a similar acid bath, until only the "Benefit" of the old heritage remained. If only he could purge the decay from New England so that the region could regain its eighteenth-century preeminence. He especially yearned to burn away the "mongrel races" (all non-Aryans) who had colonized Providence: as in Salem and Boston's North End, these immigrant aliens had occupied the oldest houses in the city. By Lovecraft's day, the old houses of Benefit Street had been cut up into slum apartments for immigrants. Just as the vampire superstitions of Exeter represented the decadence of rural New England, the Jews, Negroes, Slavs and Italians of Benefit Street represented the horrifying urban present. His early sketch "The Street," a product of the 1919–20 "Red Scare," presents a Benefit Street haunted by evil anarchists and communists: "It was said that the swart men who dwelt in The Street and congregated in its rotting edifices were the brains of a hideous revolution" (*Dagon* 347). Before their nefarious plans can be carried out, the crumbling tenements collapse upon the terrorists who occupy them. In this case, the shades of Providence's glorious past overcome the decadence of its modern inhabitants, whereas in "The Shunned House" it is the modern scientific vampire hunters who extirpate the evil of its ancient, decaying tenant.

7. Lovecraft's Legacy: The Writers and the Critics

In his last years, after repeated rejections by commercial publishers, Lovecraft became disillusioned with his own weird fiction, and more and more negative about the worth of his contemporaries' writing. The harshest judgments of critics such as Edmund Wilson pale before Lovecraft's self-assessments. As he told one correspondent in 1936, "The *Cthulhu* thing [probably "The Call of Cthulhu"] is rather middling ...but full of cheap and cumbrous touches. Indeed, nothing but the *Colour out of Space* really satisfies me" (10 Nov.; *SL* 5: 348). As he grew older, Lovecraft seemed to realize that his bent for the Gothic might be the result of certain pathologies, and that other forms of literature were worthy of mention. Having grown up on Poe and Dunsany, he came to read and even praise Proust and Faulkner. In 1933, he writes "When I say that I can write nothing but weird fiction, I am not trying to exalt that medium but am merely confessing my own weakness...my slender set of endowments does not enable me to extract a compellingly acute personal sense of interest & drama from the natural phenomena of life" (29 Sept. 1933; *SL* 4: 267). Despite its outré trappings, Lovecraft's is a literature of ideas. Though published in pulp magazines, Lovecraft made few concessions to the medium's demands for one-dimensional heroes, love interest, and unrelenting action. The "natural phenomena" of sex, commerce, and the "active" life play a small role in Lovecraft's weird tales, as they did in the fantastic creations of Clark Ashton Smith, Dunsany, Blackwood, among other authors he admired, as well.

Some of Lovecraft's complaints about his own work are justified: he depends too much upon adjectives—eldritch, monstrous, hideous—to create his single effect of horror. His cosmic interlopers are too often described rather than suggested, thereby reducing unknowable mysteries to tentacled yet amorphous creatures. Lovecraft's prose style, like Poe's, has "too many superlatives and intensitives and ineffables" (H. Levin 133) to suit modern tastes. But his best stories are grounded so firmly in actual New England legends and his own psychological quirks that they are ultimately successful as Gothic fictions. For this reader, as for Winfield Townley Scott, his stories are "the most marvelous escape: dimly lit, unspeakable, moon-shadowed nothingness, fierce-breathing ancientries, corners of horror and glittering roofs of hell that yet were transformed from a region real and near him" (72). Overall, Lovecraft's failings—purple prose, undeveloped characters—are failings of the Gothic mode in literature; his strength—atmosphere evoking the single effect of horror—is that mode's strength.

Lovecraft had remarkably clear ideas on what constituted horror and how to evoke that horror in the reader, though, like Poe, he did not always follow his own philosophy in composition. In his essay on *Supernatural Horror in Literature*, which remains the standard critical survey of this genre nearly seventy years after its composition, he analyzes the continuing appeal of Gothic horror. In his method of evaluation, a story is successful if it provokes at any time primeval emotions in the reader:

> The one test of the really weird is simply this—whether or not there be excited in the reader a profound sense of dread, and of contact with unknown spheres and powers; a subtle attitude of awed listening, as if for the beating of black wings or the scratching of outside shapes and entities on the known universe's utmost rim. (*Supernatural Horror* 16)[25]

---

[25]He was fond of this formulation, having used various versions of it in earlier letters. For example, in a letter to Frank Belknap Long, (8 Nov. 1923), he praises "this force of supernatural wonder--the faint clawing of black unknown universes on the outer rim of space" (*SL* 1: 260).

194

Judging the worth of fiction by its effect on the reader is an approach long dismissed as fallacious, yet for the Gothic it remains a valid one. Criticism of Gothic fiction always comes back to the question of belief, since the narrator's uncertainties reflect those of both reader and writer. Lovecraft's Gothic fictions tend to be effective only in so far as the reader can be convinced to share his fears, to be frightened by his nightmares. Critics who remain unconvinced of his horrors are like skeptics at a magic show, deriding as mental adolescents both the artist and those who are taken in by his tricks.

While Lovecraft's prose, relying on earlier models of narrative and language, exemplifies the conservatism of the Gothic mode, the subjects of his fiction and his letters reflect the concerns of literary modernism. Lovecraft was a paradox: while considering himself an eighteenth-century gentleman, reluctant even to wear the clothing of the twentieth century, his status as life-long Outsider makes him seem an existentialist *avant la lettre*. Only recently have critics, following the lead of S.T. Joshi, begun to consider Lovecraft as part of the mainstream of twentieth-century thought.[26] Attebury notes in *Strategies of Fantasy* that fantasists like Tolkien and E.R. Eddison tend to be left out of the histories of twentieth-century literature because they did not confront the important issues of their time, unlike "the bold experiments of Pound, Eliot, Stein, and Joyce" (37). Yet Lovecraft read and wrestled with these very modernists, his opinion evolving through years of letters from puerile scorn and satire to open admiration. Attebury's "psychic bombshells" that produced the Modernist sensibility all find their echoes in the letters and fictions of Lovecraft: "Freudian psychology, Einsteinian physics, world wars, the Russian Revolution, industrialization, deracination, and a general loss of faith" (37). The last two named, I submit, are the very basis of Lovecraft's art: the art of a materialist Outsider who applied Einstein's new physics to a cosmos stripped of all human significance.

Although all his Gothic tales record encounters with what Varnado calls "the numinous," Lovecraft was not himself a believer in any cult. He dismissed everything from traditional religious faith to Theosophy and psychical research into the "paranormal" as so much superstitious bunkum. Yet because his life and sanity

---

[26]See Joshi, *H. P. Lovecraft and the Decline of the West*.

often seemed to be suspended on a slender thread over the void, he had no difficulty depicting religious and supernatural horror. He objectified his horror of the abyss, of non-existence, into the disgusting material forms, human and non-human, that fill his stories. T.E.D. Klein, a Brown University graduate who began his writing career by imitating Lovecraft, attributes the viscous horrors of Lovecraft's universe to a fear of change, of impermanence. Perhaps, too, the horrors visited upon Lovecraft's narrators (and upon the unsuspecting world) reflect his fear of personal dissolution: of insanity and of death, the ultimate change.

Lovecraft suffered several crises in youth and adolescence that resulted in mental and physical breakdowns. His mother insisted that he was delicate, a Victorian invalid too sensitive for the twentieth century. At times he resisted this self-image; indeed, his friends report that Lovecraft could outwalk the most athletic among them. Yet from the age of thirty onwards, Lovecraft referred to himself as an "aged gentleman," and signed himself "grandfather" in letters to friends who were only a few years younger. Lovecraft's consciousness in the present time was forever just on the edge of dissolving, either back into the unknown past, or out of the physical universe altogether. Even so, though he refers again and again in letters to plans for suicide when he can no longer live like a gentleman, carrying out that project was always postponed indefinitely. Instead he struggled to live on less and less money, as genteel poverty gradually became abject. Though he was prey to the most horrendous nightmares and waking anxieties, he clung tenaciously to life and consciousness. In the face of disorder within and without, he sought for knowledge and beauty; against dissolution and decline, he set up art.

Even more dramatically than was the case with Poe and Melville, Lovecraft's reputation has increased in estimation since his death: at first thanks to the work of August Derleth and the other members of the "Lovecraft Circle" of correspondents, and in the past decade because of the "new Lovecraft circle," especially the indefatigable S.T. Joshi. Joshi's survey of *H.P. Lovecraft and Lovecraft Criticism* lists six hundred and ninety-two secondary sources, "not counting unpublished papers and academic theses" (Schweitzer, "Still Eldritch" 133). Lovecraft's friends have published their memories of him, and scholars have

196

traced down every obscure reference in his stories and letters. [27]   While the tally of specialist criticism devoted to Lovecraft mounts each year, he still cannot be considered a "mainstream" literary figure. Oddly enough, only recently has he been recognized as a vital part of the Gothic tradition in fiction. Few critics of the Gothic surveyed in Chapter Two so much as mention Lovecraft. When they do, they may confuse him with his imitators. Aguirre's *The Closed Space: Horror Literature and Western Symbolism* shows that he has read Spanish translations of Lovecraft, but he seems to believe that the *Necronomicon* is a genuine medieval source. Varnado does treat Lovecraft along with more "mainstream" contributers to the Gothic mode in *Haunted Presence: The Numinous in Gothic Fiction.* Barton Levi St. Armand remains one of the few Americanists to take Lovecraft as seriously as the French critics have, placing him in the tradition of late Romanticism, hermeticism, and local history. Donald R. Burleson's recent *Lovecraft: Disturbing the Universe* applies the methods of deconstruction and other post-structuralist narrative theories to a dozen stories.   In so doing, he identifies three themes: "forbidden knowledge," "denied primacy," (humans were not first or foremost on their own planet), and "unwholesome survivals" (156–7), that can also be seen as growing out of Lovecraft's New England heritage, demonstrating the continuity of the Gothic from the Puritans into the twentieth century.[28]

Robert Bloch, the creator of "Psycho," as a teenager was part of Lovecraft's circle of correspondents. He claims, in the introduction to *The Dunwich Horror*, that "Lovecraft may well have had more influence on other writers than any contemporary except Ernest Hemingway" (xviii). The parallel is a good one: like Hemingway's, Lovecraft's influence extended beyond his friends and his own generation. Hemingway can be seen as the ancestor of American mainstream and detective fiction, depending upon whether we trace the line of descent through Raymond Carver or Raymond Chandler. Similarly, Lovecraft can be called the progenitor of American science fiction and horror. His influence has not been

---

[27]For example, see Joshi "Autobiography in Lovecraft" and *H.P. Lovecraft: Four Decades of Criticism.* The phenomenon is also discussed in Schweitzer, "Still Eldritch" 140-141 and *Dream Quest* 59-61.

[28]Much excellent criticism of Lovecraft is still available only from the small presses, just as the authoritative editions of the texts are published only by Arkham House, the small press founded by Derleth and Wandrei. Rhode Island's Necronomicon Press is the source for many critical works and editions of previously unpublished writings of Lovecraft.

limited to acolytes such as August Derleth, who was content to imitate his prose style, evoking the deities and landscapes the master had created. His influence has also extended to writers of New England regionalist horror, such as Stephen King, who may not follow Lovecraft in style or content.[29] Lovecraft's ex-wife Sonia Davis in 1948 wrote a memoir of her ex-husband in which she ventured a judgment that has since been proven correct: "Howard had the mind, taste and personality of a much greater artist and genius than that with which he had been accredited in his lifetime. He will be to the generations of readers yet unborn a legendary and mysterious figure." (21)

During Lovecraft's life he spent more time on correspondence and revising the works of others (sometimes for pay, more often, as in the case of Derleth, Long, Robert Bloch, and others, out of friendship) than he did on his own fiction. No writer could have had more devoted disciples: after the master's death, August Derleth and Donald Wandrei collected and published his stories in hardcover. Derleth labored for years to bring Lovecraft the recognition that the circumstances of his life and personality had denied him. Unfortunately, Derleth also wrote innumerable "posthumous collaborations," inspired by nothing more than phrases from Lovecraft's commonplace book. He published these stories as well; at times, thanks to the vicissitudes of copyright law, Derleth's pastiches have been more widely available than Lovecraft's originals, leading to confusion among critics and readers.

Like Robert Bloch, Stephen King wrote stories in emulation of Lovecraft before finding his own voice. As King notes in *Danse Macabre*, "it is his shadow, so long and gaunt, and his eyes, so dark and puritanical, which overlie almost all of the important horror fiction that has come since" It is not true, as Shreffler claimed in 1977, that "Lovecraft was the last American writer to guide us...on a fearful torch-light tour of witch-haunted New England" (170). On the contrary, it seems he merely began a procession that shows no sign of ending today. As Varnado notes, Lovecraft's careful evocation of his native land has attracted imitators who never lived in those states as well as those who have, "making the New England milieu a kind of stalking ground for modern Gothic writers" (126). Rather than

---

[29]King and other New England regionalists such as Citro, D'Ammassa, and Hautala are discussed in Chapter Eight.

imitating Lovecraft's idiosyncracies of style, his skeptical materialism, or his Tory attitudes, King and a new generation of horror writers have been inspired by Lovecraft's use of New England history and folklore.

Lovecraft's vivid evocation of "unspeakable horrors" in New England has convinced many readers that he, like his artist Pickman, was truly painting what he saw. Since his death, Lovecraft's fiction has taken on a strange objective life of its own. Even in the 1930s, Lovecraft would receive letters from people seeking copies of *The Necronomicon*, or asking how to find Dunwich and Arkham, locales they could not seem to trace on the map of Massachusetts. One would-be sorcerer, Bill Lumley, became a frequent correspondent. Lovecraft's view of these credulous folk is expressed in this humorous letter to Clark Ashton Smith:

> He [Lumley] is firmly convinced that all our gang—you, Two-Gun Bob [Robert E. Howard, the creator of Conan], Sonny Belknap [Frank Belknap Long], Grandpa E'ch-Pi-El [himself], and the rest—are genuine agents of unseen Powers in distributing hints too dark and profound for human conception or comprehension. We may *think* we're writing fiction, and may even (absurd thought!) disbelieve what we write, but at bottom we are telling the truth in spite of ourselves—serving unwitttingly as mouthpieces of Tsathoggua, Crom, Cthulhu, and other pleasant Outside gentry. Indeed—Bill tells me that he has fully identified my Cthulhu and Nyarlathotep...he can tell me more about 'em than I know myself! (3 Oct. 1933; *SL* 4: 271)

Lovecraft repeatedly disclaimed any semblance of belief in the horrors and wonders he so faithfully described in fiction. Like Houdini, for whom he served as ghostwriter, Lovecraft was fascinated by the innate credulousness of most people, but he considered all supernatural beliefs equally absurd. He saw no differences in quality or kind among those who believed in vampires, Santa Claus, or the Christian God.[30]

It is therefore ironic that in the popular imagination of the 1990s, the names Lovecraft and Cthulhu are apparently synonymous with Satanism and demonic possession. The 1990 film *Cthulhu Mansion* (which went directly to video in 1992) claims to be "inspired by the writing of H.P. Lovecraft," but the word

---

[30]Among other places where he expresses this thought, see letter to Emil Petaja (31 May 1935; *SL* 5: 170-173).

"Cthulhu" is the only discernible source for such inspiration. The film spins a traditional Gothic yarn of a menaced heroine and a haunted house, but the wizard's *grimoire* that summons the demons from Hell is titled "Cthulhu." Still, the producers must have felt there was commercial magic in these names, since the box containing the video boasts that it is "From the imagination of H.P. Lovecraft."

Like the sorcerer Lumley in the 1930s, some readers continue to seek the "reality" behind Lovecraft's invented deities. Competing published versions of the imaginary *Necronomicon* have served as sacred texts for genuine cults. Heavy metal bands and role-playing games have broadcast these distorted visions of Lovecraft throughout the adolescent sub-culture. One fanzine, *Lovecraft the Sorcerer*, published for "those special individuals who not only read fantastic literature, but also practice the arcane arts," equates Lovecraft with the Great Beast, Aleister Crowley. The author states that despite Lovecraft's materialism, his fiction provided a conduit for the dark forces to enter this world (Memoli). Such misapprehensions have not gone unchallenged: at the other end of the spectrum are the devotees who commemorated the Centennial of Lovecraft's birth in 1990. Through their efforts, a monument was placed at Brown University's John Hay Library, depository of his manuscripts and letters, in tribute to his life-long love affair with Providence. [31]

Though this chapter has been concerned primarily with Lovecraft's New England horror, he also wrote dream-like narratives of Otherworld quests, inspired by Lord Dunsany, the Irish fantasist. These Dunsanian tales are set beyond the bounds of New England, indeed beyond Earth, yet in the great novella "The Dream-Quest of Unknown Kadath" (1926–27), Lovecraft realizes that even here he is still writing about his home. The rhapsodic praise of New England cityscapes found in many stories arises from his favorite views of old cities at sunset.[32] Lovecraft understood as well as any psychiatrist that his vision of the ideal city, the City of God on Earth, ultimately derived from his earliest memories of childhood

---

[31] At the 1990 Centennial Conference, S.T. Joshi's concluding address defined "this strange and secret brotherhood" who are dedicated to enhancing the master's reputation, all the while secretly wishing they could keep Lovecraft away from the attentions and misinterpretations of both the academy and the average reader (*Proceedings* 80).

[32] See Klein's introduction to *Dagon* xliv-xlv; see also Peter Cannon, "Sunset Terrace Imagery in Lovecraft" in Joshi., *Four Decades of Lovecraft Criticism*.

200

before the fall. In "The Dream-Quest," The Dreamer, Randolph Carter, one of
Lovecraft's favorite personas, has lured the all-powerful Other Gods away from
their thrones to inhabit his personal dream-realm. Carter is told by their emissary
that "your gold and marble city of wonder is only the sum of what you have seen
and loved in youth...These things you saw...when your nurse first wheeled you
out in the springtime, and they will be the last things you will ever see with eyes of
memory and love" (*AMM* 400). Lovecraft often identified the view from the park
at Prospect Terrace westward over the spires and domes of Providence (discussed
above in connection with "The Case of Charles Dexter Ward") as his first epiphany.
As he predicted in "The Dream-Quest," in his last weird tale "The Haunter of the
Dark" (1935), he dramatizes the same sunset vision. His last earthly habitation sat
nearly atop College Hill, on Providence's ancient East Side, restoring to him at the
end of his life the view of the celestial city he had loved forever. Though New
England was sadly fallen, Lovecraft dreamed of finding again the ideal city he had
glimpsed in those sunset visions. Through that ultimately fruitless quest, Lovecraft
produced his most artistically-successful fiction and his most evocative prose.

> These...are your city; for they are yourself. New-England bore
> you, and into your soul she poured a liquid loveliness which cannot
> die. This loveliness, moulded, crystallised, and polished by years
> of memory and dreaming, is your terraced wonder of elusive
> sunsets; and to find that marble parapet with curious urns and carven
> rail, and descend at last those endless balustraded steps to the city of
> broad squares and prismatic fountains, you need only to turn back to
> the thoughts and visions of your wistful boyhood. ("The Dream-
> Quest," *AMM* 401)

Though ever conscious of New England's fall, Lovecraft attempted always to
preserve his memories of an ideal commonwealth, as he strove to preserve the
physical remnants of New England's past. He was a "historic preservationist"
before the concept existed. In letters to the *Providence Journal* in the 1920s, he
protested the destruction of old warehouses on the wharves, even as he lamented
the swarms of foreigners who infested that neighborhood, and even though he
realized that the warehouses, like so many things he loved, were crumbling.

Like Hawthorne, Lovecraft was not well-loved by the town he celebrated;
unlike Hawthorne, he could never bear to leave it permanently. Marred as
Lovecraft's work may have been by the constraints of commercial publication, he

understood New England as few ever have, and for good or ill he shaped a haunted image of the region that will endure. He completed what Melville once credited Hawthorne with beginning: the transformation of New England into a realm where the powers of blackness could find safe haven, if nothing else could.

Chapter Eight
Today's Gothic New England

Please do not come. There are no ghosts, no spirits, and no curse.
--Printed warning to prospective visitors of Dudleytown, Connecticut

In 1948, the *New Yorker* published a short story that confirmed its readers' darkest suspicions about the survival of medieval superstitions in New England. Shirley Jackson's "The Lottery" occasioned more comment than anything previously published by that magazine. Her brief allegory has taken its place next to Hawthorne's "Young Goodman Brown" among the most frequently-anthologized American short stories. Jackson's essay "Biography of a Story" reprints some mail from those first *New Yorker* readers, many of whom seem to have considered "The Lottery" reportage, not allegory. Though Jackson never indicates where "The Lottery" takes place, presumably, the names of the characters, their willingness to follow old customs even when they no longer understand why, and their ability to slaughter innocent scapegoats, then return to daily life as though nothing had happened, made readers assume a New England setting. As Jackson notes, "what they wanted to know was where these lotteries were held, and whether they could go there and watch" (*Come Along* 214). One reader asked "Is there some timeless community existing in New England where human sacrifices are made for the fertility of the crops?" (215). Jackson, living in Vermont at that time, could only wonder at such credulity and insist that "it was just a story I wrote" (212).

204

Twenty-five years later, Connecticut native Thomas Tryon published a novel that answers the "Lottery" reader's question in the affirmative. *Harvest Home* is set in an imaginary Connecticut village, Cornwall Coombe, which has preserved pagan rituals to ensure a bountiful harvest. Outsiders who profane the mysteries are punished, and innocent lives are sacrificed for the well-being of the community. Again, many readers thought the novel was based on fact (adding to the confusion of fact and fancy, there really *is* a village called Cornwall in western Connecticut). For today's readers, apparently, New England is a logical setting for Gothic medievalism, a place where anything *could* happen, because unthinkable, supernatural things once *did* happen there.

1. Medievalism Dark and Light

The two types of medievalism, light and dark, have never been more active in the popular culture and life of New England than they have been in the last decade of the twentieth century. The two species of Gothic superstition identified by Dr. Nathan Drake in 1804, "the terrible and the sportive," while thriving throughout the industrialized world, emerge even more clearly from the microcosm of New England.

The current triumph of the Gothic mode can be seen in the boom in horror fiction and films. The Gothic is as prominent now, when critics have declared the death of the novel, as it once was in the era of the novel's birth. With the phenomenal success of Stephen King, New England has become synonymous with horror in the popular imagination. King is not, however, the only contemporary New England horror writer. Rick Hautala, Joe Citro, and others have added deserted factories to abandoned farms and decadent villages as the appropriate setting for emotions of fear and horror.

Unlike the other novels discussed in this chapter, King's fiction has occasioned a major critical industry. In countless interviews and in his best-selling non-fiction study, *Danse Macabre,* King has analyzed his own work and that of other horror writers.[1] To aid readers in interpreting his nearly transparent prose,

---

[1]For example, see *Danse Macabre* 400-1 for a discussion of how the spectacular trajectory of King's rise to fortune is reflected in *The Stand*; for printed interviews with the other New England horror writers, see Braunbeck; Labbe; McDonald; Wiater.

works ranging from teachers' guides to annotated bibliographies to *The Shape Under the Sheet: The Complete Stephen King Encyclopedia* ($110; 800 pp.)[2] are available. King's name has been linked with the Gothic by several critics (Hoppenstand and Browne; Egan; Magistrale, *Landscape of Fear: Stephen King's American Gothic*), but rarely in this book's sense of nostalgic medievalism. Yet when King juxtaposes the monsters of the earlier Gothic—ghosts, vampires, werewolves—against a relentlessly contemporary setting, he shows the survival of the earlier fears. Indeed, his very popularity demonstrates the potency and continued appeal of supposedly "outmoded superstitions" for an international audience.

King is the quintessential "brand-name" writer, familiar even to non-readers through his appearances in television commercials and movies.[3] King has been called a "post-literate author," apparently because he appeals to those who are not otherwise accustomed to reading. A lifelong New Englander, King's rags-to-riches story has been retold in periodical interviews and in fiction by his lightly-disguised writer-protagonists. He lives in Bangor, Maine, in a Victorian Gothic mansion behind a wrought-iron fence whose gate is adorned with bats and spiders. All his Maine homes, from boyhood to the present, have figured in his books: southern Maine in the invented towns of Castle Rock and Salem's Lot, the western lakes in "The Mist" and *The Dark Half*, and Bangor in *It*.[4] He remains a faithful local colorist, whose portrayals of Maine "characters"—particularly feisty old women— ✓ in such non-supernatural works as "The Reach" and *Dolores Claiborne* put him squarely in the line of descent from Sarah Orne Jewett. His wife Tabitha is also a novelist who loves Maine voices. Her *Caretakers* (1983) and *The Trap* (1985) are both New American Gothic, grotesque though not supernatural. In *The Trap*, a brave woman is raped and tortured by a nightmarish clan who would have felt right

---

[2]See Magistrale, *The Dark Descent*; Winter for extensive bibliographies; Spignesi wrote the encyclopedia.

[3]It is impossible to determine who first tagged King with this epithet which has a double meaning. One interpretation implies that he makes "excessive use of brand names" (R. Harris) in his fiction; on another level, it means that his name has come to symbolize the horror genre. King plays upon the latter meaning in his essay "On Becoming A Brand Name" (1980), reprinted in Underwood and Miller, *Fear Itself* (15-42).

[4]See Winter 177 for more discussion of the "fictional geography" of King's Maine.

206

at home in Faulkner country. Unlike earlier Gothic heroines, Olivia rescues herself and wreaks terrible revenge.

The current generation of New England regionalists in horror would be surprised to hear themselves described as Gothic medievalists. These writers work within the conventions of modern Gothic fiction: threatened families, rather than virginal heroines; haunted houses, cars, hotels, or factories, rather than castles or monasteries; plain serviceable prose, rather than attempts to imitate the style of the Middle Ages or Lovecraft's eighteenth century. The ancient menaces of the Gothic genre, however, remain the same: demonic possession, vampires, shapechangers, spectral ministrations of all kinds.

Like King, these men came of age during the Vietnam War, often as campus activists protesting U.S. involvement. Influenced in their youth by Lovecraft and aided by the publishing success of King, they became professional writers. Mainer Rick Hautala has published ten novels and numerous short stories of New England Gothic. Still another Gothic regionalist is Christopher Fahy, who has also been compared to (and overshadowed by) King. Vermont writer Joe Citro complains that two publishers have emblazoned on his paperbacks' covers "CITRO DOES FOR VERMONT WHAT KING DID FOR MAINE" even though "no one bothered to explain exactly what I had done for—or to—Vermont, or what King did for Maine. All I know for sure is that publishers will go to any length to get King's name on my books" ("The King and I" xii).

The term New England Gothic fits most comfortably on a little-known novel that deserves more readers than its presentation (sensational cover and editor's title, *Blood Beast*) or its publisher (Pinnacle Paperbacks) will ever win it. The author, Don D'Ammassa, a Rhode Island native, is an expert critic of fantasy, science fiction, and horror.[5] Another Rhode Islander, Les Daniels, exemplifies New England Gothic in his life, if not always in his art. A pale and cadaverous-looking man, the very model of his vampire Don Sebastian, he is partial to the indoors, writes after midnight, and shuns the light of day.

The prolific Charles L. Grant, though he lives in New Jersey, graduated from Trinity College in Connecticut and set a sequence of horror novels in a

---

[5]See *D'Ammassa's Guide to Modern Horror* (Borgo 1994) and *The Encyclopedia of Science Fiction* (Prentice-Hall 1994); he had been a long-time reviewer for *Publisher's Weekly* and *Science Fiction Chronicle* before turning to fiction.

mythical New England town, Oxrun Station. Grant has created a "shared world anthology" series about a New England coastal town, in which other writers also set stories. Like Lovecraft's Innsmouth, Greystone Bay is populated by inbred sharers of dreadful secrets.[6]

While King has become known as the writer who domesticated the Gothic strain, he has never claimed to be the first to accomplish this feat. As he told his friend and biographer Douglas E. Winter, California fantasist Richard Matheson deserves the credit. King was inspired by Matheson's *I Am Legend*, a vampire story told with the trappings of science fiction: an after-the-nuclear-holocaust setting, with radiation the cause of the vampire plague. What struck King most was the novel's resolutely ordinary Los Angeles setting, "and I realized then that horror didn't have to happen in a haunted castle; it could happen in the suburbs, on your street, maybe right next door" (qtd. in Winter 20).[7] He also acknowledges the influence of the small town American Gothic settings depicted by Jack Finney and Ray Bradbury (*Danse Macabre* 310–11). The sympathetic characters and appealing settings of King's novels and those of Grant, Hautala and Citro, have attracted readers who are not necessarily connoisseurs of the terrible and numinous, as are Lovecraft's devotees.

King's second novel, *'Salem's Lot*, brought European Gothic horror home to New England. His vampire mythology is strictly from Transylvania—the book is admittedly modeled on *Dracula*—probably because at the time of its composition (1973), King was not familiar with the native vampire belief. Even so, the tale owes its power not to ancient European vampire myths, but to the verisimilitude of the down-Maine setting. King told Winter that a chance conversation about vampires invading the Watergate-era United States was the genesis of *Salem's Lot*.

> There are so many small towns in Maine, towns which remain so isolated that almost anything could happen there. People could drop out of sight, disappear, perhaps even come back as the living

---

[6]*Greystone Bay*; *Doom City*; *The SeaHarp Hotel* form the "Chronicles of Greystone Bay" so far.

[7]Matheson, a life-long Californian, has contributed to the field of New England Gothic the genuinely horrifying novel *Hell House* (1971). Like Jackson's *The Haunting of Hill House*, Matheson's novel documents a psychic investigation of what he calls "the Mt. Everest of haunted houses." Hell House sits in a mist-shrouded valley in Maine, but its horrors do not derive from local folklore.

dead.... I could create a fictional town with enough prosaic reality
about it to offset the comic-book menace of a bunch of vampires.
(qtd. in Winter 41).

In the prologue, a fictitious newspaper article compares Jerusalem's ['Salem's] Lot
to genuine New England ghost towns that have been abandoned for economic
reasons, adding verisimilitude to the fantastic narrative (xiv–xv). The town's
heroic schoolteacher, Matt Burke, identifies the real evil that has come to Maine.
Others in town are slower to believe: "One was taught that such things could not be;
that things like Coleridge's 'Christabel' or Bram Stoker's evil fairy tale were only
the warp and woof of fantasy" (*'Salem's Lot* 164). The novel's unbelievers are
punished with living death.

The town of 'Salem's Lot is based on King's boyhood home of Durham,
Maine, and the original of the haunted Marsten House which becomes the abode of
the King Vampire was "a decrepit manse on the Deep Cut Road" (*Danse Macabre*
264). King's alter ego returns to 'Salem's Lot to write about the Marsten House,
which has haunted him since boyhood "like some kind of dark idol." Like his
creator, Mears is fascinated with small Maine towns, where he finds "indifference
spiced with an occasional vapid evil—or worse, a conscious one" (*'Salem's Lot*
119).

The novel had its remoter origin in a short story "Jerusalem's Lot."[8] This
typical piece of apprentice work, written as a course requirement in 1967 at the
University of Maine, is a pure Lovecraft pastiche, using all the props and actors of
Derleth's "Cthulhu Mythos." The overwrought Lovecraftian prose of "Jerusalem's
Lot" is quite different from King's more familiar "plain style:" In *'Salem's Lot*,
written only six years later, King had found his own voice: powerful, colloquial,
fond of italics.

Vampires are notoriously difficult creatures to finish off for good. King
returned to 'Salem's Lot in a 1977 short story "One for the Road,"[9] where it is
evident that, though the town burned to the ground, things are not yet quiet in that
part of Maine. Child vampires prey upon motorists unlucky enough to lose their
way in the vicinity of the doomed town. Both Stephen and Tabitha King have

[8]Repr. in *Night Shift* 1–34.
[9]Repr. in *Night Shift* 297–312.

considered further sequels to *'Salem's Lot* (Winter 192), though Stephen King has in the past few years moved away from the conventions of supernatural horror and toward more human manifestations of evil such as wife-beating and incest.

When Rhode Islander Les Daniels turned from writing criticism to horror fiction, he created a traditional Gothic vampire, saying that he did not want to be perceived as imitating Lovecraft by employing the New England vampire belief. Despite his extensive knowledge of local folklore, he is more interested in other places and historical periods. His vampire Don Sebastian is an unreconstructed bloodsucker, not a kinder, gentler New Age man like those of Chelsea Quinn Yarbro and Anne Rice, whose Gothic creations have enjoyed wider readership.

Dark medievalism in New England literature is not confined to these heirs of Lovecraft, writing in the horror genre. Writers who may never have heard of or read Lovecraft have set haunted house or supernatural suspense stories in New England. The grotesque strain of the Gothic is also native to New England. Among these "mainstream Gothic" writers can be counted Shirley Jackson, Thomas Tryon, Howard Frank Mosher, and John Updike.

Thomas Tryon's *Harvest Home* represents a literal medieval revival. The settlers of his rural Connecticut community, he says, were from Cornwall, known for the preservation of ancient mysteries. Like Morton of Merry Mount, their leaders quickly assimilated Indian practices to the pagan customs they brought with them: corn dollies, horn dances, the Maypole. As one of Tryon's characters says, "The church and the law have learned it's a lost cause trying to censure such beliefs. How can you hope to fight them, when it's proved that the old Cornishmen arrived here with the same gods the Indians already had?" (*Harvest Home* 164–5).

Tryon's first novel, *The Other* (1971), had marked his transition from a successful film actor to a popular novelist. This exploration of the psychological or "explained" Gothic is set in the composite town of Pequot Landing, which has elements of Windsor and Farmington, Connecticut. It is a tale of the double, the other of the title. Too, it is nostalgic for a time lost; in proper Gothic fashion, it narrates the fall of the local aristocracy, "Granddaddy Perry and his father before him having been known thereabouts as the Onion King" (16). Also typical of the Gothic mode, the narrator's fall is mirrored by the fall of the good place, the Connecticut Valley's very real descent into suburban banality:

> It's gone now, they tell me. All of it, gone.... demolished and replaced by a newer, larger building. There is a television antenna on the roof. The bogs have been drained, the meadows subdivided into tracts, and where we used to wade the brooks, streets are now laid out, with light poles, sidewalks, chainlink fences, and two-car garages. Of what was, nothing is left. (15–16)

Shirley Jackson, a long-time resident of Bennington, Vermont, remains the greatest stylist of New England Gothic, though she did not draw explicitly upon local folklore. Her works encompass both the "explained" Gothic of the grotesque in *We Have Always Lived in the Castle*, as well as the classic ghost story *The Haunting of Hill House*, which never rationalizes the malignancy of its supernatural threat. Set in the decadent backwoods village of Hilldale, Hill House blights the lives of all connected with it. With its "Gothic spires and gargoyles" (32), its angles and measurements that are all "slightly wrong" (105), Hill House haunts the psychic researchers who attempt to study it as well as those who dare to read about it. Jackson's novels, along with "The Lottery," meet the primary criterion for excellence in Gothic fiction: they are as horrifying to each new generation of readers as they were at the time of their composition.

The New England regionalist Howard Frank Mosher has worked a broad vein of the Gothic into novels that are not usually classified as fantasy or horror. In *A Stranger in the Kingdom* (1989), which has often been compared to *To Kill a Mockingbird*, Mosher's attitude, expressed through the Atticus Finch figure of the novel, is very much like that of Canadian Gothic novelist Robertson Davies, amused and ironic, but accepting of a world of wonders. Ruth, the saintly mother of the story, makes Harvest Figures:

> ...a roly-poly old farmer in overalls and a battered straw hat, sitting in a chair and watching his wife toiling over my grandfather James' wooden cider press. In the farmer's crooked arm was a half-full glass gallon of hard cider, and carved on his pumpkin face was an obviously tipsy smile, while Mrs. Pumpkin-head looked on with pursed lips. On a cardboard placard around the straw woman's neck my mother had carefully stenciled the words NEW ENGLAND GOTHIC. (*A Stranger* 100)

These harvest figures are ironic and amusing rather than sinister, seemingly derived more from Grant Wood's painting *American Gothic* than from medieval horror. In Mosher's picture, the straw man is tipsy, a Vermont Bacchus, and the wife is disapproving, a straw Puritan. Yet the straw dummies that can be found propped on porches throughout New England may be descendants of the harvest sacrifice, a real example of the survival of pagan beliefs in isolated rural backwaters which was carried to such an extreme in Tryon's *Harvest Home.*

Disappearances (1977), Mosher's first novel, is hyper-realistic, yet it accepts without irony tall-tale and purely magical happenings. The jacket copy, more accurately than most, describes it well: "Part New England gothic, part fantasy, and pure rollicking adventure story." Set in the wilds of Vermont's Northeast Kingdom, *Disappearances* romps through history, especially the uneasy relationship between the United States and Canada, as unerringly as it does through legend. Though the themes may be Faulknerian—hunting as initiation, the lawlessness of an isolated region, the weight of the past—Mosher's style is unforgettably his own.

Mosher concludes that not the least of the title's disappearances is that of his Kingdom County, "gone the way of Melville's Nantucket and Hawthorne's Salem, Thoreau's Concord and Frost's New Hampshire" (217). Childhood ends, we despoil the landscape, all that is beautiful must die, yet such evocations of New England do remain alive through art. When we read this literature, we, too, can understand Mosher's contradictory assertion that "even though it has disappeared, Kingdom County is still a place of wonders" (217).

The wonders of the invisible world continue to attract the attention of New Englanders in varied ways. Like the long-ago colonists of Merry Mount, New Englanders can now be found celebrating the rites of spring by dancing around Maypoles. Morris Dance teams revive on New England soil the ancient English rituals of luck, propitiation, and good ale. With no official sponsorship or publicity, dawn on May Day in Cambridge, Massachusetts finds Morris teams leading hundreds of dancers around a maypole erected on the banks of the Charles River, close by the spot where the Mathers once burned forbidden books.

Paganism is thriving in New England, with large gatherings at Beltane, Midsummer, and other sacred seasons. Covens exist throughout the region, not only in Salem. One New Hampshire witch says she has heard estimates of 45,000 witches in her state alone, where a country witch running a Cub Scout troop was asked not to wear her pentagram: she promptly complained of religious discrimination.

Neo-Pagans believe that their practices are not modern inventions but continuations of ancient traditions or re-creations derived from the collective unconscious memory. Their worldview is that of a truly "marginalized" folk, persecuted by the monotheistic faiths and effaced from the official histories of the past. Most Neo-Pagans in New England, however, do not claim a family tradition of the craft, but rather will admit that they came to their new faith through the ecology movement, feminism, playing Dungeons and Dragons, and, above all, reading novels of horror and fantasy. Like the practitioners of "Fantastic Archaeology" described in Chapter Three, the New England Neo-Pagans share a fascination with Indian shamanism, Celts, and Vikings. Most are also writers or fans of neo-medievalist fantasy; many are members of the Society for Creative Anachronism, yet another medievalist sub-culture.

Thanks to this medieval re-enactment organization, longbowmen and crossbowmen can be found at archery ranges, and costumed knights and damsels enjoying tournaments on the greensward are common sights of the New England summer. Nor is this sort of active medievalism limited to students of that era. Renaissance fairs have become a profitable business, and the general public flocks to highly inauthentic medieval feasts sponsored by commercial enterprises such as Boston's Medieval Manor.

The "sportive" or "light" side of the Gothic revival, as in the nineteenth century, encompasses nostalgia for whatever parts of the Middle Ages are most congenial to the spirit of the reader or writer. In addition to the horror writers discussed above, New England is home to fantasists who are, like the earliest visitors to the region, more interested in the landscapes and fantastic literature of the old world than in the reality of the new one. One writing group of women, living in and around Cambridge, Massachusetts and meeting for over five years, specializes in the neo-medieval and historical fantasy sub-genres, though members also write poetry and other types of fiction. One of its members, Delia Sherman, has been particularly influenced by New England landscapes and legends of the sea. Sherman's short stories blend weird legends from the English and Scottish ballads with the folklore and history of maritime New England. "The Maid on the Shore" and "Miss Carstairs and the Merman" are among the few recent works of fiction to draw upon the legends of merfolk in the coastal waters of New England and Atlantic Canadian (described above in Chapter Three). Her haunting "Land's End" was inspired by a painting by Steve Gervais, a Rhode Island artist of the fantastic, in which, as she writes "Figureheads, dripping seaweed...clustered around the lantern like wingless and awkward moths, yearning toward the light" (156–7). The hapless lighthousekeeper in this story violates a well-known taboo: he kills an albatross, occasioning the visitation by the figureheads of ghost ships.

Many fantasy writers besides the Cambridge group make their homes in New England; some are more influenced by that place of residence than others. Esther Friesner, a prolific Connecticut fantasist, used Columbus's sighting of "sirens" recorded in his journal as the point of departure for her *Yesterday We Saw Mermaids*. Connecticut native Paul Hazel works a different vein of the Gothic, writing a dark fantasy inspired more by Poe's prose-poem "Silence" than by "The Masque of the Red Death." *Winterking* and *The Wealdwife's Tale* take place in an alternative version of his home state, where Cornwallis never surrendered and magic persists. Madeleine L'Engle, a Christian fantasist known for her young adult novels, lives in Goshen in the Northwestern corner of Connecticut. There, at her farmhouse Crosswicks, she has set *A Swiftly Tilting Planet* and *An Acceptable Time*, tales of fantastic archaeology, of Celtic-Indian contact and the legend of Prince Madoc's journey to the New World.

2. The Persistence of Belief: Sea Monsters, Witchcraft, Indian Curses

The Gothic in New England today commands a varied audience, ranging from jaded film-goers seeking visceral thrills to true believers worshiping Lovecraft's Elder Gods, dancing around Maypoles, or attempting to exorcise haunted real estate. The latter group may even outnumber the former. Like vampires, old beliefs may go underground, only to be bodied forth in new shapes that cling, tenaciously, to imaginative life. The constellation of beliefs referred to as "New Age" are in reality ancient. So popular have they become in their modern guise that the forbidden arts of divination practiced in the past by shamans, priests, and sorcerers can be tapped (for a fee) simply by attending a "psychic fair" or by calling a 900 number to dial-a-psychic. Fortune-telling, condemned by Hale and the Mathers because it led to other types of diabolism, is now legal in Connecticut, which in 1993 repealed its statute forbidding the advertising or practice of paranormal arts (Yim).

The nineteenth-century crowds who flocked to Massachusetts beaches to marvel at the sea serpent have their present-day equivalents in the summer hordes of whale-watchers. In New England mythology, the whale has evolved from fabulous beast to nemesis and object of commercial interest to, at last, awesome friend in need of protection. Yet the older iconography persists. While nearly a million passengers go on whale-watching expeditions each year, anyone who thinks that all fear of whales has vanished has never been on board one of these fragile vessels when a leviathan chooses—for whatever unknown reason—to dive underneath. The human tendency to transfer interest and symbolism to a new object while retaining the older significance and menace is evident as well in the dinosaur mania that has raged for more than a century. So determined are we to see the ancient beasts as dragons that films always show dinosaurs threatening helpless women and children, though any ten-year-old in the audience knows this is anachronistic.

Fascination with the deeps has led to whale-worship, while dread has focused on Great White Sharks. In addition, belief in the older version of the sea monster is thriving in present-day New England. Based on the observations of monster-hunter Joseph Zarzynski, Vermont novelist Joseph Citro theorizes that the Champlain Lake Monster is a cousin to the Loch Ness monster, both having been landlocked in deep glacial lakes, on the analogy with landlocked salmon (*Dark Twilight* 74; 211). Two other large glacial lakes in Vermont, Memphremagog and Willoughby, have legends of similar serpents. The International Dracontology Society of Lake Memphremagog calls its monster "Memphré." Lake Willoughby, which closely resembles a Scottish Highland loch, prefers not to publicize the existence of its serpent. Local historian Harriet Fisher reprints an account from an 1868 newspaper reporting the demise of "the great water snake at Willoughby Lake," the victim of a brave twelve-year old. It was supposed to have been 23 feet long. Perhaps this was a juvenile lake monster? Despite the reluctance to capitalize on its existence, there have been recent sightings of a large many-humped creature (Fisher 17).

In Citro's novel *Dark Twilight*, the Champlain Lake Monster is assumed to be real. The protagonist moves to Friar's Island, based on the Hero Islands in that lake, to prove the authenticity of the lake serpent. Citro's detailed history of the monster, including the 1980s photograph and video, shows how attitudes changed from dread to welcome as the monster began to be perceived as a tourist attraction:

> With this first photopgraphic evidence, the monster had come out of the closet. People began to talk about it openly, without fear of ridicule ...Someone nicknamed it 'Champ.' ...It was cute. It was E.T.
> It had become a friend! (44)

Not everyone in the novel thinks the monster is cute. This sighting of the beast resembles the account of the species given by Olaus Magnus in 1555, as a night fisherman hooks into an unpleasant surprise:

> '...this black, pointy head comes right up out of the water! The head and neck is kind of juttin' out on an angle, like the blade of a jackknife openin' up.
> 'I can see the water drippin' off it as it comes higher and higher out of the lake.... It's all black, don't ya know, and shiny...
> 'And in the moonlight I can see Cliff's nightcrawler, all white and puffy lookin', hangin' out of its mouth, and the monofil'ment line, like a strand of silver thread, trailin' off into the lake.
> 'There must of been six feet of head and neck juttin' out of the water, and I'll tell you, mister, I wasn't interested in seein' what sort of body that neck was hooked on to! (13)

The ancient fears enshrined by Josselyn and Lovecraft have by no means vanished completely. The fear of finding dragons in the deeps still haunts the shores of lake and sea in New England.

The Neo-Pagans described above deny that their religion has any connection with the Gothic vision of Satanism and necromancy, but theirs remains a minority view. For many twentieth-century New Englanders, Satanism and witchcraft are one, just as the Puritans believed. Incursions from the "Invisible World" through showers of stones and demonic possession seem to be as much of a preoccupation in the late twentieth century as in the seventeenth. Connecticut's resident exorcists Ed and Lorraine Warren believe that New England is a particular nexus of such preternatural events because of its long and tragic history. Ed Warren began his career as a ghost-hunter, but his experiences with the Invisible World convinced him of the reality of demonic possession. He now identifies himself as a demonologist. He believes that the psychic phenomena associated with haunted houses are caused by demonic forces, and that those who seek out such phenomena solely for thrills place themselves in danger of possession. Through lectures, books, and movies based on those books, Warren's views of demonic threat have become well-known in New England. He notes with some alarm the growing interest in the malign aspects of the supernatural, "devils, demons, wood ghosts, imps," rather than in benevolent saints or angels. Adults and children, he notes, love to be frightened; after all, even non-believers are attracted to the mystical and dangerous. Why? "Why do people stop at an accident?"[10]

With Lorraine acting as a medium, the Warrens investigate cases of haunting and possession, and either refer them to religious authorities or perform exorcisms themselves. Ed Warren's expert testimony in a 1990 lawsuit in Rockville, Connecticut helped establish the right of tenants to vacate haunted houses. Warren was consulted but not allowed to testify in the infamous "demon murder case." In 1981, Arne Johnson was tried for murdering his landlord in Brookfield, Connecticut; the Warrens believe that Johnson was possessed by demonic forces at the time. The judge, however, disallowed such a defense plea that came down to "the Devil made me do it" and refused to hear any spectral evidence. [11] Just as the horrors of Salem seem to have been triggered by adolescent girls who dabbled in fortune-telling, so most of the Warrens' cases stem from adolescents playing with the ouija board and summoning forces they had not expected. Warren warns that such practices can easily lead to demonic possession.

---

[10]I thank Ed Warren for his cooperation with me in a telephone interview, 14 July 1993. Though his publications are not scholarly treatises, they reflect personal experience and deeply-held beliefs. The Warrens' notoriety, in turn, may have increased the number of reported cases of hauntings and demonic possession in Connecticut.

[11] For the Warrens' account of that trial see Brittle, *The Devil in Connecticut*. Horror and suspense writer John Farris, often cited by Stephen King as one of his favorites, wrote *Son of the Endless Night* based on the Demon Murder Case as well as Connecticut's earlier "Yale/Scarsdale" murder. In Farris's version, the judge, rather than refusing to hear the possession defense, allows it. The Devil then enchants the courtroom.

"Amateur spiritualism," he says, "is tampering with something extremely dangerous." In their condemnation of divination and seances as demonic, the Warrens show themselves to be true descendants of seveneteenth-century divines such as Perkins, the Mathers, and John Hale .

While films such as *Rosemary's Baby* and *Hocus Pocus* reflect the popular view of witchcraft as demonic pact, John Updike's treatment of witchcraft in *The Witches of Eastwick* has reaffirmed the Satanic conspiracy theory of the Warrens in the minds of a more literate audience. Updike's novel may be set in Rhode Island—significantly not the site of any real witch trials—but his witches do not feel native to New England soil. Updike knows his Puritans better than this: he has twice rewritten *The Scarlet Letter,* once to give modern readers *Roger's Version* and once, in *S.,* to redress the balance and tell Hester's side of the story. Yet in *The Witches of Eastwick,* there is no punishment for sin, and the paranoia that once possessed whole towns is reduced to mild curiosity and gossip. In this novel, Updike writes of a suburbanized New England, one without threatening forests or decaying cities. Its setting is the prosperous Rhode Island coast, not the backwaters only a few miles away where the vampire belief so long held sway. Still, he provides a fine distillation of the state's weird atmosphere, a kind of bookend for Lovecraft's similar observations:

> 'The fag end of creation' and 'the sewer of New England,' Cotton Mather called the region. Never meant to be a separate polity, settled by outcasts like the bewitching, soon-to-die Anne Hutchinson, this land holds manifold warps and wrinkles ...Refuge of Quakers and antinomians, ...it is run by Catholics, whose ruddy Victorian churches loom like freighters in the sea of bastard architecture. There is a kind of metallic green stain, bitten deep into Depression-era shingles, that exists nowhere else. (9)

Updike's witches are suburban women whose witch-lore and powers of *malefica* are those confessed by the victims of the European witch-hunts. They participate in the rites of the sabbat and have witch-marks and familiars, yet they are more powerful than the novel's devil figure, Van Horne, a pathetic suburban devil, whose powers are limited and whose estate is fallen. Though the witches are able to curse and even kill, they are not denounced or persecuted by their community. Instead, they are rewarded with their heart's desires (devoted or wealthy husbands,

218

escape from Rhode Island), and their deeds occasion only a kind of "embarrassment and unease" in the collective memory (210).

New Englander Greer Ilene Gilman, a member of the Cambridge writing group, in her neo-medieval fantasy novel *Moonwise* (1991) presents witches who seem as far removed from those of the New England witch belief, learned or popular, as the sun is from the moon. They are certainly not suburban witches: they may temporarily abide in the twentieth century, but in essence they hold apart from it, for as her protagonist Ariane learns, "she was the witch, the other" (369). Though her witches may differ in every detail from those feared by learned Puritans, she comes closer to capturing the awe and terror with which the seventeenth-century viewed witchcraft than anyone since Hawthorne.

It may seem strange that the current generation of male horror writers has not treated the New England witch belief at any length. Fear of witches apparently does not have a strong hold on their imaginations. Still, as we have seen, old beliefs can reappear in new guises. Stephen King's *Carrie* and *Firestarter* can be read as twentieth-century versions of the witch belief. Instead of being called witches or victims of demonic possession, these young women are described in terms of parapsychology. They wield the powers of telepathy, psychokinesis, and pyrokinesis—ancient "wild talents" re-inscribed into the language of modern science.

The theme of the witch's curse surviving for generations, explored by Hawthorne and Lovecraft, appears in Hautala's work as well. In addition to studying folklore and mythology in college, Hautala, growing up in Rockport, was always strongly aware of nearby Salem and its history of witchcraft. In *Dark Silence* (whose epigraph is from *The House of the Seven Gables*) the sawmill is haunted because it is built on the site where a witch was hanged in 1694. Because she was denounced by those who coveted her lands, as happened in the Salem outbreak, her curse falls upon anyone not a direct descendant in the female line who acquires or subdivides her property. She declares that "'None of ye shall escape the cleansing fire of the Lord's judgment!'" (14), thus setting the novel's events in motion.

Modern-day witchcraft and necromancy are the subject of Hautala's *Dead Voices*, not New Age nature worshippers, but an actively evil wizard. The novel juxtaposes the psychiatric and the occult visions of how to deal with loss and guilt.

With its corrupt therapist, in *Dead Voices* the "talking cure" becomes just another variation on necromancy, along with ouija boards, traditional spiritualist seances, tape-recording the dead through "electronic voice phenomenon," and, of course, reanimating the dead through traditional unhallowed rites. As the protagonist works through all these methods of contacting her dead child, we are drawn to believe her madly logical rationalizations. The climactic scene of graveyard necromancy is a most credible evocation of physical horror—perhaps because Hautala harks back to Icelandic models. Just as in *Grettir's Saga*, the revenants are physically powerful as well as nauseating: the reanimator must wrestle with the reanimated demon before it will speak. These myths of Northern Europe seem perfectly at home in the Maine setting.

The ultimate study of necromancy in modern horror fiction, however, is Stephen King's *Pet Sematary*. *Pet·Sematary* has echoes of Faust as well as Frankenstein, with its doctor hero, though the machinery of its plot is derived, according to King, from "The Monkey's Paw." Unlike *Faust* or *Frankenstein*, everyone in King's novel is sympathetic or even heroic. There are no villains and for the protagonist, Dr. Louis Creed, the road into Hell is paved with only the noblest intentions. Unlike traditional necromancers, who resurrected the dead to foretell the future and to gain power over the living, this novel's heroes only want to reanimate those they love best, the untimely dead. But as King's prologue states, "Death is a mystery," and those who meddle with it court terrible punishment. Despite its jocular, colloquial tone, *Pet Sematary* embodies a morality as rigid as any Puritan sermon on the day of doom. We cannot escape the consequences of our mortality or our actions, for, as Creed discovers, *"What you buy is what you own, and sooner or later what you own will come back to you"* (374; original italics).

Like the monsters in the deep waters, transmuted into icons of ecological good, the forest devils so dreaded by some Puritans have become heroes of a New Age. Popular sentiment in the 1990s is usually on the Indians' side. In Connecticut, the Mashantucket Pequots, supposed to have been wiped from the earth in the Pequot War of 1637, have endured and triumphed. Though Moby Dick sank Melville's Pequod (a name he chose because he believed that the tribe was already extinct), nothing seems capable of sinking the fortunes of today's Mashantuckets. The gambling casino Foxwoods on the Mashantucket Pequot reservation in Southeastern Connecticut has brought great wealth to the tribe and to the region, where it has replaced the declining defense industry as a major employer.[12] Other New England tribes may also open casinos; among them are the Narragansetts and the Mohegans, who in 1994 received federal recognition as a nation. Frequent powwows revive the very rites once excoriated by the Puritans, attracting large numbers of non-Indian tourists.

Still, as with the great whales, the dread of Indians has not entirely vanished from the minds of those who inherited their land. We can see it most commonly in fears of a curse falling upon those who desecrate Indian burial grounds. Movies such as *Poltergeist* and *The Amityville Horror* have popularized the theory that curses and hauntings inevitably result for those who disturb Indian sacred spaces, even unwittingly. Here, life and art come together, for Native Americans *are* demanding restitution for the destruction of sacred places and the wholesale removal of their ancestors' skulls in the name of now-discredited archaeological theories. Faced with these outcries, institutions such as the Smithsonian are returning skeletons and artifacts for re-burial.

In this new light, New England's entire history can seem like one long desecration of Indian sacred space. One of the first acts of the Pilgrims after landing was the excavation of Indian graves, as recorded in *Mourt's Relation*. According to the narrator, the motive was not sacrilege or archaeology, but survival: the exploring party was looking for buried caches of corn, for, the author claims "we digged in sundry like places, but found no more corn, nor any thing else but graves" (28). Nevertheless, they explored the sites with an ethnologist's fascination, and had no qualms about removing any treasures they found: "we brought sundry of the prettiest things away with us, and covered the corpse up again" (28). Most shocking to modern sensibilities, the narrator understood that the Pilgrims' acts would be construed as offensive by the native people: he says that "we thought it would be odious unto them to ransack their sepulchres" (21). Yet

---

[12]As this book goes to press, the Mashantuckets are considering extending their good fortune to the city of Norwich, located a few miles from their reservation. In a reversal worthy of Greek tragedy, the city founded by John Mason, conqueror of the Pequots in 1637, today looks to that tribe as the only hope of reviving Norwich's "faded glory" (Blechman A1).

the ransacking continued unabated, as European settlers moved onto land recently emptied by plagues, into villages where corpses lay unburied, so sudden and devastating was the onset of the disease. Later on, in the nineteenth century, the excavation of a chieftain's grave containing some copper plates lent support to the theories of early European contact, whether with Vikings, Celts, or Phoenicians. The science of archaeology in New England grew out of robbing Indian graves. Today, houses must cover many ancient sacred places. If the burial ground curse theory should prove true, which of us would 'scape cursing?

In modern horror novel and movies, Indian spirits who take revenge for defiled burial grounds have become a cliché. The phrase "Sacred Micmac Burial Ground" has penetrated the national consciousness through the movie version of *Pet Sematary* and its sequel. Perhaps because the Maine Indian tribes survived in greater numbers and hung on to their traditional ways longer than those in southern New England, Maine horror writers have used Indian myths more frequently in their writings than did Lovecraft. King claims to have heard Maine Indian legends from his dowsing, story-telling Uncle Clayt (*Danse Macabre* 87). In *Pet Sematary*, the necromantic horrors are explained by reference to the legend of the Wendigo, which embodies the chilling and unsentimental side of Indians' presumed oneness with Nature. King calls it "the Wendigo, creature of the north country, the dead thing whose touch awakens unspeakable appetites" (363). The novel's title refers to the childish spelling of a real place near Orono that King transforms into the anteroom to a more dreadful burial ground, haunted by the Wendigo and shunned by the Micmacs who first created it, where those who are buried are resurrected to unholy life. The misguided souls who transgress the boundaries of life and death are visited by their re-animated loved ones, turned into monsters. "Maybe it was a zombie or a *dybbuk* or a demon. Maybe there's no name for such a thing as that, but the Micmacs would have known what it was, name or no.. . .Something that had been touched by the Wendigo" (245).

While King's Indian lore sounds authentic, it is not. According to Winter, King's Wendigo derived from Cree mythology rather than from Maine folklore (150; 271n). King explains the strangeness of finding a cairn-topped mesa in the Penobscot River valley with this rationalization: "'Micmacs sanded off the top of the hill here,' Jud said. 'No one knows how, no more than anyone knows how the

Mayans built their pyramids. And the Micmacs have forgot themselves, just like the Mayans have'" (*Pet Sematary* 115).

Hautala's *Night Stone* features another grave desecration, with similarly awful results. His Micmac Indian Billy Blackshoe explains that the ancient tribe had left behind "guardian spirits" who would avenge the outrage: "'If a tribe thought a piece of land was sacred, they'd protect it—both in this world with warriors, and in the next world with spirits...or maybe the severed hand of a sacrificial victim'" (295). The novel goes beyond clichés, however; in *Night Stone*, the motifs of standing stones, guardian spirits, and severed hands unite European and the Indian elements and lend coherence to the narrative.

Citro's *The Unseen*, set in Vermont's Northeast Kingdom, also draws on Indian lore. He provides a naturalistic explanation for sightings of the Wendigo. Harley Spooner, a former logger, knows all about the "winny-go," (his pronunciation), "any man who wintered in the loggin' camps knows about the winny-go" and feared its power to whisper a man's name and doom him to a cannibal existence. (140–141). Spooner thinks he saw the creature and even shot at it. But the "monsters" of this novel are neither the Wendigo nor Bigfoot (a theory advanced by another character): they are a species even rarer in Vermont—they are African-Americans. A true "Lost Tribe," they are descended from slaves who became separated from their conductors on the Underground Railroad. Hidden in one of Vermont's gores, genuine no-man's lands which resulted from surveyors' mistakes, they have reverted to savagery, a process which recalls Lovecraft's degenerate cults who worship the Old Ones. In Citro's novel, however, once the truth is known, the white characters attempt to preserve rather than eradicate the tribe. They prevent an anthropologist from the University of Vermont from studying their reverse evolution, thereby saving the descendants of slaves from a dreadful fate—life on "a reservation where they could do their bit to advance Vermont's tourist industry" (267).

Rick Hautala's scholarly interest in the American Indian has blended well with his ethnic heritage of Finnish myth and legend. Certainly there are close links between the two shamanistic traditions: Longfellow did not choose idly when he modeled his *Song of Hiawatha* on the meter, form, and content of the *Kalevala*. The myths of Finland seem at home in the pine forests and stone quarries of Maine. In a process that supports Jung's theory of the collective unconscious, Hautala believed he had simply composed Indian myths out of the whole cloth, only to discover that his "compositions" mirror traditions accurately. When he sat down to invent myths "from his imagination" to provide connective tissue for the short stories that comprise the sequence "Untcigahunk" in *Night Visions*, he found that the myths "almost wrote themselves," in traditional oral formulaic style.

The word "Untcigahunk" is Micmac, meaning "Younger Brother." Hautala's invented "Little Brothers" are particularly unpleasant animated killing machines. For their first appearance, in the novel *Little Brothers*, Hautala wanted a backbone of myth to explain cyclical murders coming at five-year intervals. It occurred to him that the Indians would have knowledge of these happenings. He says he does not believe he knew, consciously, that the Micmacs, like other tribes of the Algonkian group, actually *had* legends about such nature beings, almost like elves, somewhere half-way between humans and the Great Spirits.

As we have seen in Chapter Three, these *pukwudgees* were not dainty little fairies; in some Indian legends, they are inimical to gods and humans alike. They are, however, nowhere near as vicious as the monsters Hautala let loose on the Maine countryside. As he explains in his myths of origin, the "Untcigahunk" were the product of a creator working blindly in the dark, producing a dwarfed parody of a human being, with "long dangling arms" and "long curved claws" (*Untcigahunk* 200). Small wonder that the Old One is disappointed: they exist only to devour, like 17-year locusts crossed with sharks. Their single-minded viciousness is explained with a variation of the traditional Trickster myth.

Hautala fits his creation snugly into the Maine landscape, the natural caves and hollows of the hills and riverbanks. One story of the "Untcigahunk" sequence incorporates Indian petroglyphs similar to those found "below the Solon bridge, in the town of Embden" on the Kennebec River (Burleigh 53). According to Burleigh, these petroglyphs were held in "sacred awe" by Indians in her day, though they could no longer translate the symbols carved into the rocks. In another Hautala story, "The Birch Whistle," the "Little Brothers" devour canoeists on the Saco, recalling the legend of the Indian curse on that river discussed in Chapter Three. Hautala also invokes the work of Barry Fell and the mysteries of New Hampshire's Mystery Hill to add verisimilitude to his placement of menhirs and blood sacrifice in southern Maine (*Night Stone* 161; 353). Fell's theories turn up again in the short story "Love on the Rocks," when one archaeology student

224

derides another for reading significance into the rock carvings: "You're starting to sound like that guy ...who says these petroglyphs are ...are Egyptian hieroglyphics or whatever" (*Untcigahunk* 205).

Connecticut's Pequots survive in strange forms in Paul Hazel's *Winterking* (1985). Myths of origin and Indian wars underlie the events of this novel; magic and mystery coexist with the Housatonic's curving course, "as if someone on the dwindling continent had left a message for a god" (297). In this world, Puritan misconceptions about the Indians take on objective life: even after they have been destroyed, the "Pequods" persist in burning churches. Although he is far removed from Hautala in style and intentions, Hazel also draws on the brand of proofs advanced by Goodwin, Fell and the other fantastic archaeologists. In *Winterking*, an obsessed minister proves that "the first Indians, the true Indians, were Welsh" because of the evidence of stones: "Huge upright stones and root cellars.... writing on the bare rock! Not simple pictographs but whole stanzas.... In deep-cut Ogham letters!" (85–86).

The Puritan association of Indians with the dark medievalism of the Gothic is not ended, as a new generation credits the aboriginal inhabitants of New England with mystical knowledge of nature and dominion over the living and the dead. For white New Englanders, Indians remain the Other, unknowable and tied to the supernatural, for good or for ill. Since no one is more superstitious than a gambler, perhaps the Indians' recent association with the fall of the dice and fortune's wheel will spawn a new folklore linking them to the dark powers.

3. Images of The Fall: Economic Decline and Spiritual Malaise

Nowhere is the continuing vision of New England's decline and fall more apparent than in Gothic literature. Just as Faulkner's grotesques, bowed under the weight of history, exemplified Southern poverty in the American imagination, so have Carolyn Chute's Gothic Beans of Egypt, Maine come to stand for New England's rural poor. The heirs to Lovecraft's cosmic visions, however, see a more pervasive decline in a fallen New England where poverty exists not only in pockets but in entire cities and states. Through the medium of supernatural horror, they objectify the actual loss of economic influence and the spiritual malaise that accompanies such a decline from prominence.

Unlike Lovecraft, King and the other horror writers discussed here do not descend from old New England stock. King, D'Ammassa, Citro, and Hautala are products of working-class parents, the very immigrants who in Lovecraft's eyes had caused the decline of New England. The contemporary writers are more likely to see the causes of New England's decline in the willingness of Lovecraft's old-money Yankees to move that money and their businesses elsewhere, and in the gulf between the few natives and the in-comers who have succeeded and those of the same generation who never did, who are struggling in the dying towns and industries.

According to D'Ammassa, the supernatural in his fiction is both real and "a metaphor for the way all New England has been dying," especially applicable to the economic decline of Rhode Island, which during the 1980s saw a febrile activity comparable to that of a reanimated corpse, but which has since relapsed into its grave. *Blood Beast,* his first published book, faithfully depicts that decline. The title refers to a gargoyle, literally imported from Europe, together with the other trappings of Gothic romance: an old house, a reclusive builder, hideous secrets. The novel, like much of D'Ammassa's fiction, is set in the well-realized town of Managansett, Rhode Island. Filled with human and inhuman grotesques and dying even as the novel progresses, it is an emblem for New England Gothic.

A D'Ammassa short story, "Little Evils," is even more explicit in equating corporate and supernatural ills. It is set in Taunton, Massachusetts, in an abandoned factory complex, "elderly, brick faced...more or less converted to house a successor industry which had also passed away, victim of the failing economy of the Northeast" (89). While the "evils" of the title are Lovecraftian "outsider threats," crawling starfish, bugs, and worms, the successful protagonist is a ruthless female who destroys the reanimated bodies they have colonized. Such unnatural parasitic life in a dead body is an excellent image for the current trend of converting abandoned factory buildings to outlet malls while the productive work (and the jobs) are exported elsewhere.

Haunted industrial sites also appear in Stephen King's fiction, based on his work experiences before he became America's wealthiest horror writer. Two particularly frightening early stories are "The Mangler" with its demonic industrial laundry machine, and "Graveyard Shift," with its dangerous, polluting textile mill that harbors Lovecraftian mutant monsters in its sub-basement.

Rick Hautala's *Dark Silence* focuses on a haunted sawmill on Maine's Saco River, "a weathered, gray hulk that stood out against the sky like an ancient, brooding castle" (28). Like the castle in an eighteenth-century Gothic novel, this sawmill is haunted by ghosts representing generations of guilty family secrets. And like the notoriously haunted Ramtail Factory in Rhode Island, Hautala's abandoned mill features the apparition of a hanging victim (175; 365). That the Ramtail Factory was haunted was a matter of public record in the Rhode Island Census of 1885, according to local historian J. Earl Clauson (95). While Hautala's ghost was a witch hanged by a mob, the Ramtail Factory's was a night watchman who hanged himself from the bell rope. Thereafter the bell would ring by itself at midnight, and the millwheel would revolve backwards against the current. The textile mill thus haunted closed about 1870, that is, some fifty or sixty years in advance of the rest of Rhode Island's textile industry.

Hautala, like King and Citro, evokes small towns where "old witch houses" dot the landscape and ancient evils survive. His protagonists are often outsiders or exiles returning to rural Maine. When they are attacked or possessed by the ancient evil, we are reminded that the dream of making such a return can turn into a nightmare. In Hautala's zombie novel *Moon Walker*, the walking dead in the potato fields are walking objective correlatives for the decline of rural New England. As one of his characters notes, "A dead town! Wasn't that what she had called it ever since she could remember? A God-forsaken, wasted, dead town!" (284). She had left town to escape the potato fields. Under attack by the zombies, her worst fear is that she will be condemned by their master to labor in those fields forever.

Citro reworks the theme of backwoods degeneracy so familiar from Lovecraft in his Vermont novels, and concisely and with great skill in the short story "Them Bald-Headed Snays." The Snays at first seem like typical inbred trailer-dwellers, pale, with hair so "limp and sparse"..."making his head look like it was covered with hairy bugs" (268). The child protagonist quickly learns that the Snays are born victims, scapegoats who, like the poor, are always with us. His grandfather beats one to death and is restored to health. The child, however, is unable to do as his grandfather tells him: "'The Snays...you gotta give 'em your pain. You gotta give 'em your troubles. You can't hurt 'em. You can't *kill* 'em. They jest keep comin' back'" (273). This disturbing little parable reminds us not only of New England attitudes toward the rural poor, but also of more universal examinations of the problem of human pain in Dostoevsky's narrative of the "Grand Inquisitor" and in Ursula LeGuin's "Those Who Walk Away from Omelas."

No mainstream novel in this century has conveyed the economic and spiritual decline of a region as effectively as Stephen King's *It*. The novel's grandiose proportions find room for all his earlier preoccupations: the monsters of European Gothic, their American transmutations, and the dark secrets of New England's history. *It* reads as though King wanted to exhaust the registers both of horror and of Bangor folklore. The 1100+ pages of *It* has more often been seen as a coming-of-age story, or as a monster rally and zombie jamboree.[13] *It* is truly a Maine epic. As King told the Bangor Historical Society, the book is a left-handed tribute to a town he loves: "I'm afraid I've also written some fairly awful things in my book, but I hope that when local people read it, they will sense that those awful things have been informed with a larger love for the place and the people" ("A Novelist's Perspective").[14]

That love-hate relationship with the region has prompted Magistrale to compare King to Hawthorne, since both "sensed the real meanings behind the history and physical textures of a particular place." The form and style of their allegories may differ, but Magistrale believes that both deal with the "universal themes of great literature—human sin, fear, and endurance" (*Landscape* 19). Though associated with death and destruction, King is a more profoundly optimistic writer than Lovecraft. After King has harrowed hell for his readers, he allows a vision of heaven. Some good folks escape, memories of others linger on. Some people succeed in making it out of the dark, out of the mills, and away from back-road stagnation, as Tabitha and Stephen King did. Yet King is not truly one of the neo-Romantic ruralists of the past twenty years. He sees nothing admirable

---

[13]During the long years of *It*'s gestation (1980-1986), King tended to describe the work in progress this way himself. See Underwood and Miller, *Bare Bones* 191.

[14] Another reading of the novel emphasizes King's debt to Faulkner's "handling of how the past insinuates itself into the present and how the landscape reflects the corruption of human potential for love and renewal" (Dickerson 171). See also Magistrale, *Landscape* 110-111.

228

in the mere condition of being a farmer. He kills the city folks' "back to the land" dream decisively in *Cujo,* where the back-road dweller Joe Camber is as monstrous as his rabid Saint Bernard. The novel can be seen as carrying *ad absurdum* the old Maine attitude toward those "from away"—that summer people are not truly people!

Long before King, Shirley Jackson captured the tension between summer people and year-rounders in several short stories. As in all her work, she never explicitly mentions New England, but her villages and the village characters are unmistakable. In "The Renegade" (1948) and "The Summer People" (1949). cityfolk have ghastly experiences. Characteristic of Jackson's work, no overt harm is done to any of the summer people, yet both stories hint at indescribable vengeance enacted by the natives. Both stories contrast the pastoral beauty of their settings with the barely-restrained violence of their inhabitants. In Jackson's country: "Everything was quiet and lovely in the sunlight, the peaceful sky, the gentle line of the hills. Mrs. Walpole closed her eyes, suddenly feeling the harsh hands pulling her down, the sharp points closing in on her throat" ("The Renegade," *The Lottery* 13). Perry Miller, whose intellectual histories of Puritanism admit no trace of the Gothic, attributes the Mainer's contempt for tourists not to decadence and degeneracy, but to a more noble reason. In an essay on "The New England Conscience," he claims that the virtues of the Puritan inheritance, the "ethic of abstinence, self-denial, and worry about internal motives" cause true New Englanders to dismiss light-minded "summer folk" as beneath consideration (*The Responsibility* 184). In some modern Gothic fiction, the protagonists may be punished for their sins of having and flaunting wealth and happiness before those who possess neither.[15]

A different sort of conflict between natives and outsiders is dramatized in *It.* The polymorphous perversity of the title, the many-named monster who is finally and only "It" is, like Lovecraft's monsters, not native to this earth. It takes shapes of fear from the minds of its victims, and becomes so much a part of Derry, Maine, that only the novel's child heroes, a group of outcasts and misfits, suspect It is really "from away." Like the cheesy 1950s horror movie, "It Came from Outer

---

[15]For a vivid account of the conflict between native and yuppie in-comers, though with no element of the supernatural, see Christopher Fahy's short story "The Glow of Copper," part of a volume chosen by Mary McCarthy as winner of the 1987 Maine Arts Commission Fiction Competition. (*One Day*) .

Space." And again like Lovecraft's Old Ones, It is perfectly at home in New England. Mike Hanlon, the only one of the Losers' Club to remain in Derry, explains to the now grown-up children how It has become naturalized there:

> '...It's become a part of Derry, something as much a part of the town as the Standpipe, or the Canal, or Bassey Park, or the library. Only It's not a matter of outward geography, you understand. Maybe that was true once, but now It's...inside. Somehow It's gotten inside. That's the only way I know to understand all of the terrible things that have happened here....' (503)

Bangor really is a town with many secrets whose residents prefer not to be reminded of its years as a roaring, wide-open boomtown, where lumberjacks took their pleasures in "Hell's Half Acre." In his fiction, King combines the disasters and guilty secrets—"all boom and booze and balling" (883)—from Bangor's past (along with a few inventions) to lend credence to the depredations of It, who preys upon children in a 27-30 year cycle. As King says of Bangor, "the stories you hear about this town—the streets fairly clang with them" ("A Novelist's Perspective"). King's predecessors and contemporaries may have lamented the decadence of New England, but King goes further: he claims that his Outside monster *"had created a place in Its own image...Derry was Its killing-pen, the people of Derry Its sheep"* (*It* 1007; original italics).

Such monstrous evil cannot be untwined from its habitation with no consequences for Derry. At the climax of *It*, the heroes destroy the monster, but they destroy the town as well. Similarly, when King tired of his fictional southern Maine landscape, deciding that "the time had come to close the book on Castle Rock, Maine...Time to move on" (*Four Past Midnight* 609), he sent Castle Rock to Hell in *Needful Things*, yet another variation on the Faust legend. When Hawthorne was unhappy with Salem he removed himself from the place; Lovecraft destroyed only his imaginary New England places, while sparing the Providence he loved. King, apparently, has no problems with obliterating his fictional Bangor while continuing to reside in the actual city.

The fictions of King, Hautala, Citro, et al., are designed for a popular readership, as Gothic fictions have been from their origin. Just as the idealized portrait of a flowering New England presented in Emerson, Louisa May Alcott, and the Household Poets attracted the nineteenth-century's mass audience, so does the portrait of a declining New England found in these horror writers attract today's readers. Like the Puritans who endangered their souls by crowding into the haunted chambers of Mather's possessed girls, or, unable to see for themselves, bought his accounts of witchcraft and exorcism, modern readers continue to seek out the dangerous delights of the Gothic. Tales of monsters, devils, witches, and the undead remain a reliable New England export, even when other traditional manufacturing enterprises of the region have failed.

In the northwestern corner of Connecticut, in an area of intense paranormal activity that Ed Warren calls "our Bermuda triangle," lie the cellar holes and stone walls marking the site of Dudleytown, New England's most notorious ghost town. Around this abandoned hill village cluster all the associations of New England Gothic: if Dudleytown did not exist, I would surely have had to invent it. [16]

According to the legend, Dudleytown was doomed from its settlement in 1745 as part of Cornwall, Connecticut, for the Dudleys had brought with them from England an ancestral curse on attempted regicides. Several aristocratic Dudleys, including one who married Lady Jane Grey, had been beheaded for treason. It seemed at first that crossing the water might have nullified the ancient curse, for the farming village prospered, but the economic forces that led to the decline of New England stood ready to punish the descendants of the regicidal Dudleys. The depopulation of western Connecticut began early in Dudleytown, with its thin, mountain soil. The area's early iron industry faltered, after denuding the mountains and contributing to faster soil run-off. For every death by lightning or unexplained lunacy attributed to the Elizabethan curse, many more farmers simply gave up and went west. Ironically, the most famous victim of the "Dudleytown curse" may have been Mary Cheney, the wife of Horace Greeley who advised young men to leave the played-out East and "grow with the country." Mary Cheney Greeley hanged herself. Those who remained behind in the town tended to die young of consumption, and many fires were also blamed on the curse. The area's three mountains still attract an inordinate number of lightning bolts:

---

[16]The legend of Dudleytown is told by Owens in *Mysterious New England*; a slightly different version is given in Wall. Philips has an authoritative survey of its history and folklore (134-41). New articles generally appear each Halloween. The Warrens told me their experiences; similar material can be found in their *Ghost Hunters*.

during the dry summer of 1993, devastating forest fires were set by lightning strikes.

Oddly enough, the legend of Dudleytown has not been exploited in Gothic fiction. Tryon's Cornwall Coombe has nothing in common with this Cornwall. While Grant's invented Oxrun Station would appear to be situated nearby, Grant told me in an interview that he had known nothing about the abandoned town or its curse until I told him the tales: his rationale for choosing the area was simply its presumed affluence. As he told Stan Wiater in *Dark Dreamers*, "I needed a town, so to avoid comparisons to Lovecraft's Arkham, I made it an upper-class community. That's about as far away from Arkham as you can get" (Wiater 73). Grant has now realized the danger of setting stories in haunted New England, where it is never easy to shun forbidden ground.

Since the town was abandoned and the last structures crumbled or burned, the Gothic has made itself at home in Dudleytown, sometimes called "Owlsbury." Reporters, parapsychologists, and thrill-seekers following the aptly-named Dark Entry Road have encountered eerie sounds and unnatural silences; poisonous snakes; Bigfoot monsters and Lovecraftian hybrids; avenging lunatic ghosts. Such reports could not contrast more strongly with the attitude of some town officials who refuse to give further credence to the Dudleytown legend. Descendants of Dudleytown's last residents have written pamphlets debunking the legends: as one declares: "Please do not come. There are no ghosts, no spirits, and no curse" (H. Clark 7). Despite their efforts, beliefs of such ancient standing cannot be banished so easily. Dudleytown continues to attract every brand of Gothic enthusiast. The Warrens, who have held seances there, declare it a "psychic magnet." Ed Warren claims to have found idols and animal sacrifices, constituting "positive evidence of Satanism." Thus, "even if there weren't demonic forces at work" in Dudleytown in the past, motorcycle gangs holding rituals on the mountain have ensured demonic infestation (*Ghost Hunters* 182). The curse may have claimed the last of the Dudleys, and wilderness the town they founded, but the Gothic legacy of New England continues.

After patiently following the downward spiral this far, the gentle reader may ask, "is this the *true* picture of New England at the close of the Second Millennium?" It may seem as if I have been leading a quest for Darkman's Land, with intentions as single-minded and incorrect as those of the nineteenth-century enthusiasts who sought to transform the New World into Whiteman's Land. Of course, neither represents a complete picture. Both, however, share something with the grand quests of life and art. We may no longer believe in the Fortunate Isles, the Seven Golden Cities, or the Fountain of Youth, but once nearly everyone did. Those who did believe ardently pursued those quests, and in pursuing them, they altered history and, as if by accident, brought our world into being.

Studying the Gothic in New England may have transformed me into a darker image of Emerson's sage, one who finds weird inscriptions on stones, spooks in every nook, and bad in everything. Nevertheless, this portrait of New England, like those of Mather, Hawthorne, Lovecraft, or King, is valid though it may not be true. The novel *Ægypt* by John Crowley, a fantasist now residing in Massachusetts, sets out to convince us that there is another country, not the Egypt of the Pharaohs and the archaeologists, but *Ægypt*, whence come the Gypsies, the secret powers of pyramids, and all magic. There is, Crowley says, another history of the world, existing side by side with the history we are taught in schoolbooks. In another world history, I believe, New England road maps are marked "here be monsters," with symbols for sea serpents carefully drawn in the Chain Lakes and Lake Champlain, off Cape Ann, and Nantucket, and those for mermen marked in Penobscot Bay and the Thimble Islands. In the gores of Vermont, the hills of the Connecticut Valley, the back roads of Maine, the second-growth woods and abandoned fields of western Rhode Island, inbred tribes worship the dark powers. In this New England, witches *were* burned at Salem, rightfully, and mobs still light their torches to punish necromancers who bargain with the Devil. The crumbling slums and abandoned factories of Bridgeport, Providence, Lowell, Fall River are haunted by evils more ancient than crack and unemployment. Forbidden books, psychic seers, and exorcists furnish the only protection against the darkness. Here, at this intersection of history, fantasy, magic, and art, I have planted my New England. The wonders and horrors recounted may not have been native to New England, but here they have found a local habitation and a name.

Works Cited

Abbot, Abiel. *History of Andover from its Settlement to 1829.* Andover, 1829.

Abbot, Katharine M. *Old Paths and Legends of New England.* New York: Putnam, 1903.

Aguirre, Manuel. *The Closed Space: Horror Literature and Western Symbolism.* Manchester and New York: Manchester UP, 1990.

Alger, Abby L. *In Indian Tents: Stories Told by Penobscot, Passamaquoddy and Micmac Indians.* Boston: Roberts, 1897.

Altman, Lawrence K. "For Most, Risk of Contracting Tuberculosis Is Seen as Small." *New York Times* 1 January 1992: 1+

Anderson, Jeannine. Typescript Collection of Maine Folklore, 1962. Northeast Archive 3.

Ankarloo, Bengt and Gustav Henningsen, eds. *Early Modern European Witchcraft: Centres and Peripheries.* Oxford: Clarendon, 1990.

Attebery, Brian. *Strategies of Fantasy.* Bloomington: Indiana UP, 1992.

---. *The Fantasy Tradition in American Literature.* Bloomington: Indiana UP, 1980.

Babcock, William H. *Legendary Islands of the Atlantic: A Study in Medieval Geography.* New York: American Geographical Society, 1922.

Bacon, Edwin M. *The Connecticut River and the Valley of the Connecticut.* New York: Putnam, 1906.

Bailey, Sarah Loring. *Historical Sketches of Andover, Massachusetts.* Boston: Houghton, Mifflin, 1880. Repr. Andover Historical Society, 1974.

Baker, Margaret. *Folklore of the Sea.* Newton Abbey, London: David & Charles, 1979.

Baldick, Chris. Introduction. *The Oxford Book of Gothic Tales.* Oxford: Oxford UP, 1992.

Barber, John Warner. *Connecticut Historical Collections.* New Haven, 1856.

Barber, Paul. *Vampires, Burial, and Death: Folklore and Reality.* New Haven: Yale UP, 1988.

Barron, David P. and Sharon Mason. *A Guidebook to "The Greater Gungywamp."* Noank: The Gungywamp Society, 1991.

Batchelor, Rev. George. "Salem." *History of Essex County Massachusetts, with Biographical Sketches of many of its Pioneers and Prominent Men.* Ed. D. Hamilton Hurd. 2 vols. Philadelphia: J.W. Lewis, 1888.

Beck, Horace. *Folklore and the Sea.* [Pub. for Marine Historical Association, Inc. Mystic Seaport] Middletown: Wesleyan UP, 1973.

---. *Folklore of Maine.* Philadelphia: Lippincott, 1957.

Beckwith, Henry L.P. *Lovecraft's Providence and Adjacent Parts.* 2nd Ed. West Kingston: Donald M. Grant, 1986.

Bell, Michael. *The Face of Connecticut: People, Geology and the Land.* Bulletin 110. State Geological and Natural Historical Survey of Connecticut, 1985.

Bellantoni, Nicholas. Personal interview. 17 March 1992.

Birkhead, Edith. *The Tale of Terror: A Study of the Gothic Romance.* New York: Russell & Russell, 1921.

Blackington, Alton. *Yankee Yarns.* New York: Dodd, Mead, 1954.

Blechman, Andrew. "City Plan in the Cards/ Hayward: 'We Said We Would Invest in the Area.'" *Norwich Bulletin* 20 Nov. 1993: A1+.

Bleiler, Everett. *The Guide to Supernatural Fiction.* Kent: Kent State UP, 1983.

Bolté, Mary. *Haunted New England.* New York: Weathervane, 1972.

Bonewits, P.E.I. *Real Magic.* New York: Berkeley, 1971.

Botkin, B.A. *A Treasury of New England Folklore.* New York: Bonanza, 1965.

Bourgaize, Eidola Jean. "Supernatural Folklore of Rhode Island." M.A. thesis, University of Rhode Island, 1956.

Boutwell, George S. "The Decadence of New England." *Forum* 10 (Oct. 1890): 142–51.

Boyer, Paul S. and Stephen Nissenbaum, eds. *The Salem Witchcraft Papers: Verbatim Transcripts of the Legal Documents of the Salem Witchcraft Outbreak of 1692.* 3 vols. New York: Da Capo, 1977.

---. *Salem Possessed: The Social Origins of Witchcraft.* Cambridge: Harvard UP, 1974.

Brainard, John G.C. *The Literary Remains.* Ed. John Greenleaf Whittier. Hartford, 1832.

-----. *The Poems.* Hartford: Edward Hopkins, 1841.

Bradford, William. *History of Plymouth Plantation 1620–1647* 2 vols. N.p.: Massachusetts Historical Society, 1912.

Braude, Ann. *Radical Spirits: Spiritualism and Women's Rights in Nineteenth-Century America.* Boston: Beacon, 1989.

Braunbeck, Gary A. "Into the Dark Decayed: Joe Citro and the Perfection of the Hideous." *Tekeli-li! Journal of Terror* Fall 1991: 61–63; 78–79.

Briggs, Katharine. *The Vanishing People: Fairy Lore and Legends.* New York: Pantheon, 1978.

Brittle, Gerald. *The Demonologist: The Extraordinary Career of Ed and Lorraine Warren.* Englewood Cliffs: Prentice-Hall, 1980.

---. *The Devil in Connecticut.* New York: Bantam, 1983.

Brooks, Van Wyck. *The Flowering of New England.* New York: Dutton, 1957.

Brown, Raymond Lamont. *Phantoms of the Sea: Legends, Customs and Superstitions.* New York: Taplinger, 1972.

Bryant, Alice. Typescript Collection of Maine Folklore, 1959. Northeast Archive 23.

Burleigh, Elsia Holway. "The Indian Ledges at Solon." *Maine Writers* 53–57.

Burleson, Donald. "H.P. Lovecraft: The Hawthorne Influence." *Extrapolation* 22.3 (Fall 1981): 262–269.

---. *Lovecraft: Disturbing the Universe.* Lexington: UP of Kentucky, 1990.

Burr, George Lincoln, ed. *Narratives of the Witchcraft Cases 1648–1706.* 1914. New York: Barnes and Noble, 1959.

Cahill, Robert Ellis. *Haunted Happenings.* Salem: Old Saltbox, 1992.

---. *New England's Ghostly Haunts.* Collectible Classics #2. Peabody: Chandler-Smith, 1983.

---. *New England's Marvelous Monsters.* Collectible Classics #3. Peabody: Chandler-Smith, 1983.

---. *New England's Witches and Wizards.* Collectible Classics #1. Peabody: Chandler-Smith, 1983.

Calef, Robert. *More Wonders of the Invisible World, or The Wonders of the Invisible World Displayed in Five Parts.* 1700. Fowler, v–373.

Canfield, Dorothy [Fisher]. *Hillsboro People.* New York: Henry Holt, 1915.

Carpenter, Lynette and Wendy K. Kolmar, eds. *Haunting the House of Fiction: Feminist Perspectives on Ghost Stories by American Women.* Knoxville: U of Tennessee P, 1991.

Carter, Margaret L. *Specter or Delusion? The Supernatural in Gothic Fiction.* Ann Arbor and London: UMI, 1987.

Cave, Alfred. "Indian Shamans and English Witches in Seventeeth-Century New England." *Essex Institute Historical Collections* 128.4 (Oct. 1992): 239–254.

Citro, Joseph A. *Dark Twilight.* New York: Warner, 1991.

---. Personal interview. NECON at Bryant College, North Smithfield RI. 20 July 1991.

---. "The King and I." Foreword to Magistrale *The Dark Descent* xi–xiv.

---. "Soul-Keeper." *Lovecraft's Legacy.* Ed. Robert E. Weinberg and Martin H. Greenberg. New York: Tor, 1990: 142–156.

---. "Them Bald-Headed Snays." *Masques III.* Ed. J.N. Williamson. New York: St. Martin's, 1989. Rpt. in. *The Year's Best Fantasy and Horror.* Ed. Ellen Datlow and Terri Windling. New York: St. Martin's, 1990: 274.

---. *The Unseen.* New York: Warner, 1990.

Clark, Harriet Lydia. *True Facts About Dudleytown.* Cornwall: Cornwall Historical Society, 1989.

Clark, James W., Jr. "The Recurrence of Salem Witchcraft in American Literature." A paper given at the Essex County History Conference, 20 June 1972. Typescript in the collection of the Essex Institute, Salem, MA.

Clark, Kenneth. *The Gothic Revival: An Essay in the History of Taste.* Rev. Ed.

New York: Scribner's, 1950.

Clauson, J. Earl. *These Plantations*. Providence: n.p., 1937.

Coatsworth, Elizabeth. "Daniel Webster's Horses." *Fire and Sleet and Candlelight*. Ed. August Derleth. Sauk City: Arkham House, 1961. 55–6.

Condé, Maryse. *I, Tituba, Black Witch of Salem*. Trans. Richard Philcox. [*originally published as Moi, Tituba, Sorcière ..Noire de Salem*]. CARAF. Charlottesville: UP of Virginia, 1992.

Cook, Albert B. "Damaging the Mathers: London Receives the News from Salem." *New England Quarterly* 65.2 (June 1992): 302–308.

Costello, Peter. "American Lake Monsters." *Mysteries of Mind Space & Time: The Unexplained*. Vol. 1. Westport: Stuttman, 1992. 93–105.

Cowley, Geoffrey. "A Deadly Return." *Newsweek* 16 March 1992: 53–57.

Crawford, Mary C. *The Romance of Old New England Rooftrees*. Boston: Page, 1902.

Cronon, William. *Changes in the Land: Indians, Colonists, and the Ecology of New England*. New York: Hill & Wang, 1983.

Crowley, John. *Ægypt*. New York: Bantam, 1987.

Cthulhu Mansion. Film. Screenplay and Directed by J.P. Simon. Filmagic, 1990. Republic Pictures Home Video, 1992.

Curran, Ronald, ed. *Witches, Wraiths & Warlocks: Supernatural Tales of the American Renaissance*. Greenwich: Fawcett, 1971.

Currier, John McNab. "Contributions to the Folk-Lore of New England." *Journal of American Folk-Lore* 2 (July-Sept. 1889): 291–3.

---. "Contributions to New England Folk-Lore." *Journal of American Folk-Lore* 4 (July-Sept. 1891): 253–256.

Dailey, Barbara Ritter. "Beyond Salem Village: New Perspectives on the Witch Hunt of 1692." Typescript deposited in the Andover Historical Society Library of Memorial Lecture, Andover Historical Society, 25 March 1992. N. pag.

D'Ammassa, Don. *Blood Beast*. New York: Pinnacle, 1988.

---. "Little Evils." *Chilled to the Bone*. Ed. Robert T. Garcia. Niles: Mayfair Games, 1991: 87–100.

Daniels, Les. Personal interview. NECON at Roger Williams College, Bristol, R.I. 20 July 1990.

---. "Grave Undertakings." *The* [Providence] *Eagle* 29 Oct. 1981: 3.

da Silva, Manuel Luciano. *Portuguese Pilgrims and Dighton Rock: The First Chapter in American History.* Ed. Nelson D. Martins. Bristol, R.I.: privately printed, 1971.

Davis, Sonia H. [Lovecraft]. *The Private Life of H.P. Lovecraft.* [ed. from unpublished ms.typescript]. West Warwick: Necronomicon, 1985.

Day, William Patrick. *In the Circles of Fear and Desire: A Study of Gothic Fantasy.* Chicago: U of Chicago P, 1985.

DeCamp, L. Sprague. *Lost Continents: The Atlantis Theme in History, Science, and Literature.* New York: Dover, 1970.

---. *Lovecraft: A Biography.* New York: Ballantine, 1976.

"The Decay of New England." Editorial. *The Nation* 8 (27 May 1869): 410–11.

De Champlain, Samuel. *Voyages 1604–1618.* Ed. W.L. Grant. *Original Narratives of Early American History.* New York: Scribner's, 1907.

DeForest, John W. *History of the Indians of Connecticut from the Earliest Known Period to 1850.* 1851. Hamden: Archon, 1964.

DeLaMotte, Eugenia. *Perils of the Night: A Feminist Study of Nineteenth-Century Gothic.* New York: Oxford UP, 1990.

Demos, John Putnam. *Entertaining Satan: Witchcraft and the Culture of Early New England.* New York: Oxford UP, 1982.

Derleth, August. *Some Notes on H.P. Lovecraft.* Sauk City: Arkham House, 1959.

Dickerson, Mary Jane. "Stephen King Reading William Faulkner: Memory, Desire, and Time in the Making of *It*." Magistrale, *The Dark Descent* 171–186.

Donovan, Josephine. *New England Local Color Literature: A Women's Tradition.* New York: Continuum, 1983.

Doris, Virginia Louise. "The Stephen Harris Mansion at #135 Benefit St. Providence RI 1764–1964 which is "The Shunned House" a Tale by Howard Phillips Lovecraft." Typescript. John Hay Library, Brown University.

Dorson, Richard M. *America in Legend.* New York: Pantheon, 1973.

---. "Aunt Jane Goudreau, *Roup-Garou* Storyteller." *Western Folklore* 6 (1947):

13–27.

---. *Buying the Wind: Regional Folklore in the United States*. Chicago: U of Chicago P, 1964.

Drake, Samuel Adams. *The Heart of the White Mountains: Their Legend and Scenery*. New York: Harper, 1882.

---. *New England Legends and Folk-Lore*. New, Rev. ed. Boston: Little, Brown, 1906.

Drake, Samuel G. *Annals of Witchcraft in New England and Elsewhere in the United States from their First Settlement, Drawn up from Unpublished and Other Well Authenticated Records of the Alleged Operations of Witches and Their Instigator, The Devil*. 1869. New York: Blom, 1967.

Dresser, Norine. *American Vampires: Fans, Victims, Practitioners*. New York: Norton, 1989.

Dufresne, Beth. "'Discovering Ellis Ruley.'" *New London Day* 19 Dec. 1993: C1+.

Earle, Alice Morse. *Customs and Fashions in Old New England*. New York: Scribner's, 1894.

Earle, Edna. "The Passamaquoddy Indians." Maine Writers 115–122.

Early English and French Voyages Chiefly from Hakluyt. Ed. Henry S. Burrage. Original Narratives of Early American History. New York: Scribner's, 1932.

Eckstorm, Fannie Hardy. *Old John Neptune and Other Maine Indian Shamans*. Portland: Southworth-Anthoensen Press, 1945.

Egan, James. "'A Single Powerful Spectacle': Stephen King's Gothic Melodrama." *Extrapolation* 27.1 (Spring 1986): 62–75.

Ehrenfeld, Tom and John Engstrom. "Selling Satan." *Boston Globe* 26 Oct. 1986: 18+.

Eisenach, Emlyn. "The Devil, the Witch, and the Community in an Alpine Valley, 1504–5." A paper given at Session 273, "Popular Elements in European Witch Beliefs: Beyond Margaret Murray." Sponsored by the Society for Reformation Research. 28th International Congress on Medieval Studies. Kalamazoo, Michigan. 6–9 May 1993.

Emrich, Duncan. *Folklore on the American Land*. Boston: Little, Brown, 1972.

"EXHUMED THE BODIES/Testing a Horrible Superstition in the Town of Exeter/ Bodies of Dead Relatives Taken From their Graves." *Providence Journal*. 19 March 1892: 3.

240

Facts and Fancies Concerning North Kingstown, Rhode Island. Pettaquamscutt
Chapter Daughters of the American Revolution. North Kingstown, 1941.

Fahy, Christopher. *Dream House.* New York: Zebra Books, 1987.

---. *One Day in the Short Happy Life of Anna Banana and other Maine Stories.*
Thomaston: Coastwise Press, 1988.

Farber, Norma. *Mercy Short: A Winter Journal, North Boston, 1692–3.* New
York: Dutton, 1982.

Farmer, Sarah Bridge. "Notes and Queries: Folk-Lore of Marblehead, Mass."
Journal of American Folk-Lore 7 (July-Sept. 1894): 252–3.

Farrington, Deborah. "Witches Do Stalk Our Rhody." *Providence Evening
Bulletin* 31 Oct. 1968.

Farris, John. *Son of the Endless Night.* New York: Tor, 1986.

Fedorko, Kathy A. "Edith Wharton's Haunted Fiction: 'The Lady's Maid's Bell'
and *The House of Mirth.*" Carpenter and Kolmar 80–107.

Fell, Barry. *America B.C.: Ancient Settlers in the New World.* New York:
Quadrangle/The New York Times, 1976.

---. *Bronze Age America.* Boston: Little, Brown, 1982.

Felt, Joseph B. *The Customs of New England.* Boston, 1853.

Fiedler, Leslie A. *Love and Death in the American Novel.* 2d ed. 1966. London:
Paladin, 1970.

"A Final Resting Place." *The Salem Evening News* 4 Aug. 1992: 1+.

Fisher, Harriet F. *Willoughby Lake Legends and Legacies.* Brownington: Orleans
County Historical Society, 1988.

Flint, Valerie I.J. *The Imaginative Landscape of Christopher Columbus.*
Princeton: Princeton UP, 1992.

---. *The Rise of Magic in Early Medieval Europe.* Princeton: Princeton UP, 1991.

Forbes, Esther. *A Mirror for Witches.* 1928. Chicago: Academy Chicago
Cassandra Editions, 1985.

Fowler, Samuel P. *Salem Witchcraft; Comprising More Wonders of the Invisible
World, collected by Robert Calef; and Wonders of the Invisible World, by
Cotton Mather.* Salem: H.P. Ives and A.A. Smith, 1861.

Fox, Denton and Hermann Palsson, trans. *Grettir's Saga.* Toronto: U of Toronto

P, 1974.

Frank, Frederick. *Guide to the Gothic: An Annotated Bibliography of Criticism.* Metuchen: Scarecrow Press, 1984.

Freneau, Philip. "The Indian Burying Ground." *The American Tradition in Literature.* 7th Ed. Shorter Ed. in one Vol. Ed. George Perkins et al. New York: McGraw-Hill, 1990. 241–2.

Friesner, Esther. M. *Yesterday We Saw Mermaids.* New York: Tor, 1993.

Furneaux, Rupert. *Ancient Mysteries.* New York: McGraw-Hill, 1977.

Gardiner, George W. "Swamptown—A Queer Locality." *Facts and Fancies Concerning North Kingstown, Rhode Island.* 70–73.

Garrett, Edmund H. *Romance and Reality of the Puritan Coast.* Boston: Little, Brown, 1897.

Germann, George. *Gothic Revival in Europe and Britain: Sources, Influences and Ideas.* Trans. Gerald Onn. Cambridge: MIT Press, 1972.

Gilman, Charlotte Perkins. *The Living of Charlotte Perkins Gilman.* New York: Appleton-Century, 1935.

Gilman, Greer Ilene. *Moonwise.* New York: Roc [NAL], 1991.

---. Personal interview with Gilman and Delia Sherman. Cambridge, Massachusetts. 26 June 1991.

Ginzburg, Carlo. "Deciphering the Sabbath." Ankarloo and Henningsen 121–138.

---. *The Night Battles: Witchcraft & Agrarian Cults in the Sixteenth & Seventeenth Centuries.* Trans. John and Anne Tedeschi. Baltimore: Johns Hopkins UP, 1983.

Goodwin, William B. *The Ruins of Great Ireland in New England.* Boston: Meador, 1946.

Gould, John. *The Jonesport Raffle.* Boston: Little, Brown, 1969.

Grant, Charles L., ed. *Doom City: The Second Chronicle of Greystone Bay.* New York: Tor, 1987.

---. *Greystone Bay.* New York: Tor, 1985.

---. *The SeaHarp Hotel: The Third Chronicle of Greystone Bay.* New York: Tor, 1990.

Greene, J.R. *Strange Tales from Old Quabbin.* Athol: privately printed, 1993.

242

Gross, Louis S. *Redefining the American Gothic: From* Wieland *to* Day of the Dead. Ann Arbor: UMI, 1989.

Hale, John. *A Modest Enquiry into the Nature of Witchcraft Boston in N.E. 1702.* Harris, et al.

Hall, David D., ed. *Witch-hunting in Seventeenth-Century New England: A Documentary History 1638–1692.* Boston: Northeastern UP, 1991.

---. *Worlds of Wonder, Days of Judgment: Popular Religious Belief in Early New England.* New York: Knopf/Random House, 1989.

Hansen, Chadwick. "Andover Witchcraft and the Causes of the Salem Witchcraft Trials." *The Occult in America: New Historical Perspectives.* Ed. Howard Kerr and Charles L. Crow. Urbana: U of Illinois P, 1983. 38–57.

---. *Witchcraft at Salem.* New York: NAL, 1969.

Hard, Walter R. Jr. and Janet C. Greene, eds. *Mischief in the Mountains.* Montpelier: Vermont Life, 1970.

Harris, Marguerite, Miles F. Harris, Eleanor V. Spiller, and Mary Carr. *John Hale, a Man Beset by Witches.* Beverly: privately printed, 1992.

Harris, Robert R. "Brand-Name Horror." *New York Times Book Review* 27 Nov. 1983: 43.

Hartt, Rollin L. "A New England Hill Town. Part I. Its Condition." *Atlantic Monthly* 83 (April 1899): 561–574.

Haskell, Raymond I. "The Great Carbuncle." *New England Quarterly* 10 (Sept. 1937): 533–5.

Hauptman, Laurance M. and James D. Wherry, eds. *The Pequots in Southern New England: The Fall and Rise of an American Indian Nation.* 1990. Norman and London: U of Oklahoma P, 1993.

Hautala, Rick. *Dark Silence.* New York: Zebra, 1992.

---. *Dead Voices.* New York: Zebra, 1990.

---. *Little Brothers.* New York: Zebra, 1988.

---. *Moon Walker.* New York: Zebra, 1989.

---. *Night Stone.* New York: Zebra, 1986.

---. *Untcigahunk: Stories and Tales of the Little Brothers. Night Visions #9.* N.p.: Dark Harvest, 1991.

---. Letter to the author. 21 July 1992.

---. Personal interview. NECON at Bryant College, North Smithfield RI. 19 July 1992.

---. Personal interview. Westbrook, Maine 15 June 1993.

Hawthorne, Nathaniel. *The Complete Novels and Selected Tales*. Ed. Norman Holmes Pearson. New York: Modern Library, 1937.

---. *The House of the Seven Gables*. Hawthorne 243-438.

---. *The Marble Faun*. Hawthorne 589-858.

---. *The Scarlet Letter*. Hawthorne 85-242.

--- *Twice-Told Tales and Other Short Stories*. Intro. Quentin Anderson. New York: Washington Square Press/ Pocket Books, 1960.

Hazard, Thomas Robinson. *The Jonny-Cake Papers of 'Shepherd Tom' Together with Reminiscences of Narrangansett Schools of Former Days*. Boston: n.p., 1915.

---. *Recollections of Olden Times: Rowland Robinson of Narragansett and his Unfortunate Daughter*. Newport, 1879.

Hazel, Paul. *The Wealdwife's Tale*. New York: Morrow/AvoNova, 1993.

---. *Winterking*. Boston: Atlantic Monthly, 1985.

Heller, Terry. *The Delights of Terror: An Aesthetics of the Tale of Terror*. Urbana: U of Illinois P, 1987.

Henningsen, Gustav. "'The Ladies from Outside': An Archaic Pattern of the Witches' Sabbath." Ankarloo and Henningsen 191–217.

Heuvelmans, Bernard. *In the Wake of the Sea-Serpents*. Trans. Richard Garnett. New York: Hill and Wang, 1968.

Higginson, Thomas Wentworth. *Tales of the Enchanted Islands of the Atlantic*. 1898. New York: Macmillan, 1930.

Hill, Charlotte T. "Who Are the Indians?" Maine Writers 160–66.

Holman, Mabel Cassine. *Old Saybrook Stories*. Connecticut State Library, 1949.

Hoppenstand, Gary and Ray B. Browne, eds. *The Gothic World of Stephen King: Landscape of Nightmares*. Bowling Green: Bowling Green State U Popular P, 1987.

"How Did Andover Resolve the Witchcraft Tragedy?" *Andover Historical Society Newsletter* 17.3 (Autumn 1992): 1–2.

Hurd, D. Hamilton, compiler. *History of Essex County Massachusetts, with Biographical Sketches of many of its Pioneers and Prominent Men.* 2 vols. Philadelphia: J.W. Lewis, 1888.

Hyde, Virginia. "From the 'Last Judgment' to Kafka's World: A Study in Gothic Iconography." Thompson 128–149.

Hyles, Vernon. "Freaks: The Grotesque as Metaphor in the Works of Stephen King." Hoppenstand and Browne 56–63.

Ingstad, Helge. *Westward to Vinland: The Discovery of Pre-Columbian Norse House-Sites in North America.* Trans. Erik Friis. New York: St. Martin's, 1969.

Jacobus, Donald Lines, compiler. Typescript of the New Haven County Court Records of the Wtchcraft Trials of Winfred Benham. Donated to the Essex Institute by Thelma Benham Boyle, a descendant. No pagination.

Jackson, Shirley. *Come Along With Me: Part of a Novel, Sixteen Stories, and Three Lectures.* Ed. Stanley Edgar Hyman. New York: Viking, 1968.

---. *The Haunting of Hill House.* 1959. New York: Penguin, 1986.

---. *The Lottery and Other Stories.* New York: Farrar, Straus, Giroux, 1949.

---. *The Witchcraft of Salem Village.* New York: Random House, 1956.

[Johnson, Edward]. *Johnson's Wonder-Working Providence 1628–1651.* Ed. J. Franklin Jameson. *Original Narratives of Early American History.* New York: Scribner's, 1910.

Johnson, Kirk. "28 Graves Giving Up Secrets of the 1700's." *New York Times* 10 September 1992: B7.

Jones, Gwyn. *The Norse Atlantic Saga: Being the Norse Voyages of Discovery and Settlement to Iceland, Greenland, America.* London: Oxford UP, 1964.

Joshi, S.T. "Autobiography in Lovecraft." *NECON Stories.* 142–159.

---. *H.P. Lovecraft: The Decline of the West.* Mercer Island: Starmont, 1990.

---., ed. *H.P. Lovecraft: Four Decades of Criticism.* Athens: Ohio UP, 1980.

---. ed. *The H.P. Lovecraft Centennial Conference Proceedings.* West Warwick: Necronomicon, 1991.

---, and Marc Michaud. *Lovecraft's Library: A Catalog.* West Warwick: Necronomicon, 1980.

Josselyn, John. *John Josselyn, Colonial Traveler: A Critical Edition of Two Voyages to New-England.* Ed. Paul J. Lindholdt. Hanover: UP of New England, 1988.

Jung, C.G. *Psychology of the Unconscious: A Study of the Transformations and Symbolisms of the Libido. A Contribution to the History of the Evolution of Thought.* Trans. Beatrice Hinkle (c. 1916). New York: Dodd, Mead, 1963.

Kammen, Michael. "The Problem of American Exceptionalism: A Reconsideration." *American Quarterly* 45.1 (March 1993): 1–43.

Karlsen, Carol F. *The Devil in the Shape of a Woman: Witchcraft in Colonial New England.* New York: Vintage/ Random House, 1989.

Kieckhefer, Richard. *European Witch Trials: Their Foundation in Popular and Learned Culture, 1300–1500.* Berkeley: U of California P, 1976.

Kiely, Robert. *The Romantic Novel in England.* Cambridge: Harvard UP, 1972.

Kinder, Nancy. "The 'Vampires' of Rhode Island." *Mysterious New England.* Ed. Austin Stevens. Dublin: Yankee, 1971. 211–215.

King, Stephen. *Carrie.* New York: Doubleday, 1974.

---. *Cujo.* New York: Viking, 1981.

---. *Danse Macabre.* 1981. New York: Berkley, 1983.

---. *The Dark Half.* New York: Viking, 1989.

---. *Dolores Claiborne.* New York: Viking, 1993.

---. *Firestarter.* New York: Viking, 1980.

---. *Four Past Midnight.* New York: Viking, 1990.

---. *It.* New York: Viking, 1986.

---. *Needful Things.* New York: Viking, 1991.

---. *Night Shift.* New York: Signet, 1979.

---. "A Novelist's Perspective on Bangor." *Black Magic and Music: A Benefit for the Bangor Historical Society.* Program Book. 27 March 1983. N. pag.

---. *Pet Sematary.* Garden City: Doubleday, 1983.

---. *'Salem's Lot.* New York: Signet/NAL, 1975.

---. *Skeleton Crew.* New York: Putnam, 1985.

King, Tabitha. *Caretakers*. New York: Macmillan, 1983.

---. *The Trap*. New York: Macmillan, 1985.

Kittredge, George Lyman. *Witchcraft in Old and New England*. 1929. New York: Russell & Russell, 1956.

Klaniczay, Gabor. "Hungary: The Accusations and the Universe of Popular Magic." Ankarloo and Henningsen 219–256.

Kliger, Samuel. *The Goths in England: A Study in Seventeenth and Eighteenth Century Thought*. Cambridge: Harvard UP, 1952.

Kolodny, Annette. "Among the Indians: The Uses of Captivity." *New York Times Book Review* 31 Jan. 1993: 1+.

Labbe, Rodney A. "Rick Hautala: Maine's 'Other' Horror Novelist." *Footsteps* 9 (July 1990): 72–76.

Larkin, Jack. *The Reshaping of Everyday Life 1790–1840*. New York: Harper & Row, 1988.

Larner, Christina. *Enemies of God: The Witch-hunt in Scotland*. Baltimore: Johns Hopkins UP, 1981.

L'Engle, Madeleine. *An Acceptable Time*. New York: Farrar Straus Giroux, 1989.

---. *A Swiftly Tilting Planet*. New York: Farrar Straus Giroux, 1978.

Leventhal, Herbert. *In the Shadow of the Enlightenment: Occultism and Renaissance Science in Eighteenth-Century America*. New York: New York UP, 1976.

Levett, Christopher. *A Voyage into New England Begun in 1623 and ended in 1624*. London, 1628. Repr. as *Maine in the Age of Discovery: Christopher Levett's Voyage, 1623–1624 and A Guide to Sources*. Maine Historical Society, 1988.

Levin, David. "Salem Witchcraft in Recent Fiction and Drama." *New England Quarterly* 27 (Dec. 1955): 537–546.

Levin, Harry. *The Power of Blackness: Hawthorne, Poe, Melville*. New York: Vintage, 1958.

Lévy, Maurice. *Lovecraft*. Paris: Union Général d'Editions, 1972.

---. Trans. S.T. Joshi. as *Lovecraft: A Study in the Fantastic*. Detroit: Wayne State UP, 1988.

---. *Le Roman "gothique" anglais 1764-1824*. Toulouse: Faculté des Lettres et Sciences Humaines de Toulouse, 1968.

Libby, Sam. "Cemetery Holds Tales of Vampires." *New York Times* 16 Feb.1992: CN 8.

Liberman, Ellen. "Its Secrets Unearthed, Family is Reburied." *New London Day* 10 September 1992: A1+.

Lovecraft, H.P. *At the Mountains of Madness and Other Novels*. Texts Ed. S.T. Joshi. Sauk City: Arkham House, 1964 [corrected sixth prtg.; *AMM*]

---. *Dagon and Other Macabre Tales*. Texts Ed. S.T. Joshi. Sauk City: Arkham House, 1965 [corrected fifth prtg.; *Dagon*]

---. *The Dunwich Horror and Others*. Texts Ed. S.T. Joshi. Sauk City: Arkham House, 1963 [corrected eighth prtg. 1984; *DH*]

---. *Selected Letters I 1911-1924*. Ed. August Derleth and Donald Wandrei. Sauk City: Arkham House, 1965. [*SL* 1]

---. *Selected Letters II 1925-29*. Ed. August Derleth and Donald Wandrei. Sauk City: Arkham House, 1968. [*SL* 2]

---. *Selected Letters IV 1932-34*. Ed. August Derleth and James Turner. Sauk City: Arkham House, 1976. [*SL* 4]

---. *Selected Letters V 1934-37*. Ed. August Derleth and James Turner. Sauk City: Arkham House, 1976. [*SL* 5]

---. *The Shunned House*. Preface by Frank Belknap Long, Jr. Athol: W. Paul Cook, The Recluse Press, 1928. Copyright 1936 by R.H. Barlow.

---. *Something About Cats and Other Pieces*. Collected by August Derleth. Sauk City: Arkham House, 1949.

---. *Supernatural Horror in Literature*. 1945. Intro. E.F. Bleiler. New York: Dover, 1973.

Magistrale, Tony, ed. *The Dark Descent: Essays Defining Stephen King's Horrorscape*. Contributions to the Study of Science Fiction and Fantasy 48. Marshall Tymm, Series Editor. New York: Greenwood, 1992.

---. *Landscape of Fear: Stephen King's American Gothic*. Bowling Green: Bowling Green State U Popular P, 1988.

Maine Writers Research Club. *Maine Indians in History and Legend*. Portland: Severn-Wylie-Jewett, 1952.

Malin, Irving. *New American Gothic*. Carbondale: Southern Illinois UP, 1962.

Malleus Maleficarum. Heinrich Institoris and Jakob Sprenger. (ca. 1485). Ed. and Trans. Montague Summers. 1928. New York: Blom, 1970.

Map, Walter. *De Nugis Curialium (Courtier's Trifles).* Trans. Frederick Tupper and Marbury Bladen Ogle. London: Chatto & Windus, 1924.

Marsh, George P. *The Goths in New England: A Discourse Delivered at the Anniversary of the Philomathesian Society of Middlebury College, August 15, 1843.* Middlebury, 1843.

Massé, Michelle A. *In the Name of Love: Women, Masochism and the Gothic.* Reading Women Writing, a series. Shari Benstock and Celeste Schenck, eds. Ithaca: Cornell UP, 1992.

Masters, Anthony. *The Natural History of the Vampire.* London: Rupert Hart-Davis, 1972.

Mather, Cotton. *Magnalia Christi Americana or, the Ecclesiastical History of New England.* 2 vols. Hartford, 1820. First American Ed. from First London ed., 1702.

---. *Selected Letters of Cotton Mather.* Ed. Kenneth Silverman. Baton Rouge: Louisiana State UP, 1971.

---. *The Wonders of the Invisible World: Being an Account of the Tryals of Several Witches Lately Executed in New-England and of Several Remarkable Curiosities therein Occurring.* 1693. Fowler 377–446.

Mather, Increase. *Remarkable Providences Illustrative of the Earlier Days of American Colonisation.* 1684. London: Reeves and Turner, 1890.

Matheson, Richard. *Hell House.* 1971. New York: Bantam, 1972.

Matthews, Caitlin, ed. *Voices of the Goddess: A Chorus of Sibyls.* England: Aquarian Press, 1990.

MacAndrew, Elizabeth. *The Gothic Tradition in Fiction.* New York: Columbia UP, 1979.

McDonald, T. Liam. "American Neo-Gothic: Profiles in Terror. T. Liam McDonald Interviews Rick Hautala." *Cemetery Dance* 4.4 (Fall 1992): 42–49.

McFarland, Gerald. *The "Counterfeit" Man: The True Story of the Boorn-Colvin Murder Case.* New York: Pantheon, 1990.

McMillen, Persis. *Currents of Malice: Mary Towne Esty and Her Family in Salem Witchcraft.* Portsmouth: Peter Randall, Publisher, 1990.

---. Letter to the author. 17 June 1993.

McNally, Raymond T. *A Clutch of Vampires*. New York: Bell, 1974.

Meisel, Perry. "Freudian Trip." Review of *Freud, Jung, and Hall the King-Maker* by Saul Rosenzweig. *New York Times Book Review* 24 Jan. 1993: 1+.

Memoli, Paul. *Lovecraft the Sorcerer*. Issue #2 of *Deus Irae*. Fanzine ca. 1979 deposited in John Hay Library, Brown University.

Merrifield, Ralph. *The Archaeology of Ritual and Magic*. New York: New Amsterdam, 1988.

Messent, Peter B. *Literature of the Occult: A Collection of Critical Essays*. Englewood Cliffs: Prentice-Hall, 1981.

Midelfort, H.C. Erik. *Witch Hunting in Southwestern Germany 1562–1684*. Stanford: Stanford UP, 1972.

Miller, Arthur. *Collected Plays*. New York: Viking, 1957.

Miller, Noreen. "Salem Witches' Magic Money Spell." *Sun* 27 April 1993: 26–7.

Miller, Perry. *The New England Mind: The Seventeenth Century*. New York: Macmillan, 1939.

---. *The Responsibility of Mind in a Civilization of Machines*. Ed. John Crowell and Stanford J. Searl, Jr. Amherst: U of Massachusetts P, 1979.

Mills, Lewis Sprague. *Legends of Barkhamsted Lighthouse and Satan's Kingdom in New Hartford*. Hamden: Shoe String Press, 1961.

Mitchell, Edwin Valentine. *It's an Old New England Custom*. New York: Vanguard, 1946.

Morton, Thomas. *New English Canaan or New Canaan*. Amsterdam, 1637.

Mosher, Howard Frank. *Disappearances*. New York: Viking, 1977.

---. *A Stranger in the Kingdom*. New York: Doubleday, 1989.

Mourt's Relation: A Journal of the Pilgrims at Plymouth. 1622. Ed. Dwight Heath. Cambridge: Applewood Books, 1986.

Muchembled, Robert. *Popular Culture and Elite Culture in France 1400–1750*. Trans. Lydia Cochrane. Baton Rouge: Louisiana State UP, 1985.

---. "Satanic Myths and Cultural Reality." Ankarloo and Henningsen 139–160.

Murray, Will. "Dagon in Puritan Massachusetts." *Lovecraft Studies* 11 (1985): 66–70.

---. "Lovecraft's New England: Haunted Backwaters" *H. P. Lovecraft Centennial*

250

Guidebook. Ed. Jon B. Cooke. Pawtucket: privately printed, 1990.

"My Old Home Town: Regionalism in Horror." Panel discussion with Rick Hautala, Joseph Citro, R. Patrick Gates, and Elizabeth Massie at NECON, Roger Williams College, Bristol, R.I. 21 July 1990.

Mydans, Seth. "Child-Molesting Case Raises Old Questions in San Diego." *New York Times* 22 Sept. 1993: B10.

Mysteries of Mind Space & Time: The Unexplained. Vol. 1. Westport: H.S. Stuttman, 1992.

Necon Committee. *NECON Stories.* Providence: Three Bobs Press, 1990.

Nevius, John. *Demon Possession and Allied Themes. Being an Inductive Study of Phenomena of our Own Times.* 3rd Ed. Chicago: Fleming Revell, [c.1896].

Nolan, John. *History of Taftville, Connecticut.* Norwich: Bulletin Press, 1940.

Nott, Charles C. "A Good Farm for Nothing." *The Nation* 49 (21 Nov. 1889): 406–408.

O'Connell, Shaun. *Imagining Boston: A Literary Landscape.* Boston: Beacon, 1990.

O'Keefe, Daniel Lawrence. *Stolen Lightning: The Social Theory of Magic.* New York: Continuum, 1982.

Orians, G. Harrison. "New England Witchcraft in Fiction." *American Literature* 2 (March 1930): 54–71.

Otten, Charlotte F., ed. *A Lycanthropy Reader: Werewolves in Western Culture.* Syracuse: Syracuse UP, 1986.

Owens, Joseph A. "Dudleytown Never Had a Chance." *Mysterious New England.* Ed. Austin Stevens. Dublin: Yankee, 1971. 312–315.

Palfrey, John Gorham. *History of New England.* 3 vols. 1865. New York: AMS, 1966.

Parker, Derek. *Familiar to All: William Lilly and Astrology in the Seventeenth Century.* London: Jonathan Cape, 1975.

Perkins, William. *Discourse of the Damned Art of Witchcraft, So farre forth as it is revealed in the Scriptures, and manifest by true experience.* Cantrell Legge, Printer to the University of Cambridge, 1618.

Petry, Ann. *Tituba of Salem Village.* New York: Crowell, 1964.

Philips, David. *Legendary Connecticut.* Hartford: Spoonwood Press, 1984.

Phillips, Daniel L. *Griswold Cemeteries History and Inscriptions 1724–1918.* Bound typescript, presented to Otis Library, Norwich CT., 1918.

---. *Griswold—A History: Being a History of the Town of Griswold Connecticut from the Earliest Times into the World War in 1917.* N.p.: Tuttle, Morehouse & Taylor, 1929.

Physiologus. Trans. Michael J. Curley. Austin: U of Texas P, 1979.

dePina, Eloise. "A Mania for the Macabre." *Boston Globe* 21 July 1983: 43–44.

Pohl, Frederick Julius. *The Lost Discovery: Uncovering the Track of the Vikings in America.* New York: Norton, 1952.

---. *Prince Henry Sinclair: His Expedition to the New World in 1398.* New York: Clarkson Potter, 1974.

---. *The Viking Settlements of North America.* New York: Clarkson Potter, 1972.

Pratt, Pinehas. *A Declaration of the Affairs of the English People that First Inhabited New England.* 1622. Ed. Richard Frothingham. Boston, 1858.

Praz, Mario. *The Romantic Agony.* 2d ed. 1951. New York: Oxford UP, 1970.

Punter, David. *The Literature of Terror: A History of Gothic Fiction from 1765 to the Present Day.* London: Longman, 1980.

Purchas, Samuel. *Hakluytus Posthumus or Purchas His Pilgrimes.* 20 vols. Glasgow: n.p., 1906.

Pyle, Howard. "The Salem Wolf." Waugh et al. 93–106.

Railo, Eino. *The Haunted Castle: A Study of the Elements of English Romanticism.* New York: Dutton, 1927.

Reeve, Clara. *The Progress of Romance through Times, Countries and Manners.* 1785. New York: Garland, 1970.

Reynard, Elizabeth. *The Narrow Land: Folk Chronicles of Old Cape Cod.* Boston: Houghton Mifflin, 1934.

Ringe, Donald A. *American Gothic: Imagination and Reason in Nineteenth-century Fiction.* Lexington: UP of Kentucky, 1982.

Roberts, George S. *Historic Towns of the Connecticut River Valley.* Schenectady: Robson and Adee, 1906.

Robinson, Enders A. *Salem Witchcraft and Hawthorne's House of the Seven Gables.* Bowie: Heritage Books, 1992.

Russell, Jeffrey Burton. *Witchcraft in the Middle Ages.* Ithaca: Cornell UP, 1972.

St. Armand, Barton L. *Facts in the Case of H. P. Lovecraft.* Pawtucket: Lovecraft Philatelic Group, 1990. [first pub. in Rhode Island Historical Society Quarterly, *Rhode Island History*, Feb. 1972].

---. *The Roots of Horror in the Fiction of H. P. Lovecraft.* Elizabethtown: Dragon Press, 1977.

---. "The Roots of Horror in New England." Part of the panel "Lovecraft and New England" at the H.P. Lovecraft Centennial Commemoration, Brown University, 18 August 1990.

---. "The 'Mysteries' of Edgar Poe: The Quest for a Monomyth in Gothic Literature." Thompson 65–93.

Sargent, Epes. *Peculiar.* New York: Carleton, 1863.

Sawyer, Faith. Typescript Collection of Maine Folklore, 1964. Northeast Archive 377.

Scarborough, Dorothy. *The Supernatural in Modern English Fiction.* New York: Putnam, 1917.

"The Search for Spectral Ghoul in the Exeter Graves/ Not a Rhode Island Tradition but Settled Here." *Providence Journal.* 21 March 1892:

Schweitzer, Darrell. *The Dream Quest of H.P. Lovecraft.* The Milford Series: Popular Writers of Today 12. San Bernardino: Borgo, 1978.

---. "H.P. Lovecraft: Still Eldritch after all these Years." *NECON Stories* 131–41.

Scott, Winfield Townley. *"His Own Most Fantastic Creation*: Howard Phillips Lovecraft" *Exiles and Fabrications.* Garden City: Doubleday, 1961.

Sherman, Delia. "Land's End." *Fantasy & Science Fiction* March 1991: 143–58.

---. "The Maid on the Shore." *Fantasy & Science Fiction* October 1987: 37–51.

---. "Miss Carstairs and the Merman." *Fantasy & Science Fiction* January 1989.

Sherman, Sarah Way. *Sarah Orne Jewett, an American Persephone.* Hanover: UP of New England, 1989.

Shreffler, Philip A. "H.P. Lovecraft and an American Literary Tradition." Messent 156–170.

Silverman, Kenneth. *The Life and Times of Cotton Mather.* 1984. New York: Columbia UP, 1985.

Simister, Florence Parker. *A Short History of Exeter, Rhode Island.* Exeter Bicentennial Commission, 1978.

Simmons, William S. "The Mystic Voice: Pequot Folklore from the Seventeenth Century to the Present." *The Pequots in Southern New England.* Ed. L. Hauptman and J. Wherry. Norman: U of Oklahoma P, 1993. 141–175.

---. *Spirit of the New England Tribes: Indian History and Folklore, 1620–1984.* Hanover: UP of New England, 1986.

Sinclair, Andrew. *The Sword and the Grail.* New York: Crown, 1992.

Skelton, R.A., Thomas E. Marston and George D. Painter. *The Vinland Map and the Tartar Relation.* New Haven: Yale UP, 1965.

Skinner, Charles M. *Myths and Legends of Our Own Land.* 2 vols. Philadelphia: Lippincott, 1896.

Sledzik, Paul. Curator, National Museum of Health and Medicine. Telephone interviews. 24 and 25 March 1993.

Smith, Charles C. "Whodunit?" *Massachusetts.* Summer, 1991: 24–27.

Snow, Edward Rowe. *Ghosts, Gales and Gold.* New York: Dodd, Mead, 1972.

---. *Incredible Mysteries and Legends of the Sea.* New York: Dodd, Mead, 1967.

---. *Legends of the New England Coast.* New York: Dodd, Mead, 1957.

---. *True Tales and Curious Legends.* New York: Dodd, Mead, 1969.

Sontag, Susan. *Illness as Metaphor.* New York: Farrar, Straus, Giroux, 1977.

Speare, Elizabeth George. *The Witch of Blackbird Pond.* Boston: Houghton Mifflin, 1958.

Spignesi, Stephen J. *The Shape Under the Sheet: The Complete Stephen King Encyclopedia.* Ann Arbor: Popular Culture, Ink, 1991.

Spofford, Harriet P., Louise Imogen Guiney, Alice Brown. *Three Heroines of New England Romance.* Boston: Little, Brown, 1895.

Stanko, Dieter. "When Courts Grappled With the Devil." *New York Times* 1 November 1992.

Starkey, Marion L. *The Devil in Massachusetts: A Modern Enquiry into the Salem Witch Trials.* 1949. Garden City: Doubleday-Dolphin, 1961.

---. *The Tall Man from Boston.* New York: Crown, 1975.

---. *The Visionary Girls.* New York: Dell, 1973.

Stephens, Rockwell. "The Vampire's Heart." *Mischief in the Mountains.* Ed.

Walter R. Hard, Jr. and Janet C. Greene. Montpelier: Vermont Life, 1970. 71–80.

Stetson, George R. "The Animistic Vampire in New England." Reprinted from *American Anthropologist* 9.1(1896): 1–13. Washington, D.C.: Judd & Detweiler, 1896.

---. Three autograph unpublished letters to Sidney Rider, Esq., dated Dec.11, 1896; Dec. [?], 1896; and Aug. 13, 1897. In the John Hay Library, Brown University, Providence, RI.

Stevens, Austin, ed. *Mysterious New England.* Dublin: Yankee, 1971.

Stevens, Gifford. Typescript Collection of Maine Folklore, 1967. Northeast Archive 390.

Stone, Edwin M. *History of Beverly: Civil and Ecclesiastical from its Settlement in 1630 to 1842.* Boston, 1843.

Stone, Lincoln R. "An Account of the Trial of George Jacobs for Witchcraft." *Essex Institute Historical Collections* 2 (1860): 49–57.

Stowe, Harriet Beecher. *Oldtown Fireside Stories.* Boston: James Osgood, 1872.

---. *Oldtown Folks.* 1869. Boston: Houghton Mifflin, 1886.

---. *The Pearl of Orr's Island.* 1862. Boston: Houghton Mifflin, 1892.

Sturtevant, Celia. "The Story of the Saco River." Maine Writers 149–50.

Summers, Montague. *The Gothic Quest: A History of the Gothic Novel.* 1938. New York: Russell & Russell, 1964.

---. *The History of Witchcraft and Demonology.* London: Kegan Paul, Trench, Trubner, 1926.

---, ed. and trans. *Malleus Maleficarum.* Heinrich Institoris and Jakob Sprenger. (ca. 1485). New York: Blom, 1928. Repr. 1970.

Teachout, Terry. "Mencken Unsealed." Review of *My Life as Author and Editor* by H.L. Mencken. *New York Times Book Review* 31 Jan. 1993: 9–10.

Tedeschi, John. "Inquisitorial Law and the Witch." Ankarloo and Henningsen 83–118.

Thompson, D.P. *Locke Amsden, or The Schoolmaster.* 1847. New York: Lovell, Coryell, n.d.

Thompson, G.R., ed. *The Gothic Imagination: Essays in Dark Romanticism.* Pullman: Washington State UP, 1974.

Thoreau, Henry David. *The Writings of Henry David Thoreau. Journal* Vol. 9; *Journal* Vol. 10. Ed. Bradford Torrey. Boston: Houghton Mifflin, 1906.

Three Sovereigns for Sarah. Film. Night Owl Productions. Directed by Philip Leacock. Written and produced by Victor Pisano. 150 mins. 1986.

Todorov, Tzvetan. *Introduction a la littérature fantastique.* Paris: Editions du Seuil, 1970.

Tomlinson, R.G. *Witchcraft Trials of Connecticut.* Hartford: privately printed, 1978.

Trask, Richard B. *"The Devil Hath Been Raised": A Documentary History of the Salem Village Witchcraft Outbreak of March 1692.* Danvers: Danvers Historical Society, 1992.

Tree, Christina. *How New England Happened: The Modern Traveler's Guide to New England's Historical Past.* Boston: Little, Brown, 1976.

Tryon, Thomas. *Harvest Home.* New York: Dell, 1973.

---. *The Other.* New York: Fawcett, 1971.

Twitchell, James B. *The Living Dead: A Study of the Vampire in Romantic Literature.* Durham: Duke UP, 1981.

Underwood, Tim and Chuck Miller, eds. *Bare Bones: Conversations on Terror with Stephen King.* New York: McGraw-Hill, 1988.

---. *Fear Itself: The Horror Fiction of Stephen King.* San Francisco: Underwood-Miller, 1982.

---. *Feast of Fear: Conversations with Stephen King.* New York: Carroll & Graf, 1992.

Updike, John. *Roger's Version.* New York: Knopf, 1986.

---. *S.* New York: Knopf, 1988.

---. *The Witches of Eastwick.* New York: Knopf, 1984.

Varma, Devendra. "Quest of the Numinous: The Gothic Flame." Messent 40–50.

Varnado, S.L. *Haunted Presence: The Numinous in Gothic Fiction.* Tuscaloosa: U of Alabama P, 1987.

Vaughan, Alden T. *New England Frontier: Puritans and Indians 1620–1675.* Boston: Little, Brown, 1965.

Verill, A. Hyatt. *Along New England Shores.* New York: Putnam, 1936.

Wall, Richard. "Curse or Coincidence?" *Connecticut's Finest*. Winter 1989: 5–6.

Warren, Ed, Demonologist. Telephone interview. 14 July 1993.

Warren, Ed and Lorraine, with Robert David Chase. *Ghost Hunters: True Stories from the World's Most Famous Demonologists*. New York: St. Martin's Paperbacks, 1989.

---. *Graveyard: True Hauntings from an Old New England Cemetery*. New York: St. Martin's, 1992.

Watkins, Charles. "The Coming of Pamola." Maine Writers 169.

---. "The Story of John Neptune." Maine Writers 170–1.

---. "Why Katahdin." Maine Writers 167–68.

Waugh, Charles G., Martin H. Greenberg and Frank D. McSherry, Jr., eds. *Yankee Witches*. Emmaus: Yankee Books, 1988.

Weisman, Richard. *Witchcraft, Magic, and Religion in 17th-Century Massachusetts*. Amherst: U of Massachusetts P, 1984.

White, Glenn E. *Folk Tales of Connecticut*. 2 vols. Meriden: Journal Press, 1977; 1981.

Whittier, John Greenleaf. *The Poetical Works of John Greenleaf Whittier*. Boston: Houghton Mifflin, 1891 (?).

---. *The Supernaturalism of New England*. 1847. Ed. Edward Wagenknecht. Norman: U of Oklahoma P, 1969.

Wiater, Stanley. *Dark Dreamers: Conversations with the Masters of Horror*. New York: Avon, 1990.

---. "The Joseph A. Citro Interview." *Tekeli-li! Journal of Terror* Fall 1991: 58–60.

Wilkins, Mary E. [Freeman]. *Silence and Other Stories*. New York: Harper, 1898.

Wilkins-Freeman, Mary. *Collected Ghost Stories*. Intro. Edward Wagenknecht. Sauk City: Arkham House, 1974.

Williams, Roger. *The Complete Writings of Roger Williams*. 7 vols. New York: Russell & Russell, 1963.

Williams, Selma R. and Pamela Williams Adelman. *Riding the Nightmare: Women & Witchcraft from the Old World to Colonial Salem*. 1978. New York: Harper Perennial, 1992.

Williams, Stephen. *Fantastic Archaeology: The Wild Side of North American Prehistory.* Philadelphia: U of Pennsylvania P, 1991.

Winerip, Michael. "On Sunday: Rikers Fights an Epidemic Cell by Cell." *New York Times* 24 May 1992: 35.

Winter, Douglas E. *Stephen King: The Art of Darkness.* Rev. Ed. New York: Signet, 1986.

Winthrop's Journal "History of New England" 1630–1649. 2 vols. Ed. James Kendall Hosmer. New York: Scribner's, 1908.

Wolf, Jack C. and Barbara Wolf, eds. *Ghosts, Castles, and Victims: Studies in Gothic Terror.* Greenwich: Fawcett, 1974.

Wood, William. *New Englands Prospect.* 1634. The English Experience Its Record in Early Printed Books Published in Facsimile 68. Amsterdam and New York: Da Capo Press/ Theatrum Orbis Terrarum, 1968.

Wright, Dudley. *The Book of Vampires.* 1924. New York: Causeway Books, 1973.

Wright, Lawrence. "Remembering Satan: Parts I and II." *New Yorker* 17 May 1993 and 24 May 1993: 60–81; 54–76.

Yim, Eli. "Spiritualism Growing in Popularity/ Psychic Fair: Fun for Some, Serious for Others." *New London Day* 22 July 1993: A1+.

Zelz, Abigail Ewing and Marilyn Zoidis. *Woodsmen and Whigs: Historic Images of Bangor, Maine.* Virginia Beach: Donning, 1991.

Index

264

Stamford, CT 96
Staples, Mary, accused witch 95
Starkey, Marion 129
Stetson, George 139, 143-144, 148-149, 153, 189
Stoker, Bram 20, 143-144, 207-208
Stowe, Harriet Beecher 19, 51
Supernatural in New England 8-10, (See also New England Gothic, definition of)
supernatural, belief in 26-32, 194, 198-199, 213-219, 224, 230-232
Swampscott, Mass. 44
Sysladobosis Lake 47
Tantaquidgeon, Chief Harold 59
Tantaquidgeon, Gladys 60, 63
Taunton, Mass. 225
Thames River 59
Thimble Islands (See Branford, CT)
Thompson, D.P., Locke Amsden 31-32, 125
Thoreau 2, 44-45
Three Sovereigns for Sarah 126
Tituba, accused witch 98, 99, 103, 105, 107, 108, 129, 130
Todorov, Tzvetan 27-28
Tom, Mt. 64
Trask, Richard 133
trials, witch (See witchcraft, trials for)
Tryon, Thomas
Harvest Home 204, 209, 231
The Other 209
tuberculosis
linked to vampires 137, 138-139, 144, 145, 146-148, 149, 151, 152, 153, 155-156, 189-190
Tuckey, Job, convicted witch 90, 103
Twain, Mark 18
Twin Lakes 47
Uncasville, CT 59
Updike, John
Witches of Eastwick 217-218
urban belief stories (See belief stories, urban)
vampires 8, 26, 28, 206, 207-208, 209
in European tradition 139-140
native belief 8, 137-156, 188-191
Vikings 35
Vikings, presence in New England

69-70
Walcott, Mary, witchcraft accuser 114
Walpole, Horace 3, 4, 21, 26, 73, 164, 176
Waltham, Mass. 40
Walton cemetery
vampire excavation 145-148, 180
Wampanoag 51
Wardwell, Samuel, convicted witch 93, 112
Warren, Ed and Lorraine 216-217, 230-231
Warren, Ed, demonologist 66, 216
Warren, Mary, witchcraft accuser 117
Webster, Daniel 2, 45-46
Webster, Mary, convicted witch 97
Wells, Maine 108
Wendigo 53, 221, 222
Wenham, Mass. 126
werewolves (See loup-garou)
West Greenwich, R.I. 150
West Indies 99, 106
Westerly, R.I. 124, 125
Westford, Mass. 70
Weston, CT 65
Wethersfield, CT 89
Wharton, Edith 19
Whitbourne, early explorer 49
Whitby, Yorkshire 61
White Mountains 64
Whiteman's Land 67, 68, 70, 232
Whittier, J.G. 16, 17, 79, 97, 128
Supernaturalism of New England 17, 124, 149
Wiesel, Elie 120, 134
Wilbraham, Mass. 185
Wilkins Freeman, Mary 19, 29, 128-129, 171
Williams, Abigail, witchcraft accuser 114, 116
Williams, Roger 55, 59, 63, 71, 79
Williamstown, Mass. 184
Windham frog fight (See mass delusions)
Windham, CT 80
Winslow, Edward, early explorer 58
Winsted, CT 53
Winter, Douglas E. 207, 221
Winthrop, John 55, 65, 79, 81, 91
witchcraft

CPSIA information can be obtained at www.ICGtesting.com
Printed in the USA
BVOW05s0212180315

392219BV00001B/42/P